FAMILY THERAPY SUPERVISION IN EXTRAORDINARY SETTINGS

Family Therapy Supervision in Extraordinary Settings showcases the dynamism of systemic family therapy supervision/consultation as it expands beyond typical and historical traditions. In this unique collection, contributors write about their innovations, unexpected learnings, and "perfect accidents" in the context of systemic therapy. These essays highlight creative approaches to supervision, present a wide variety of clinical cases and therapy settings, and demonstrate how training takes place in real time.

Each chapter illustrates increasingly diverse settings in which systemic family therapy services are delivered, whether in public mental health care for families across high-, low-, and middle-income countries, in areas of armed conflict or instability due to political violence or war, or stable, liberal democracies with robust public mental health systems. Each setting of supervision is extraordinary in the way it supports family therapy service delivery. Given the wide variation in access to systemic family therapy services, and the diverse settings in which systemic family therapy services are delivered, a set of brief, specific, and lively cases is called for that focus on the dynamic nature of a family therapy supervision and consultation interaction and its influence on clients, trainees, and supervisors.

Working as a family therapist in the world today, an era of global mental health, is as full of wonder and challenge as it was in the time family therapy originated as a profession. It is thus no accident that supervision and consultation work is just as extraordinary. This book will be essential reading for family therapy and counseling supervisors, as well as a helpful reference for supervisees.

Laurie L Charlés, Ph.D., L.M.F.T., implements systemic family therapy practice in international humanitarian relief contexts, in low- and middle-income countries, and with vulnerable populations in conflict-affected states. She is the author and co-editor of several books in family therapy and qualitative research, including *Family Therapy in Global Humanitarian Contexts: Voices and Issues from the Field*, with Dr. Gameela Samarasinghe. Laurie has delivered family therapy training content and provided systemic, clinical supervision support to public mental health professionals living and working in such diverse places as Guinea during the 2014 Ebola outbreak, post-conflict Kosovo, Syria, the Central African Republic, Cameroon, Burundi, Libya, the Democratic Republic of Congo, Sri Lanka, the Philippines, Egypt, and Uzbekistan. A 2017–2018 Fulbright Global Scholar and a graduate of the Fletcher School of Law and Diplomacy, Laurie lives in Boston, Massachusetts.

Thorana S. Nelson, Ph.D., is an Emerita Professor of Marriage and Family Therapy in the Department of Family, Consumer, and Human Development at Utah State University. She developed and has taught the Fundamentals of Supervision and Supervision Refresher courses for the American Association for Marriage and Family Therapy. She chaired the AAMFT Task Force that reviewed the AAMFT Approved Supervisor standards and made recommendations for changes. She also teaches solution-focused brief therapy (SFBT), SFBT supervision, and other workshops, including *SFBT With Families*, also a Routledge book. She has published numerous articles, book chapters, and books in the areas of family therapy, family therapy supervision, and solution-focused brief therapy. She is a Clinical Fellow and Approved Supervisor for AAMFT and lives in Santa Fe, New Mexico, with her husband.

FAMILY THERAPY SUPERVISION IN EXTRAORDINARY SETTINGS

Illustrations of Systemic Approaches in Everyday Clinical Work

Edited by Laurie L. Charlés and Thorana S. Nelson

Routledge
Taylor & Francis Group

First published 2019
by Routledge
52 Vanderbilt Avenue, New York, NY 10017

and by Routledge
2 Park Square, Milton Park, Abingdon, Oxon, OX14 4RN

Routledge is an imprint of the Taylor & Francis Group, an informa business

Library of Congress Cataloging-in-Publication Data
A catalog record has been requested for this book

ISBN: 978-1-138-48034-6 (hbk)
ISBN: 978-1-138-48038-4 (pbk)
ISBN: 978-1-351-06302-9 (ebk)

Typeset in Bembo
by Deanta Global Publishing Services, Chennai, India

CONTENTS

CONTRIBUTORS

Alexandra E. Alfaro, M.S., L.M.F.T., is a doctoral candidate in marriage and family therapy at Nova Southeastern University. She has experience in school-based settings, blossoming from Therapist Intern to Graduate Assistant Supervisor. As a Graduate Assistant, she worked with full-time faculty professor, Dr. Anne Rambo, to further build her supervisory skills and to collaborate on publications and presentations. She currently works as an ESE Family Counselor at Pine Ridge Education Center, an elementary behavior change school in Broward County, FL.

Vjollca Berisha Avdiu graduated with a Master of Arts degree in Clinical Psychology at the University of Prishtina Kosova. She completed postgraduate training in Clinical Psychology and Psychotherapy. She works at the Child and Adolescent Mental Health Centre in Prishtina. Vjollca teaches psychology courses at the "Dardania" College in Prishtina. She is experienced in working with children in foster-care and with foster-parents. Vjollca has participated in the Kosova Systemic Family Therapy Training Program, implemented by Kosovo Health Foundation, where she was trained by the International Family Therapy Trainers. She participated in many training modules in the field of trauma and she has earned a DIRFloortime Certificate of Proficiency.

Saliha Bava, Ph.D., L.M.F.T., is an Associate Professor of Marriage and Family Therapy at Mercy College. She serves on the International Certificate Program in Collaborative-Dialogic Practices Board, on the advisory board of Taos Institute, and as a doctoral advisor for the Taos Ph.D. and Diploma Programs. She is an AAMFT Approved Supervisor, served on the American Family Therapy Academy Board (2012–2017), and co-founded the *International Journal of Collaborative-Dialogic Practices*. As the Director of Research with the International Trauma

Studies Program, NYC, she has researched theater, community resiliency, and psychosocial practices. Her focus on performative practices, dialog as socially just, and on hyperlinked identities is part of her academic activism where she questions the dominant discourses of research methodology, training, social justice, and identity. Drawing on her relational play consultancy, she co-authored *The Relational Book for Parenting*. Originally from India, Saliha lives and works in NYC.

Monte Bobele is an Emeritus Professor of Psychology at Our Lady of the Lake University (OLLU) in San Antonio, Texas and Faculty of the Houston Galveston Institute in Houston, Texas. He is a licensed Psychologist and an AAMFT Clinical Fellow and Approved Supervisor. He co-edited (with Arnold Slive) *When One Hour is All You Have: Effective Therapy for Walk-In Clients*. He is also co-editor (with Hoyt, Slive, Young, and Talmon) of *Single-Session Therapy by Walk-In or Appointment*. He was the recipient of the Texas Psychological Association's 2012 Outstanding Contribution to Education Award, and OLLU's 2013 Fleming Award for Teaching Excellence. He teaches graduate courses in strengths-based approaches to therapy and supervises graduate students in the university's Community Counseling Service. He has published several articles and book chapters on postmodern approaches to family therapy. He presents internationally on approaches to brief therapy. He makes his home in San Antonio, Texas.

Roshan Dhammapala has a master's degree in Clinical Psychology from the University of Zimbabwe. She is currently a Visiting Lecturer and Course Coordinator for the M.Phil. degree in Clinical Psychology at the Faculty of Graduate Studies, University of Colombo. She has spent the past few years installing and strengthening a peer support and supervision mechanism program and providing in-service training for counselors employed within Sri Lanka's public services as part of a consultancy with the Asia Foundation. Her practice experience is drawn from her work in Zimbabwe's public health system and academia, Australia's community mental health services, and Sri Lanka's academia, nongovernment psychosocial services, and clinical practice. Roshan lives in Colombo but regularly escapes the urbanscape to restore her equilibrium.

Amalka Edirisinghe, M.Phil., in Clinical Psychology, is a Clinical Psychologist and the former Director of Programs at the Family Rehabilitation Centre, Colombo, Sri Lanka. She has provided clinical supervision to the Psychosocial Workers and conducted capacity building in the areas of violence related trauma, individual and group counseling skills, and on routine outcome measures. Further, she conducted lectures for students enrolled in the Masters of Philosophy in Clinical Psychology program at the University of Colombo, Sri Lanka. Amalka was a member of the consultative group to review and finalize the draft Mental Health Policy of Sri Lanka and a member of the working group to create and finalize the Scheme of Recruitment to absorb Clinical Psychologists into the public health system in Sri Lanka. Amalka is currently studying for her second master's degree and is enrolled in the Master of Cognitive Behavior Therapy program offered by Flinders University, Australia. She lives in Adelaide with her husband, Ruchira and son, Chenula.

Gizem Erdem, Ph.D., is an Assistant Professor in the Department of Psychology at Koc University and a licensed marriage and family therapist. She was a Postdoctoral Researcher at University of Illinois at Chicago from 2014–2015. She held summer visiting positions at Harvard University, Cambridge, Massachusetts, and ISCTE University Institute of Lisbon. She serves as the National Council on Family Relations Family Therapy Section secretary/treasurer. She teaches clinical area courses and Introduction to Couple and Family Therapy for senior undergraduate students at Koc University. She supervises master's students in clinical psychology and couple and family therapy programs from various Turkish universities, and trains probation officers in systemic family therapy. She has published scientific articles on substance abuse, juvenile delinquency and probation, and efficacy of family therapy and youth mentoring to intervene with at-risk youth and their families. She and her husband, Burak, live in Istanbul, Turkey.

Mihiri Ferdinando is an experienced Development Practitioner with over 15 years of experience in research and technical support for psychosocial programs. She is currently Senior Program Manager at The Asia Foundation for its Mental Health and Psychosocial Support Programs. In this capacity, she is responsible for all program activities, working closely with government agencies, donor organizations, and field partners. Prior to this assignment, she served as an Assistant Lecturer in Sociology at the Department of Sociology, University of Colombo, Sri Lanka. In 2016, she was elected as an Independent Expert to the Council of the International Refugee Council for Torture Victims. She has published locally. She holds M.Phil. and B.A. (Hons) degrees in Sociology from the University of Colombo.

Chrystal Fullen, M.S., is a doctoral student at Our Lady of the Lake University in San Antonio, Texas. She is completing her clinical internship at the South Texas Veterans Healthcare System. She has worked extensively in the community providing psychotherapy services to children, adults, and families at multiple training clinics. She currently lives with her family in San Antonio, Texas.

Shelley Green, Ph.D., is a Professor of Family Therapy at Nova Southeastern University, a Clinical Fellow and Approved Supervisor with the American Association for Marriage and Family Therapy, and a licensed family therapist in the state of Florida. She serves as the co-director with Dr. Douglas Flemons of Context Consultants, Inc., where she specializes in working with couples regarding issues of sexuality and intimacy. She is co-editor with Dr. Flemons of *Quickies:*

The Handbook of Brief Sex Therapy (Norton, 2018—3rd Edition). Dr. Green has published and presented widely on her relational approach to equine facilitated psychotherapy.

Anagi Gunasekara, M.Phil., in Clinical Psychology, is a Clinical Psychologist at the Family Rehabilitation Centre, Colombo, Sri Lanka. She is involved in the tasks of providing clinical supervision to psychosocial workers who are engaged in providing counseling for those impacted by violence-related trauma while capacitating the staff and other stakeholders on the same. Anagi is also involved in the coordination of the rehabilitation programs implemented by the Family Rehabilitation Centre. She is also serving as a visiting lecturer and resource person for many diploma, undergraduate, and postgraduate psychology degrees in Colombo, Sri Lanka. Anagi currently lives in Colombo, Sri Lanka with her family.

Brittany Henry, Ph.D., L.M.F.T., works with the Seminole Tribe of Florida as a Family Therapist and Program Director, providing school-based consultation and services. During her master's and doctoral programs, she worked with Dr. Anne Rambo at the PROMISE program as a therapist intern and later as a graduate assistant supervisor. She has consulted with schools and orphanages in South Africa and India. She completed a research project on the use of solution-focused techniques with children in school in South Africa.

Brittany Houston is a doctoral candidate at Our Lady of the Lake University in San Antonio, TX. She has provided services to clients in a variety of settings that include schools, Veterans Administrations, private practice, primary care, and non-profit agencies. Brittany has provided supervision to psychology trainees and medical residents in the delivery of psychological interventions. Her interests include "whole person care," training and education, cultural competence, and integrated primary care. She enjoys good humor, cartoons, sports, dancing, and spending time with family and friends.

Elizabeth M. Jarquin, M.S., L.M.F.T., is a doctoral candidate in Marriage and Family Therapy at Nova Southeastern University. During her master's and Ph.D. programs, she worked alongside Dr. Anne Rambo at the PROMISE Program as a therapist intern, and later as a graduate assistant supervisor. Presently, Elizabeth works as a School Counselor at a charter school in Miami, Florida that offers concurrent instruction in Greek and in English. Elizabeth has a special interest in immigration issues. She coauthored an article related to immigration and the PROMISE Program and hopes to conduct further research on this topic.

Saeid Kianpour, Ph.D., holds a doctoral degree from Virginia Tech University; when he was offered to contribute the chapter for this book, he was a Behavioral Science Doctoral Intern at the Indiana University School of Medicine. After he earned his doctorate, Saeid recently moved to Canada where he is establishing a private clinical practice. He worked with refugee families in Indianapolis, IN and wrote his dissertation on how Syrian refugee fathers perceived their identity and family dynamics in the US after displacement. His clinical and research interests are international family therapy, refugee families, and cultural humility in family therapy.

Paula Leech is a licensed Marriage and Family Therapist, Certified Sex Therapist, and Certified Supervisor of Sex Therapy with the Association of Sexuality Educators, Therapists, and Counselors (AASECT). She leads workshops, teaches courses, and trains therapists in sex therapy at various institutes, universities, and online. She supervises students from all over the US and Canada pursuing sex counseling or sex therapy certification through AASECT. She lives in Boston, Massachusetts with her husband and young son.

marcela polanco is an African, Muisca, and European Colombian immigrant in the US. She is part of the faculty team of the Master's in Family Therapy program at San Diego State University. As a Family Therapist, marcela situates her research, teaching, supervision, and practice geopolitically. In her immigrant English, she is strongly influenced by the social justice politics and literary framework of Narrative Family Therapy. In her Colombian Spanish, she has been immersing herself into the politics, epistemologies, and ontologies of the work of Andean decolonial academic and social activists. Additionally, she borrows from the work of Latin American literary writers of magical realism, particularly Gabriel García Márquez. marcela's work is driven by academic activism searching for inter-cultural and inter-language encounters of knowledge fair trades between Eurocentrism and decoloniality. She is interested in the development of coexisting alter narratives that would support the integrity of the construction of new pluriversal and deracialized responses to social suffering and the systems of power that support it.

Adelina Ahmeti Pronaj is a Child Psychiatrist who works at the University Clinical Center in Prishtina, Kosova, as a Child Psychiatrist. She is an assistant at the University Clinical Center of Prishtina-Department of Neuropsychiatry. Adelina provided supervision to SOS-Kinderdorf educators. She lectured courses at the "Dardania" College in the field of social welfare and was an assistant in the Master's in Family Counseling Program. She has participated in the Kosova Systemic Family Therapy Training Program, implemented by KHF, where she was trained by the International Family Therapy Trainers. She earned a DIRFloortime Certificate of Proficiency.

Anne Rambo, Ph.D., L.M.F.T., has taught in a COAMFTE-accredited family therapy program for 29 years, and has worked with graduate interns in schools for

18 of those years. She is the author of numerous articles and book chapters, three books on the supervision and training of family therapists, and one book for parents who need help negotiating the school system. It has been a great joy for her to see her former students move into careers in schools both in the US and internationally.

Lina Hussein Sadek, M.A., in Psychology, is Guidance and Counseling Specialist at the National Employment Office at the Ministry of Labor in Lebanon. She has worked as a Psychosocial Support Program Coordinator for schools of the United Nations Relief and Works for Palestine Refugees in Lebanon; as MHGap technical supervisor for primary health care centers in Beirut, Mount Lebanon and in the South at the National Mental Health Programme, Ministry of Public Health; and as a Psychosocial Support Program Coordinator in Haret-Hreik Primary Health Care Center and as head of the Social Municipal office at the Municipality of Haret-Hreik. She contributed to the revision of MHGap HIG, Arabic version, and to testing the second version of MHGap Job Aids at primary health centers in Lebanon. She has contributed to the revision of a number of psychosocial support manuals in Lebanon and was a team leader and co-supervisor for a systemic family therapy project in Lebanon. She lives with her husband and her four children in Beirut.

Fatmire Shala-Kastrati holds a master's degree in Clinical Psychology at the University of Prishtina, Kosova. She currently works at the Institute of Forensic Medicine-Ministry of Justice in Prishtina where she works as a Psychosocial Support Officer for Family Members of Missing Persons in Kosova. She participated in many training modules in the field of trauma where she was trained by international trainers. She is a coauthor of the published article, "Posttraumatic Growth among Family Members with Missing Persons from War in Kosova: Association with Social Support and Community Involvement," as well as several published books in the area of missing persons and their family members in Kosova. She, her husband, and two of her sons live in Prishtina, Kosova.

Cindy Silitsky is an Associate Professor and Director of the Family Therapy Program at St. Thomas University (STU), in Miami Gardens, Florida. She is a licensed marriage and family therapist in the state of Florida, practicing in the community for over 20 years, specializing in couple's therapy, grief and loss, and medical family therapy. She is a state-approved supervisor for MFT and MHC, and an AAMFT (American Association for Marriage and Family Therapy) Approved Supervisor and Clinical Fellow. Prior to her position at STU, she taught internationally in Jamaica and the Bahamas. Her research interests include gender in couple's therapy, service learning, HIV/AIDS, and the study of systems theory. She is a published author and conference presenter.

Muriel Singer, Ph.D., began her career as a registered nurse working with adolescents in a psychiatric and substance abuse facility. This experience inspired her passion for the practice of systemic family therapy. Muriel is an Associate Professor and Department Head of the Couples and Family Therapy Program at Kean University in Union, New Jersey. She's an Approved Supervisor with the American Association for Marriage and Family Therapy. In addition to teaching and her administration duties, Muriel supervises clinicians working toward licensure throughout the US.

April Trejo, M.A., L.P.C., is a doctoral candidate in Counseling Psychology in the department of Psychology at Our Lady of the Lake University (OLLU) in San Antonio, TX. She enjoys supervising at various community clinics and teaching solution-focused brief therapy (SFBT) to graduate students throughout San Antonio. She also teaches undergraduate psychology courses at OLLU. April has a passion for SFBT, single-session, and walk-in therapies. She has presented at various conferences about strengths-based therapies with Latino and disabled communities. Currently, she runs a family-owned community rehabilitation agency and private practice with her mother in San Antonio where she lives with her husband and four children.

PREFACE

The idea for this book began germinating for me (Laurie) in 2014 while I supervised live family therapy practica at the Community Counseling Service as a faculty member at Our Lady of the Lake University. At the time, I was also providing distance supervision support to public mental health professionals in Syria for a set of projects within the World Health Organization (WHO). The combination of the two worlds of supervision happening side by side in real time—the context of discussions with new trainees in COAMFTE training programs as well as seasoned Syrian professionals learning about family therapy for the first time while living in the midst of the war—created a powerful dynamic for me as a supervisor. Every family therapy clinical case in the work I was privy to in both settings seemed to tell a story, and the stories were as much about supervision as they were about the clinical work.

As I watched some of my supervisees (in both places) do amazing work, I noticed how my supervision practices from one place filtered into and informed the other. I think perhaps this is how the "ordinary/extraordinary" idea took hold. The clinical cases of the supervisors I was supporting in Syria were graphically violent, and painful, but also, full of hope and resourcefulness. The same was true for the clients of the supervisees I was training in San Antonio.

However, the intensity of the process of my consultation with each group was vividly different. In Texas, it was routine, fairly calm, ordered. In my Syrian world, virtual through the use of information and communication technologies, it was anything but; we had no control over the conditions in the country, and so the nature of the Syrians' clinical work with their own supervisees and my supervision support of that work took on a similar pattern. Nevertheless, I often found my stories from Texas useful to share with the Syrians; and similarly, the intensity of the work in Syria brought a new dimension to the conversations I had with my

San Antonio trainees. There was a symmetry. I knew I was experiencing something truly "extraordinary"—but also, very ordinary, too. As ordinary as systemic family therapy processes can be, that is.

I was busy readying my portfolio for tenure, working on projects in other countries, and developing various grants, papers, and so on. So, I put a mental bookmark on the ordinary/extraordinary idea. But I kept writing notes on all I was observing as it was happening.

After the Syria projects had ended, after I'd earned tenure and left OLLU, I finally reached out to Rana about co-writing with me a proposal for a book that showcased what I was thinking of at the time as "Family Therapy Supervision 2.0." I had in fact shared Rana's book, *The Contemporary Relational Supervisor* (Lee & Nelson, 2014) with the Syrians, for whom I had developed a supervision curriculum. Although Rana and I had never worked together before, I had an intuitive sense that she could help me bring to fruition a book that illustrated the kind of dynamism I was observing in my work across the globe, specifically showcasing the very ordinary extraordinariness of the supervision process. The showcase expanded to include consultation as we learned more about the kinds of support that were happening with our contributors. We also did our best to create a forum for voices that are, literally and metaphorically, doing systems work in multiple languages front and center.

Here, our contributors have written for us in English. However, many of them have translated their work from their native tongues including Arabic, Albanian, Sinhala, Farsi, Spanish, and Turkish. The mesmerizing, compelling stories of supervision/consultation, as shared here, are beyond even what we could have foreseen.

Contemporary family therapy supervision and consultation is in a dynamic state of change as family therapy services expand beyond typical and historical traditions. Our authors' contributions showcase that dynamism from the different points on the globe where they work and within the set of resources available to them in their settings. Our contributors present examples of how systemic family therapy clinical work, via its supervision and consultation process, is adapted to fit the context and the variety of forms in which family therapy and family focused psychosocial support takes place. We find these settings both ordinary and extraordinary.

The chapters focus on many types of settings and many approaches to systemic work with families. Our contributors' work highlights the combination of the innovation of systemic supervision that can happen unexpectedly in challenging situations, whether it is live in the therapy room, behind the mirror with a set of trainees and colleagues, or in the supervision office. However, in some stories presented here, there is no supervisor to be found. In such cases, professionals who work with families create their own networks of support—peer supervision under mango trees, or with çaj (tea) and colleagues at the kitchen table, or on their own, through their writing or other creative endeavor that can serve as both self-care and self-supervision. Supervision and consultation of family therapists takes on a different shape in countries where the field of family therapy is a regulated profession, and where supervisors are ubiquitous. Creativity is no less present here, however. Rather, the problem set of issues for families is different, and thus, so is the supervision and consultation. Wherever they occur, the examples here highlight specific cases that illustrate the dynamic nature of a family therapy supervision and consultation, and its influence on clients, trainees, and/or supervisors.

In this era of global mental health, the work illustrated here by our contributors showcases the dynamism of systemic family therapy work as it expands beyond typical and historical traditions. In contemporary family therapy in the U.S. and across the globe, there is wide variation in access to systemic family therapy services, and increasingly diverse settings in which systemic family therapy services are delivered. Part of this is due to increased focus on access to public mental health care for families across low- and middle-income countries, or in areas of armed conflict or instability due to political violence or war. However, even stable, liberal democracies with robust public mental health systems are extraordinary in their own way when it comes to family therapy service delivery. Working as a family therapist in the world today is as full of wonder and challenge as it was in the time family therapy originated as a profession. It is thus no accident that supervision and consultation work is just as extraordinary.

Reference

Lee, R. E., & Nelson, T. S. (2013). *The contemporary relational supervisor.* New York, NY: Routledge/Taylor & Francis Group.

1

EN DEFENSA DE SPANGLISH FAMILY THERAPY SUPERVISION IN THE ERA OF ENGLISH

marcela polanco

I am in the U.S., *en* San Diego, California. It is the fifth state where I have made my home since I migrated *de Colombia hace 18 años*. I arrived here in California less than a month ago after joining the faculty of the Master's in Marriage and Family Therapy (MFT) program *en* San Diego State University with the prospect of developing a bilingual (Spanish-English) MFT training track that includes supervision in Spanish. The university is located on the land of the Kumeyaay. I am in front of my office *del* North Education Building. I am relishing the company of the comforting San Diegan weather; *me recuerda al clima de Colombia.* I am sitting on a wooden bench. It is painted with an image of a paved road heading toward a white orb of sunshine high above the point directly above where the road ends. On the left-hand side of the road, words, alternately red and white, declare: "concentration," "perseverance," "graduation," and "expectations." And, on the right, equally assertively: "optimism," "determination," and "grades." These could very well be considered to summarize the tenets of the Western, U.S., Eurocentric, neoliberal rhetoric of *desarrollismo* or developmentalism (Escobar, 2007), expressed in an education that promises progress and success in the era of English (Mizumura, 2015).

I am seated on the left side of the road. I am persevering in my attempts here to take *otros caminos como* alternative winding roads whereby I can switch from one to the other. I am seeking to convey the advantages of the complexities, both cultural and linguistic, of bilinguality within the context of MFT live supervision that often lead to destinations *other* than a *white* orb of sunshine located high above the point where the road ends, but not against it. I draw from other sources rather than only neoliberal ones to inform my MFT Spanglish supervision in order to capture the aesthetics of our bilingual games (Sommer, 2003, 2004). I consider bilinguality in supervision to afford a substantive advantage to the relational and contextual tenets of family therapy practice, given that we bilinguals live and breathe linguistic relationality and contextual shifts. But most importantly, I consider bilingual MFT supervision as a matter of language justice (polanco, 2016a). I emphasize language games at the borders of supervision, disallowing linguistic purists and prudes (Sommer, 2003) who infringe on our rights to our Spanglish*es* on the grounds that these games are the "mutilation of Spanish" (Anzaldúa, 1987, p. 35). *Entre ellxs estan quienes protegen con su vida la virginidad de los idomas.* As a note, I situate bilingualism as Spanish and English, considering my own linguistic social locations and the context of my work in Hispanic-serving institutions with a significant representation of Spanish-speaking MFT trainees. However, I anticipate that what I write may apply to a certain extent to MFT supervision with trainees who subscribe to other languages as well as English.

I hope to engage a monolingual, bilingual, or polylingual family therapy readership in defense of Spanglish MFT training. To English monolinguals more specifically but implicitly, from an ethical stance, I problematize their seeming supervision when having no access to the language in which the therapeutic conversation is taking place even if translated. I aspire to recruit their support to advocate for the implementation of bilingual training in MFT as an ethical imperative. Parallel to my supervision, here I seek to engage the reader in a fashion whereby I can maintain the integrity of my message to defend linguistic rights in supervision. I do so by freely shifting from one language to the other, and by means of the untamed, descriptive, detailed, and nonlinear storytelling aesthetics of the Africana, Indigenous, and European Colombian heritages of the oral traditions of my culture alongside the cultures of various Latin American communities that feature prominently in bilingual therapy and its supervision. *La cosa no es nada fácil; sin duda!* I discuss elements that have become critical to my Spanglish supervision, including: (a) addressing the coloniality of language and its discriminatory effects spilling over our work; (b) claiming Spanglish in supervision; (c) incorporating street translation with consideration to the incommensurability of language; and (d) discerning the particular oral traditions culturally negotiated in each language that make us listen differently.

Attempting to breathe life into my hopes, I have with me my laptop and headphones that are plugged into my phone. With one ear I listen to ChocQuibTown, Sylvio Rodriguez, Natalia Lafourcade *y* Calle 13, and with the other, I remain connected to what is around. I am sipping a cup of tea amidst concrete buildings lost in their uniform and plain, featureless architecture. The faraway sound of traffic rebounds off the nearby hills. Strong, tall, and entitled trees that have taken up residence in irrigated grass that has escaped from the fierce droughts so familiar in California stare me down. They house, in turn, various birds that I can't see but hear distinctively as a symphony. As the morning routine unfolds, the traffic of people passing by increases. I overhear snatches of their conversations in a polyphony of languages that find expression outside the anglophone classrooms. These include Spanish and others I cannot recognize. Some of the people pass me by on foot and others on wheels, speedily rolling through the various paths in a dance; their bodies, moving artfully, seem rooted on their skateboards avoiding everything and everyone around them to head toward their destinations. The wailing sound coming from the wheels in contact with the cement joins the birds' symphony.

Someone approaches at a brisk pace and catches my attention. I would locate this person as a white male, perhaps quite a bit older than me—although I must admit that my judgment on others' ages falls short of anything amounting to even a minimum of reliability. He passes about six feet from me and is carrying a suitcase. He loses his balance and trips over one of the few small rocks on the ground. His body brakes his fall before mine could react. He regathers himself and picks up the rock. He swings his arm aiming at a trash can on the opposite side of the bench I am seated on. He makes a clean score in LeBron James style. I hear the forceful impact of the rock as it strikes the bottom of the trashcan. My imagination prologues the rock's utterance joining the symphony creating a menacing but dramatic background score. Notwithstanding that this man did what could very well be considered an act of kindness by disposing of obstacles in his path and for pedestrians who might follow his footsteps, I couldn't help myself wondering, at what cost? In this case, a substance from nature—a remnant of the settling of a Western academic institution on Kumeyaay land—is discarded as garbage.

The Coloniality of Language: Language Discrimination Effects in Supervision

Within the particular historical, economic, social, and political relations between the U.S. and Latin America—incarnated *en carne y hueso* in our immigration experience—those of us MFTs of various generations of migrants from various Spanish-speaking Latin American countries have been confronted at times with those who mistake bilinguality as a deficiency in our speaking and writing. Our bilinguality is approached as a rock in the middle of the road that needs to be disposed of, cleared, or ironed out so our "development" as family therapists is not impeded, or we do not impede the development of others by "interrupting national arrangements" (Sommer, 2003, p. 9). As Sommer (2003) wrote, "in a powerful United States where it's enough to speak one language, because less powerful foreigners must learn to speak English [,]…monolingualism sounds normal" (p. 3).

Our communications split us "between jokester and butt of the joke, an alienating thrill that bilinguals learn to survive" (Sommer, 2003, p. 9). Our accented pronunciations and linguistic aesthetics are questioned by correction and counsel based on what it is considered normal, correct, proper, and an educated language treatment, both socially and professionally. This is so that monolingual eyes and ears remain intact in their troubling efforts to understand us in our "failures." Then we could go on through our paths, on foot or on wheels, toward a white orb of sunshine, persuaded by a professional and social rhetoric to pursue monolingual ideals of success in this country as respectable MFTs.

Our languages are organized according to monolingual parameters of nationalism (Platt & Natrajan-Tyagi, 2014) and to a colonial hierarchy of a normalized, linguistically-arranged social order whereby rights to legitimacy are warranted to certain identities (white), languages (English), and knowledges (Eurocentric; Quijano, 1992) high above the point directly above where the road ends. At the bottom, in its periphery, its dark side has constituted for over 500 years *other* racialized identities (African, Asian, Indigenous, Mestizx, Zambxs, Mulatxs, Chicanxs), with our languages (in this case, Spanish and borderland variations such as Spanglish, Pocho, Chicano, Tex-Mex, Pachuco, etc.) and knowledges (in this case decolonial; Mignolo, 2005/2012).

The well-intended acts of kindness when "helping" us and "correcting" us in our assumed linguistic failures, inadvertently display shameless and at times merciless discriminatory intolerance (Sommer, 2003) with tangible colonial effects that clearly feature in supervision. *Lamentablemente,* intolerance instills in us a shameful relationship with our own borderland Spanish*es*, which petrifies our creativity and imagination in our therapy practices. Furthermore, it results in our colonial internalization of the same well-intended acts of kindness to shame one another's bilinguality in its accented expressions by following the same "normal" or "correct" linguistic criteria rooted within the rhetoric of professionalism. This is, given that we have been humiliated in our bilingual, accented aesthetics, newly-coined words at the intersection of both languages, and code switching. This means that we have been humiliated in our social and cultural renderings of our worlds *considerando que nuestros idiomas le corresponden a nuestros modos de vivir* (Anzaldúa, 1987, p. 35).

Español e Inglés Junticos y Revueltos: Claiming Spanglish in Supervision

I now join the symphony around me in solidarity. I don't want to let go of the rock's utterance echoing in my imagination. When it begins to fade away, my fingers begin to play on my laptop's keyboard to articulate my response to the effects of merciless discriminatory experiences that feature in my supervision. This is for supervisees who still remain connected to their Spanish in their professional lives. Some heritage speakers who learned the language at home from parents and/ or grandparents refuse to speak Spanish in their professional lives, giving little to no consideration to any recruitment efforts for MFT bilingual training in turn. They anticipate the replication of the same educational (Cooper Stein, Wright, Gil, Miness, & Ginanto, 2018) and social patterns that have contributed to a long-standing sense of linguistic inadequacy, no longer feeling completely safe to speak Spanish outside their homes. Language shame is all too familiar to native Spanish speakers as well but in terms of our accented immigrant Englishes.

Language shame shows up in group supervision in various forms. It is not uncommon that native and heritage speakers compare their proficiency against one another to measure each other up linguistically. In the work, it shows up in the form of an invasive preoccupation with the use of correct or appropriate vocabularies in the therapy session. It often suffocates almost all room for MFT theoretical or practical reflexivity during the conversation. Fear of coming across as linguistic failures that may put their "professional credibility" at risk in front of families is also not uncommon. Therefore, in my supervision, first and foremost, I pay considerable attention to these matters and make efforts to address them.

My efforts have come through my own apprenticeship, having received no training during my MFT studies, and in collaboration with supervisees, a majority of whom have been women of color of Mexican descent who were training in the Psychological Services for Spanish Speaking Populations (PSSSP) certificate at Our Lady of the Lake University[1] in Texas where I worked for the past six years. I learned about the significance of engaging conversations to articulate our ungracious responses to monolingual and language purists who approach us with their intolerant "help." Our conversations include exposing the incarnated effects of their help through critical, friendly yet fierce provocations, as I am doing in this chapter, called upon by the very tangible colonial effects of linguistic discrimination. We situate our sense of linguistic inadequacy in supervision and therapy in the context in which it belongs: coloniality. We storytell our relational experiences of discrimination and our responses to make visible the power relationships that have racialized our languages. We dedicate ourselves to a spirit of solidarity that comes with mitigating the negotiations around power also implicated in the institutionalized roles of supervisor and supervisee for these conversations to take place as safely as we find it to be possible. This comes about when building a sense of community *y lazos de solidaridad* from reciprocal learnings among supervisees and supervisors. This is performed in the tellings of our intersecting experiences as bilingual people of color in the U.S., hence insiders of the colonial experience. This is also well nourished with tacos, pan dulce, and chocolate cake.

Throughout these conversations, I came to claim Spanglish as the preferred language in supervision. *Somos terapeutas y también terapistas.* Spanglish serves as a legitimate territory to articulate the linguistic borderlands where our laments of the tangible effects of well-intended yet intolerant acts in the era of monolingual English (Mizumura, 2015) play out into the power of action. I implement Spanglish communicative guidelines at the outset of supervision. These include a requirement for all team members to refrain from problematizing or humiliating one another's bilinguality. Furthermore, they include a politics of linguistic imperfection during our consultations. We refrain from "correcting" our pronunciations or translations and rather support the multiple vocabularies of our Spanishes, Englishes, and Spanglishes. We strive to experience the thrill of being only the jokesters rather than the butt of jokes. We rigorously subscribe to linguistic disobedience. We keep from restricting ourselves to a single, mono, official, *virgen* or purist Spanish and English that would tame the linguistic imaginative games and creativity of our practice that comes with the borderland territories of our bilinguality. In Gabriel García Márquez' (2014) terms, we strive to humanize our linguistic arrangements on the fringe of grammatical rules *al hacerlo "algo humano, familiar o afable" y sin ser ningún pecado* (para 2). *Además, sin que "suframos con sus camisas de fuerza y cinturones de castidad[,]…apelamos a la sabiduría callejera" (para 13), y simplificamos reglas arbitrarias que terminan por simplificarnos y deshumanizarnos.*

I invite supervisees to bring into the therapy room the linguistic imperfection of their bilingual aesthetics, making it overt and also part of the therapeutic process. As in supervision, supervisees begin therapy sessions by taking their time introducing their language backgrounds in detail. They also interview each family member about their language locations, preferences, and translation practices at home or in their communities when applicable, so that the therapeutic conversation follows the same language patterns as much as it is possible. They keep a decolonial eye to discern possible colonial patterns that may have had an impact on family members' position to abstain from speaking either language in their family and social life even though they know how to.

Supervisees share the particularities of the geocultural backgrounds of their Spanishes to families. They do so to mark possible linguistic differences (rather than sameness) from where they can learn from one another. This happens even with families who may share their same nationality of origin or ancestry. We understand that national languages have regional variations added to the immigration, educational, social class, and other experiences, whereby our Spanishes undergo transformations in nuanced ways. Furthermore, supervisees make explicit the borderland origins of their Spanishes to heighten the likelihood that although the session may take place in Spanglish, Spanish, and English, depending on the family's language patterns, they may be required to interrupt one another for translation within their Spanishes to reach vocabulary clarity. This has added therapeutic value. Families are alerted to the supervisees' bilingual training experience and consequent potential of their not knowing some words in Spanish or making up others that may not be recognizable to all. Hence, supervisees ask families for permission to consult them for vocabulary assistance. This is an interesting practice because families lend supervisees a hand in considering vocabularies for questions they will follow up once they arrive at a vocabulary consensus. To the surprise of some supervisees, more often than not, families respond in very appreciative and supportive ways and are highly interested in helping supervisees with their bilingual training, engaging in a solidarity sort of fair-trade exchange of knowledge. This has had a significant impact in diminishing supervisees' senses of linguistic shame and inadequacy, in turn heightening their creativity in therapy.

Apelando a la Sabiduria Callejera: Street Translation in Supervision

By re-engaging supervisees' creativity in therapy, we can get to work with the play of language. Bilinguality is no longer that which needs to be brief but to join in its vast coexistence and aesthetic maneuverings. With considerations on how languages are globally arranged hierarchically in a colonial pattern of power— English centered at the top and Spanglishes at the peripherical bottom—we strive to make language justice (polanco, 2016b). We are attentive to how languages enter into communication with one another justly and via translation. Parallel to the politics of language, this work also has been supported by my own MFT training as a bilingual, which I have documented elsewhere (polanco, 2010, 2016a, 2016b) and my research on translation since my dissertation work (polanco, 2011). I have come to better understand what I believe is at the heart of bilinguality, easily disregarded from monolingualism: the incommensurability of languages and the consequent impossibility of translation.

Bilinguals understand that what we say in one language does not mean the same as what we say in the other or must necessarily have its equivalent (polanco, 2009). Crossing over linguistic borders means dislocation and relocation, hence meaning reinvention, rearticulation, or redefinition through bicultural maneuverings that often involve something far more complex and intricate than just a Google quickie translation. From this postmodern perspective (Tymockzo, 2010), languages are, after all, untranslatable. Hence, learning MFT in English and practicing it in Spanish is far more complicated, more so when ascribing to an aspiration of cultural integrity; otherwise, patterns of the coloniality of knowledge come into play. Such impossibility of translation makes translation a possible act of transformation and origination, rather than knowledge transfer. Transformation is constituted by difference as contextual shifts that reveal a multiplicity of implicit vocabularies in cultural negotiations whereby a power twist occurs in relation to the hierarchy of languages.

Therefore, I track with a keen ear equal bilanguage participation in supervision and therapy and the borderland linguistic crossings/rearticulations, or lack thereof. When supervisees reflect upon their work in English upon a session that took place in their Spanishes, I intervene. I do so to assure the entrance of Spanish as well and the border crossings in between. I invite them to rearticulate, hence reinvent what they just said but now in their preferred Spanglishes *¿y ahora cómo dirías eso en tu Español o Tex Mex or Mexicano, and so forth?* The times when a word seems to get stuck in monolingualism, often about an MFT theory concept they learned in English and has not found its way to an equivalent in their Spanglish when they ask, "how do you say this?," I also intervene. I do so by inviting their street translation skills before or instead of any official translation. Yielding far more excitement via a street translation, we draw upon our culturally forged imaginations of our collective street cred and that of the families we work with to rearticulate our practice in our borderland terms, *embarrándonos de lenguaje hasta la cabeza.* I engage their culturally forged imaginations through inquiry *¿Al considerar este término en Inglés ahora cruzando la frontera hacia tu cultura Espanglish, qué te corre por la mente; qué imágenes te evoca, sabores, colores, símbolos, figuras, sentidos, palabras o cualquier otra cosas que puedas describir, dibujar o actuar? Y, ¿qué significado tiene esto ahora* *tras haber migrado, en relación con tu cultura (y no con la cultura de la palabra al otro lado de la frontera en el Inglés? ¿Qué aprendizajes sacas de ésto que te sean útiles para tu práctica de MFT en tu Espanglish, Tex Mex, Pocho, etc.).* These conversations in supervision alert supervisees to the importance of assuring entrance of both languages in their therapeutic conversations as well as the bridging between both to engage in an experience of reinventing families' responses to their sufferings given that nonsuffering in English is not the same as it is in Spanish.

By comparing differences between the versions of their reflections in their Englishes and Spanishes, it is possible to discern the possibilities that bilinguality offers to coin a polyphony of MFT contextual meanings that did not exist before; we have learned that "bilingual wit has the particular virtue of attesting to the kind of intelligence that invents relationships where there had been none" (Sommer, 1999, p. 95). Our Eurocentric MFT learnings become unhinged of their English meanings where they rightfully belong, to twist their intentions for their renewal, playfully, with our flavors, rhythms, sounds, tastes, and accents that often bring us to laughter and even hilarity at times, even, or more so, when addressing our sufferings and the ones of the families we serve. We make mischief with meaning; laughter, wholeheartedly agreeing with Sommer (2004), makes us better citizens.

How to Listen: The Heart is in the Detail *¡Déjame y Te Cuento!*

Although bilinguals understand that what we say in one language is not the same as what we say in another, discerning *how* what we say in one language is not *how* we say it in the other requires a bit more supervisory assistance. The point of entrance to this distinction usually comes when discussing matters of rhetoric length. This shows up in consultations in a wide range of frustrations or puzzlements, at first when working with Spanglish-speaking families that "talk a lot," breathlessly, and sometimes seemingly without directly answering the question *después de un chorro de historias.* This sense of frustration frequently recruits the supervisee in a kind of game on how to skillfully and respectfully interrupt the family. Although certainly a useful skill to develop, if it is the only consideration, greater cultural and linguistic considerations may be missed. I am referring here to an additional kind of cultural and linguistic dislocation to vocabulary incommensurability. That is, the contextual qualities of how experience is culturally constituted in the particular, therefore, heterogeneously in each language whereby realities are languaged in their unique corresponding grammatically arranged paradigms.

We have established in our supervisory consultations that lengthy responses are not a matter of overinflated word count or punctuation failure. It is, rather, a matter of ontology. Commonly, realities come into existence in our Spanishes in tellings that are storied in the form of circular chronologies where time and space collapse into one distinction; dialogues of who said what that are conveyed in faithful transcriptions of conversational turns *"yo le dije…, y ella luego me dijo…, y entonces yo le respondí…y ella me respondió";* and very detailed and particular descriptions of events that can only be uttered if in tandem with their surroundings because they are part of what makes an experience an experience, including descriptions like the wood bench one is sitting on, the pedestrians passing by, the kinds of drinks, and the music played. Additionally, and quite distinctively, although not exclusively to Latin American oral traditions, non-human descriptions feature in our storytellings in an unquestionably mythic sort of way, for example, rocks utter messages and entitled trees stare us down. I have explored this last matter through a framework of magical realism in therapy elsewhere (polanco, 2010, 2016a).

When becoming attuned to the ontological matters of each language, frustration or puzzlement switches into curiosity about families' oral traditions, which brings to life that which a single Eurocentric, modern paradigm of the era of English MFT may not render available. Now we can resist the pressures of only listening from a place of homogeneity embedded in MFT Eurocentric values of concrete, behavioral, succinct, and measurable descriptions of experience that culturally may not be coherent with our borderland oral traditions.

Final Commentary: Join the Polylingual Symphony; *Vamos* MFT!

Rather than problematizing bilinguality in MFT supervision as something that needs to be overcome, the time has come to problematize instead the academic MFT systems that we bilinguals have had to overcome when our bilinguality is discarded to the periphery at the bottom of the program's budget and accrediting curricular plans, if at all. Bilingual trainees have had to leave our Spanishes in the periphery of Eurocentric, English MFT training. Furthermore, we are called to the center to provide services in Spanish to Spanish-speaking families when we are needed or when monolinguals need us to serve them as translators. Yet, we receive no training whatsoever to do so, or receive the support of bilingual supervisors who lack as much appropriate training as ourselves. Hence, bilingual supervisees are asked to sort out on our own what is instead a highly cultural and linguistic complex task, as I hope to have articulated here, in matters of seconds at the very moment the therapy session starts. This is, ethically, concerning to me.

Without question, it is a critical time for linguistic diversity in MFT given the increase of highly polylingual contexts in the U.S. that dizzy the hegemony of monolingual English. Therefore, what has gradually become an ordinary phenomenon requires with great urgency extraordinary ethical attention, which— with very few exceptions *que se pueden contar con los dedos de una mano*—has not been given properly, sufficiently, and seriously to the extent required. The ordinary phenomenon: the increase of family therapy trainees in the U.S. who traffic life at the borderlands between their Latin American-infused Spanish*es* and their U.S. English*es*, in this case. The extraordinary considerations: the match or rather integrity between the Spanish*es* spoken by the family served; by the family therapist trainee who delivers the service; by the supervisor who supervises the encounter between the former two; and by an MFT bilingual training curriculum that incorporates, seriously and rigorously, the theoretical and practical foundations that support the cultural-linguistic interconnections between the former three. Throughout my experience training bilingual MFTs, I have come to learn that the stakes are high if any of the above linguistic extra-ordinary considerations are put under the rug *o si nos hacemos lxs locxs* for whatever institutional reasons that may be, for example, political, budgetary, or otherwise. It is not only an academic but a social and an ethical responsibility.

Marriage and Family Therapists are well versed in the notion of language being the milieu where our identities, relationships, and worldviews are constituted. This has oriented us to promote the rights of families to have access to services in their preferred languages. It has not taken us quite yet to promote the rights of bilingual trainees to receive an education that contributes to our own cultural understanding of our languages, which will help us better support the rights of families' access to services of care. Hence, bilinguals stand for services that protect the rights of communities we serve while being asked to compromise our own by not having been given an education that contributes to our own understanding of the prestige of our borderland-languaged lives and worlds. I can only hope MFT programs proceed to join the symphony.

Note

1 To learn more about the PSSSP and its development, the reader can read Biever, Gómez, González & Patrizio (2011) and Biever & Santos (2016). These authors document their task of developing what became the first rigorous official bilingual training graduate certificate in the U.S. for family therapists and counseling psychologists in San Antonio and Houston, Texas. Interestingly enough, this certificate was developed 20 years ago by euroamerican monolinguals, Joan Biever, Glenn Gardner, and Monte Bobele, who took their time to listen to the experiences of bilingual trainees and investigated beyond their monolinguality into the complex cultural and linguistic nuances of bilingualism of trainees and local families they were serving to take action, engaging ongoing institutional support to develop the certificate.

References

Anzaldúa, G. (1987). *Borderlands-La frontera: The new mestiza* (2nd ed.). San Francisco, CA: Spinsters/Aunt Lute.

Biever, J., Gómez, J. P., González, C. G., & Patrizio, N. (2011). Psychological services to Spanish-speaking populations: A model curriculum for training competent professionals. *Training and Education in Professional Psychology, 5*(2), 81–87.

Biever J. L., & Santos J. C. (2016). Ofreciendo terapia en el idioma de preferencia del cliente: El modelo de preparacion profesional calificada en dos idiomas de OLLU.

In L. L. Charlés & G. Samarasinghe (Eds.), *Family therapy in global humanitarian contexts* (pp. 51–64). New York, NY: Springer Briefs Series.

Cooper Stein, K., Wright, J., Gil, E., Miness, A. & Ginanto, D. (2018). Examining Latina/o students' experiences of injustice: LatCrit insights from a Texas high school. *Journal of Latinos and Education, 17*(2), 103–120.

Escobar, A. (2007). *La invención del tercer mundo: La construcción y deconstrucción del desarrollo.* Caracas, Venezuela: La Fundación Editorial el perro y la rana.

García Márquez, G. (2014). *Entrevista sobre la gramática.* Retrieved from https://ciudadseva. com/texto/entrevista-sobre-la-gramatica/

Mignolo, W. D. (2005/2012). *La idea de América Latina: La herida colonial y la opción decolonial* (S. Jawerbaum & J. Barba, Trans.). Barcelona, Spain: Editorial Gedisa. (Original work published 2005).

Mizumura, M. (2015). *The fall of language in the age of English.* New York, NY: Columbia University Press.

Platt, J., & Natrajan-Tyagi, R. (2014). Preparing global-minded systemic supervisees for an international context. In T. C. Todd & C. L. Storm (Eds.), *The complete systemic supervisor: Context, philosophy, and pragmatics* (2nd ed., pp. 61–84). New York, NY: John Wiley & Sons.

polanco, m. (2010). Rethinking narrative therapy: An examination of bilingualism and magical realism. *Journal of Systemic Therapies, 29*(2), 1–14.

polanco, m. (2011). Autoethnographic means to the end of a decolonizing translation. *Journal of Systemic Therapies: Special Edition, 30*(3), 73–87.

polanco, m. (2016a). Language justice: Narrative therapy on the fringes of Colombian magical realism. *International Journal of Narrative Therapy and Community Work, 3*, 68–76.

polanco, m. (2016b). Knowledge fair trade. In L. Charlés & G. Samarasinghe (Eds.), *Family therapy in global humanitarian contexts: Voices and issues from the field* (pp. 13–26). New York, NY: Springer Briefs Series.

Quijano, A. (1992). Colonialidad y modernidad/racionalidad. *Perú Indígena, 13*(29), 11–20.

Sommer, D. (1999). *Proceed with caution, when engaging by minority writing.* Cambridge, MA: Harvard University Press.

Sommer, D. (2003). *Bilingual games: Some literary investigations.* New York, NY: Macmillan.

Sommer, D. (2004). *Bilingual aesthetics: A new sentimental education.* Durham, NC: Duke University Press.

Tymockzo, M. (2010). Translation, resistance, activism: An overview. In M. Tymockzo (Ed.), *Translation, resistance, activism* (pp. 1–22). Amherst, MA: University of Massachusetts Press.

2

FROM CRIME AND PUNISHMENT TO EMPATHY AND ACCEPTANCE

Family Therapy Training and Supervision with Turkish Juvenile Probation Officers

Gizem Erdem

"You are being called from the Attorney General's Office of the Turkish Republic. Please hold while we transfer you to the Office of External Affairs of the Probation and Parole" said the mechanic voice on the phone. I waited in confusion. It felt like a really long wait.

My mind was full of questions. *Am I being sued? Are they going to ask me to testify for a case? Is there something missing in my resettlement documents?* I had just moved from the United States to Turkey, following nine years of graduate education and post-doc work in the Midwest. It was a transition and an acculturation process in progress. I was now an assistant professor of psychology, teaching couple and family therapy, doing research with substance abusing adolescents and their families.

> Professor Erdem, we are a team working on improving probation services and we arrange trainings for our staff. We need your guidance in youth substance abuse and juvenile delinquency. We heard you are also a family therapist. We really want to provide the best service we can for the youth and we hope you can give us trainings.

He was speaking with such enthusiasm and excitement that it was unreal. He sounded like he found the secret remedy for all problems in the world of probation and it was called *family therapy!*

This is how our story began.

In the past three years, my colleagues and I at Koç University have given trainings and supervision to probation officers in Istanbul as well as in other cities of Turkey. We work in collaboration with the Turkish Ministry of Justice through which we recruit, inform, train, and support the officers. It has been both a challenging and an inspiring journey for me to translate sacred models of the US-based family systems therapy to the Turkish Probation system. How do you explain concepts of "an identified patient" or "triangulation" to a probation officer who deeply believes these youth and/or families are untreatable? How do you motivate officers when families shut doors to their faces and will not let them in for a family visit? How do you engage a father to attend a family counseling session in a context where parenting is perceived as a solely "feminine" task?

This is how our story evolved.... But before we dive into this, let me tell you the story of the probation system in Turkey.

Probation and Parole in Turkey: Background and Current Characteristics

Probation refers to a correctional practice where convicted criminal defendants serve their sentences in the community rather than jail. Probation practices incorporate supervision of the offender along with case management and rehabilitative services (Phelps, 2013). Probation was implemented in Turkey in 2005 as an urgent remedy to the skyrocketing numbers in the prison population around the country (Işık, 2016; Kamer, 2008). Although probation eased the pressure from the prison system, the rehabilitation services offered in the probation system have been too limited to be a true alternative to incarceration (Kamer, 2008). This dilemma puts the probation system in limbo, and the probation officers in Turkey acutely feel the sense of ongoing role conflict; they report feeling confused over their roles in rehabilitation as opposed to law enforcement (Erdem, Tuncer, Safi, Çankaya, Ergin, & Aydoğan, 2018).

The Turkish Ministry of Justice (2017) estimated that adult cases under probationary supervision reached almost half a million within a decade. By contrast, juvenile offenders are estimated at 12,133 and there is currently no separate juvenile probation system.[1] Probation officers often work heavily with adult offenders and have limited time and resources to address the unique needs of the juvenile delinquents. They also do not receive much specialized training in adolescent development, risk behavior, or evidence-based practices geared specifically for adolescents and their families (Erdem et al., 2018).

Experiences of Youth, Families, and Officers in the Probation System

In the past three years, we have run several studies with juvenile offenders and their families as well as probation officers, directors, and prosecutors to assess juveniles' needs and experiences (Erdem et al., 2018; Erdem, Tuncer, Çankaya, & Ergin, 2016; Tuncer, Erdem, & de Ruiter, 2018a, 2018b). Our research revealed that what mattered most for youth was probation officers' attitude and approach. If officers were open to understanding youths' needs and built alliances and trust, youth were more motivated to participate in substance abuse treatment or other rehabilitative services. The parents, on the other hand, raised concerns over being stigmatized once their youth was involved in the criminal justice system and were reluctant to seek any rehabilitative services. They felt blamed or judged for not being "good enough parents" and were worried about their reputations in their communities if they attended any meetings. There were also barriers around accessibility of the bureau because low-income parents could not afford transportation and/or were working during office hours and did not have the option to have leave from work to attend meetings with probation officers.

Similarly, probation officers and directors in focus groups complained about the reluctance of families, but also emphasized the unintended harmful consequences of families' resistance. Parents, as legal guardians of minor offenders, are legally obligated to attend at least one meeting with the POs at the institution. After the first missed appointment, a youth and his/her family receive an official warning, but the second missed appointment counts as a violation of probation and the youth's case is reevaluated, which may result in the youth being sent to juvenile prison. Therefore, there is an ongoing dance between youth, families, and the probation officers with one step forward and another one backward, each actor keeping its distance from the other because of fears, worries, shame, anger, and sometimes hopelessness.

Moving Toward a Family-Centered Rehabilitative Approach

Clearly, the punitive-oriented probation system neither works well to engage families nor keeps the youth motivated to be involved in substance abuse intervention groups. The key here is to connect families and officers around a common goal and an overarching theme. In the context of probation, the common theme becomes a collaboration of the parties for rehabilitation of the youth and promotion of his/her well-being through building trust and alliance.

The story of our project unfolds here: the family becomes a targeted system for an intervention through which we advocate for acceptance of the youth and transform the meaning of his/her conviction of "crime" to a relational process. In that way, our goal is to shift focus from the "delinquent youth" (actor) to the "dysfunctional reactions to family distress" (actions). The first offense of the youth indicates an underlying unresolved issue in the family system (in other words, a presenting symptom) and the youth involved in crime is the symptom carrier. This line of systemic thinking immediately moves us toward a non-blaming and non-labeling language/perspective of the youth and the family as a whole.

More importantly, we use the power of relationships to facilitate youth's rehabilitation process. We wanted youth and families to be engaged in rehabilitation services through their connection to the probation officers, rather than the fear of violation of parole/probation and its consequences.

The idea of building alliances and mutual trust to engage clients in therapy is not new to us as psychotherapists, but it is tremendously difficult for officers who are overwhelmed with an increasing caseload, dealing with repetitive experienced adult offenders, and having no training in systemic therapeutic interventions. Officers typically have little hope for the system-involved youth. Teaching officers *how to steal hearts of young offenders and their families, rather than punishing, blaming, and shutting hearts down* is the part that is most challenging and fruitful for supervising family therapy in the probation setting.

The ÇAM Project

Stealing hearts came up as part of a larger intervention that integrated coaching, individual and group sessions, recreational activities, home-based family therapy, and an establishment of a center for youth and their families. Engaging families in the rehabilitation process via mobile teams and home visits was the novel contribution of the project to the already existing probation practices. The project was funded by the Istanbul Foundation Agency and was implemented from 2016 to 2017. The "ÇAM" acronym refers to "*Çocuk ve Aile Merkezi*" (Center for Children and Families) and also means *pine tree* in Turkish. Because the pine tree is resilient to harsh weather conditions and requires minimal effort to continue growing in different climates, the name symbolizes the capabilities and competence of crime-involved youth and their families and their ability to bounce back from stressful life events and conditions. The newly established center served youth ages 14 to 29 and included individual meeting rooms, seminar rooms, a library, and youth-friendly spaces for indoor activities. Overall, the project reached 180 youth and families in its first year and the center continues to operate under the Istanbul Bureau of Probation even after the funding ended. I was involved in the substance abuse treatment and family therapy training/ supervision parts of the project.

A Case Illustration of Supervision

Following two full days of training,[2] probation officers made family visits in mobile teams of two staff, consisting of a probation officer and a case manager. Given families' worries over being shamed and exposed in the neighborhood, we made an extra effort to make the vehicles anonymous (free of Ministry of Justice logos).

I had supervision sessions with teams as follow up to their training; we met in groups of six probation officers and discussed cases. In an attempt to illustrate our supervision work, here is a case example compiled of several different cases of youth in probation.

Ayşe was a 28-year-old woman working as a probation officer for four years. She firmly believed in the value of rehabilitative probation practices. She had been to several clinical workshops to advance her skills and she was motivated and curious to learn more. During the training, she was outspoken and assertive.

She came with questions and participated in the case formulations and role-play exercises.

From a family systems perspective, our client is the relationship, not the individuals. Hence, I was observing relationships of the probation officers with one another and also with me during the trainings. My observations gave me a sense of a relational pattern of each officer, which referred to one's role in significant relationships and associated ways of interacting with significant others through which one builds, maintains (or breaks), and fosters relationships. I thought once I identified a relational pattern of an officer, I was more informed to predict challenges they may face later in their work with youth in probation.

Although Ayşe was very competent in both academic and social skills, she was pushing too hard to earn admiration and acceptance in the group (and from me), which, in turn, created tension among colleagues and an unnamed hierarchy (as if "she is the most educated one, others are not"). This tension triggered a higher need to belong in Ayşe, and an urge to break the distance with others. It was a perfect example of circular causality; the more she pushed for acceptance and admiration, the more her colleagues felt looked down upon and pushed back. The more her colleagues distanced, the more she pursued them, and the cycle continued.

As a supervisor, I saw her role as the overachiever and a golden child. She was diligently saving other officers from the responsibility of participating in discussions and role plays and she was the first one speaking up while others were shy. It served a function to keep the training going and all officers complied with that pattern. Some colleagues were, in a way, proud to have such a member in the group—a systemic process similar to the families where they are proud to have an overachiever. If a member is too hardworking, the others have some space to do less. But for some officers, that process made them feel constrained; they felt they did not have the option of *becoming* hardworking—that role was taken from them.

These interactions early in the training signal patterns that may occur later in family visits as well as supervision sessions. In the sessions, Ayşe, as expected, struggled with joining with the families. Ironically, the family felt pressured and pursued (a similar process to the experience of the colleagues in the trainings) and the youth felt he had to balance the relationship between the family and the officer (similar to the triangulation process that I experienced as a trainer). Ayşe also found herself in the "hero trap": she wanted to fix everything and address all issues.

Ayşe was well-prepared prior to the supervision. She brought in all the paperwork, her notes on the case, and her training slides. She was working with a 16-year-old adolescent, Ahmet, who was sentenced to probation due to committing drug offenses and theft. It was his first offense and Ayşe deeply believed that he could be "saved" from repeated criminal behavior. Ahmet presented issues of substance abuse and his drug of choice was Spice. He was living with his family in a slum at the outskirts of Istanbul and his father was unemployed. His older brother was in a boarding school in another city and was continuing his education on financial scholarships. Ahmet also had three younger siblings. Ayşe gathered all that information through individual interviews with Ahmet. When she went for a home visit, the door was shut in her face. She felt locked out, disappointed, and crushed. "I am different," she said; "I don't understand why they do not trust me; I am one of the idealistic officers." Ahmet tried to convince his family to meet Ayşe because it was mandatory, but they declined. Both parents were very angry at Ahmet and felt violated by the officer.

In the eyes of the family, Ayşe was not a motivated idealistic helper, nor was she their ally. They perceived Ayşe simply as another representative of the state, an officer, and a symbol of institutional punishment. Her presence reminded them of the crime their son committed and all issues related to those crimes: poverty, discrimination, substance abuse, and safety issues in the neighborhood. It was painful to face all of that. They were struggling in their own lives and they did not want an outsider to tell them what to do, so they pushed back as much as they could.

In supervision, we talked about Ayşe's struggles to engage the family and discussed how she could *steal* their hearts.

Ayşe: I don't understand. I did everything right. I was nonjudgmental, I gave them a call to confirm my visit, I was polite and professional. I even had Ahmet help me out.

Supervisor: You really want to help them and fix everything they are going through. If you do things right, you feel it will go well for everyone.

Ayşe: Yeah, I do! But, to be honest, I want to help the kid most. They are adults and they can take care of themselves, but Ahmet is only 16 years old; there is a life ahead of him.

Supervisor: You have done a good job in building an alliance with Ahmet. He trusts you and participates in his meetings regularly. I wonder how his parents feel about your relationship with him?

Ayşe: I don't know... Ahmet told me several times that his parents are always angry at him. I don't think they know anything about the probation process at all.

Supervisor: Sometimes family members present as angry because they want to protect their boundaries and their integrity. Under that anger there may be years of pain, hurt, and disappointment.

Ayşe: I think they are just selfish and live in their own shell!

Supervisor: It looks like their shell is hard to break in; it may have taken years to build it—and it is hard to trust anyone to risk being broken again. Maybe someone broke that shell earlier and they do not want to let it happen again.

Ayşe: But I am trustworthy!

Supervisor: Then, how can you get them to believe that trust can grow between you two?

In this segment, we can sense in Ayşe's language that she was building a coalition with the adolescent, Ahmet, against the parents. She had built an empathic understanding of Ahmet's situation. He was isolated and scapegoated in the family. Ayşe wanted to relabel Ahmet's role in the family and reframe his actions, but the family was resistant to even meet her. They felt pressured and looked down on. Through a series of relational questions and reframes, I worked with Ayşe to understand the family's process and the true meaning of their "resistance." Every time she talked about family members as actors, I changed the topic to actions and focused the conversation on relational patterns, dynamics, and emotions.

The more we talked about the case, the more we unfolded the emergence of "crime," "deviance," and "substance abuse" in the system. When Ahmet's older brother left home for the boarding school, Ahmet became the eldest child (and a son!) in the household. It was also around the same time his dad was fired from his job. This was not only a family struggling with poverty; it was also a system where there were traditional gender roles and expectations about the financial responsibilities of men to take charge and provide for the family. Men in that family had to be strong and not show any vulnerability. Emotional distance between son and father was a way of making sure there was a sense of authority, hierarchy, and power. All those family processes (eldest son moving, financial stress, traditional gender role expectations, and distant son-father relationships) created anxiety in the system. From a systemic perspective, one way of dealing with that anxiety was to bring in a third actor to balance all relationships (triangulation). Necmi, Ahmet's paternal uncle, became more involved in the family and regulated the relationship between Ahmet and his father. Necmi became a role model and a mentor for Ahmet and financial and emotional support for the parents. The whole process was congruent with traditional gender roles because Necmi was a brother of the father and it was acceptable.

Nevertheless, several issues emerged from that triangulation process. Over time, the parents became uneasy with Ahmet's getting too involved with Necmi and his lifestyle. Necmi was dealing drugs in the neighborhood and Ahmet was hanging out with him all the time. Ahmet's parents blamed Necmi for taking advantage of Ahmet to deal drugs. Because Ahmet was a minor, he was less likely to be convicted of drug offenses and his parents were worried about his future. When the parents found out Ahmet was arrested due to theft and drug possession, they cut ties with Necmi, called him the "poisonous blood," and set a strict curfew for Ahmet to stay home in parental supervision. Having lost his mentor and role model, Ahmet rebelled and started to run away from home and violate rules. His father perceived Ahmet's reactions as a violation of trust and a sign of allying with Necmi. "You are taking his side, so you are also poisonous blood!" he said. Ahmet's mother stayed quiet and Necmi did not accept Ahmet in his house. Ahmet felt he did not belong anywhere.

While we were working on a systemic case conceptualization in the supervision, Ayşe thought the real actor to blame in this story was Ahmet's paternal uncle:

Ayşe: Necmi is the real deal here, he is a drug dealer and obviously has a bad influence on Ahmet. I am making sure that Ahmet does not have any contact with him. The parents also did not do their best to intervene; they should have protected Ahmet. I will refer them for psychoeducation groups for parenting skills.

In this segment, we see Ayşe was blaming Necmi for all of Ahmet's troubles and wanted to maneuver the situation by taking charge. This is problematic on multiple levels. On one hand, one goal of probation is deterrence and prevention of future crime. It is crucial that an adolescent understand the consequences of his/her criminal behavior as well as its effects on others (and the public) and takes accountability and responsibility for what s/he has done. On the other hand, responsibility comes with an opportunity for growth. Probation officers need to work with youth to identify their needs for further resources to prevent future crime.

For Ahmet, crime emerged as a way of connecting with his uncle; it was a shared experience that made him feel connected to a family member. Although crime was dysfunctional and harmful, it had an emotional and a relational meaning for Ahmet. All attempts to cut ties with his uncle, therefore, were in vain. Instead, we focused on treatment planning to engage the family and conduct sessions to restore and heal family relationships, especially the one between the father and the son. Once their relationship was closer, they would neither need a third party (Necmi) to regulate their emotions nor would Ahmet engage in deviant groups or behaviors to fulfill the need to belong.

One potential way of engaging that family was addressing the feelings of *guilt*. The parents let Necmi in their system and it had unexpected harmful consequences for Ahmet. Another process was *feelings of betrayal* and *violation of trust*. The parents, especially the father, felt Necmi took advantage of their situation and felt betrayed in a time they needed support as a family. They also felt betrayed when Ahmet wanted to stay in touch with Necmi. They were heartbroken and disappointed. Ahmet, on the other hand, felt he did not belong and was marginalized in his family as "poisonous blood." He thought there was something wrong with him and felt guilty for being the "bad one."

In supervision, we identified those relational themes in the family and came up with strategies to address them. Promoting hope and empowerment and addressing their crucial roles as parents were key to engage both parents in therapy. When Ayşe went to their door, she said "You are important for Ahmet, you all mean so much to him. I am here to support you to listen to each other, that is all. You let me in when you are ready." And she waited.

When the door was opened half way through, she knew it was on! Ayşe engaged the father through her nonblaming stance and acknowledgment of his efforts: "You have done so much for this family. There were times it worked, there were times it did not, but you survived and kept it all together as a family." Once

Ayşe started thinking systemically, she gave up on finding someone to blame in the family. Instead, she focused on the guilt, disappointment, and the need to connect with others.

In fact, all family members wanted to be accepted as they were but it was difficult to say it. We reframed the "poisonous blood" that runs among men in the family: "It looks like deep down you feel what connects you all (you, your son, your brother) is your blood. Blood is vital for your survival; therefore, it hurts so much if it runs bad because they are part of you and you are part of them."

This is how we connected them...

Conclusion

Ayşe gained insight through the supervision meetings and realized it was impossible to solve all the problems of the family or create any miracles. She was not a hero, a saver, or a fixer. Instead, she realized she could work with the family to reconnect them emotionally, to rebuild their trust with one another so that they survive in the context of adversity by supporting each other. There was still hope and she did not have to be an overachiever to promote it.

Ayşe's journey implies a story of supervision and family therapy training in the context of probation in Turkey. Family meetings in the probation system are non-traditional in nature by default; the process in probation is extremely brief. In the ÇAM project, officers had only three home-based meetings with the youth and their family members, and an additional 3–12 individual meetings with the youth. The brevity of the family intervention undeniably forces the officers to join with the family, do a systemic and relational assessment, and implement brief interventions right away. Therefore, my training and supervision goal was to provide systemic toolkits for officers to utilize in those meetings so they could rely on engagement strategies and interventions. There was little room for self-of-therapist issues, self-care of the officers, or any issues related to the treatment planning and termination process. The goal was to use three family sessions as efficiently as possible and refer families to services if needed. In that manner, we can consider family therapy in the probation setting as a brief targeted intervention for low to moderate risk families and a triage system for high risk families who are in need of more comprehensive services. The brevity of the intervention and constraints of the probation practices do not negate the fact that we can still *plant a seed* in the family system. A relational reframe may not change the view of the adolescent completely in the eyes of the family members all of a sudden, but it is a targeted intervention to shift the way the system operates in the future.

Despite cultural differences[3] and our perspectives on youth rehabilitation, there also are universal aspects of relationships that we can work with. We all have the need to belong, trust, and build meaningful relationships—we want to love and be loved. The beauty of family therapy is to collect broken pieces of hearts of family members and heal them through hope, connection, loyalty, trust, acknowledgment, and empathy.

At the end of the day, it is relationships that heal or break us.

Acknowledgments

I would like to sincerely thank my collaborators Esra Tuncer, Rengin Işık, and Dinçer Kocalar, and probation officer Ramazan Aydoğan for their enthusiasm to organize those comprehensive trainings, and the Ministry of Justice and Istanbul Agency of Development for their financial support. I applaud probation officers for their interest in learning new skills and advocating for the rehabilitation of juvenile delinquents.

Notes

1 Although there is a well-established juvenile court, juvenile police, juvenile prosecutor, and advocacy system for minor offenders with separate legislation and law enforcement systems, there is no juvenile probation system in Turkey. Juvenile delinquents meet the same probation officers in the same governmental buildings as adults. There is an ongoing discussion on structurally separating the juvenile probation system, but it has not been implemented.
2 The training included five modules focusing on adolescent development, risk behavior and substance abuse, family systems theory, family interviewing skills, and systemic intervention skills. The training was experiential in nature with small group activities, role plays, and case conceptualization examples.
3 The early family therapy models were based in the US context, taking for granted that parenting is a dyadic process between both parents (e.g., Structural Family Therapy) or that differentiation is key for healthy family processes (i.e., Bowen Family Systems Therapy). In Turkey, family is centered around children and their well-being, parenting tasks are defined strictly within traditional gender roles, and growing children have to balance connectedness and separateness. Therefore, it becomes vital to be loyal to the systemic framework but also to tailor it to meet the cultural norms and expectations.

References

Erdem, G., Tuncer, A. E., Safi, O. A., Çankaya, B., Ergin, M., & Aydoğan, R. (2018). The professional experiences and training needs of probation officers in Turkey. *Journal of Social Work, 0*(0), 1–23. doi: 10.1177/1468017318768181
Erdem, G., Tuncer, E., Çankaya, B., & Ergin, M. (2016). *Program evaluation of a psychoeducational program targeting officers at Istanbul Bureau of Probation and Parole.* Paper presented at the National Addiction Convention, Antalya, Turkey. (in Turkish, İstanbul Denetimli Serbestlik memurlarına yönelik geliştirilen eğitim programının etki değerlendirmesi).
Işık, E. (2016). Türkiye'de denetimli serbestlik uygulamaları. In *Türkiye'de denetimli serbestlik 10. yıl uluslararası sempozyumu bildiri kitabı* (pp. 3–7). Istanbul, Turkey: Adalet Bakanlığı Ceza ve Tevkifevleri Genel Müdürlüğü.
Kamer, V. K. (2008). Ceza adalet ve infaz sistemi içinde denetimli serbestlik sisteminin önemi. *Adalet Dergisi, 31*, 69–80.

Phelps, M. S. (2013). The paradox of probation: Community supervision in the age of mass incarceration. *Law & Policy, 35*, 51–80. doi: 10.1111/lapo.12002

Tuncer, A. E., Erdem, G., de Ruiter, C., & Çankaya, B. (2018a). *Attitudes toward probationers and organizational trust as predictors of burnout among Turkish probation officers*. Turku, Finland: European Association of Psychology and Law Annual Conference.

Tuncer, A. E., Erdem, G., & de Ruiter, C. (2018b). *The impact of an RNR-based intervention training program on Turkish juvenile probation officers' role orientations and recidivism risk perceptions*. European Association of Psychology and Law Annual Conference, Turku, Finland.

Turkish Ministry of Justice (2017). 2017 yılı haziran ayı istatistikleri. Retrieved from http://www.cte-ds.adalet.gov.tr/istatistik/2017/haziran_2017.pdf

3

A STRENGTHS-BASED TEAM APPROACH TO HOLISTIC WELLNESS

Using Live Supervision to Expand the Boundaries of Traditional Mental Health

Chrystal Fullen and Brittany Houston

Chrystal (CF): As a psychology doctoral student, supervision was undoubtedly the most influential component in my training. My experiences in supervisory relationships encouraged my personal and professional growth. I learned many lessons during live supervision through my interactions with clients as well in my conversations about supervision. Later in my degree program, my supervision of other trainees reinforced my belief in the strengths-based approach to supervision and the need for flexibility when adopting a model of supervision. One of the more impactful lessons that continues to guide my practice is the knowledge that clients' problems are not limited to mental health concerns: they are exacerbated by other health and systemic factors. This chapter is my first experience in discovering how to integrate holistic approaches in mental health treatment.

Brittany (BH): Similar to Chrystal's experience, the supervision experience as the supervisee and later as a supervisor was a crucial component of my professional development. In my time as a master's student, I learned which supervision styles promoted my growth and which did not. Experiencing both positive and negative styles reinforced my belief in appropriate scaffolding, collaboration, and a strength-based perspective. Additionally, the uniqueness of live supervision amplified my confidence as a beginning therapist through the support of my supervisor and colleagues. Much of my own experiences have influenced the way that I approach and engage supervisees in supervision as a doctoral student. When reflecting upon the case example in this chapter, it reminds me to encourage the integration of client systems into my own and my supervisees' considerations for interventions in total wellness. When reviewing how initially foreign the ideas in this case were to me, I'm reminded of the importance of promoting the biopsychosocial model and the impact of social determinants of mental and physical health in client care.

A Strengths-Based Approach

Our counseling psychology program was developed with strengths-based and systemic emphasis. The strengths-based model inspired a unique stance to our interactions with professors, peers, and clients. As psychologists-in-training inside the therapy room and as co-supervisors observing from outside the therapy room, we adopted this model wholeheartedly after experiencing its positive effects in our own training and development. This model focused on the resilience, adaptability, and inherent assets we see in our clients. Similarly, these are the features we, as co-supervisors, intend to amplify and highlight in our supervisees. As supervisees, these are the interactions that built our confidence in the therapy room and nurtured our own intuition as practitioners. The strengths-based perspective invites supervisors and supervisees to co-create an environment in which strengths can be shared, observed, and learned from one another.

Our counseling psychology program provided both master's and doctoral students with a live supervision model at a university training clinic that offers therapy services to the local community. The clinic serves a predominantly lower-income minority population seeking services for a wide range of difficulties. The spirit and culture located within the walls of this little clinic attached to a local doctor's office is derived from the people we serve. We trained at the clinic for five years as clinicians at the time of the case we present in this chapter; we had also just begun our training as supervisors. In the case we present below, we illustrate how our teamwork unfolded, while our supervisor in the team encouraged our experience as both team members and supervisors in training.

Therapy Teams

The program adopted a team approach to our training. Each team had four to six students, all varying in levels of training (master's, doctoral, first-year master's, second-year master's, and so forth). The variety of training levels in each team was a phenomenal approach to encourage learning from each other. Conversations in these teams took on multiple important topics including professional development, case conceptualization, systemic factors, and good old-fashioned brainstorming. Clients who attended the clinic for services signed informed consent forms that explained our approach to services and training. Our clinic provided modern-day behind-the-mirror live supervision for students. Each therapy room was equipped with video and sound recording, which would be displayed in a separate team room. The teams met in those rooms and were provided with opportunities to observe their fellow team members in session and to consider what they would do or not do if they were in the room.

The session structure included a mid-session break where, at 30–40 minutes into the session, the co-therapists would return to the therapy room to consult with their team and supervisor. This model provided a check-in for the co-therapists to share their conceptualization of the case and discuss next steps. Additionally, in the spirit of our strengths-based approach, teams would discuss both co-therapists' and client/s' strengths and provide this feedback during the mid-session consultation. Clients were made aware of this approach and often enjoyed the feedback from the multiple perspectives on the team that the co-therapists took back to them when returning to the therapy room for the remainder of the therapy hour.

Different teams had different training focuses such as bilingual therapy services, single-session/walk-in services, and psychological assessment. We liked to think that our team used advanced therapeutic techniques because our supervisor at the time always encouraged us to "think outside the box," applying our collective knowledge in sessions, and embracing the strengths-based perspective to our communication with each other and our clients. We strived to think outside the four walls of the "boxy" therapy room and bring in strengths, knowledge, and ideas that did not happen in the context of therapy. Reaching beyond the borders of psychology, we brought in perspectives from other disciplines (e.g., art, technology, nutrition).

Our team adopted the practice of joining the client in the therapy room to inspire client self-efficacy and promote mastery. Further, this approach ensured we brought our personalities into the room and promoted genuineness and the integration of personal and professional identities. No topic was taboo. Our supervisor encouraged an environment where we would respect self-disclosure and provide one another with respectful feedback and confidentiality. The rule was to always respect first and we built a relationship as a team by creating an environment that was inclusive. We asked each other the questions we asked our clients. We discussed how culture and our personal histories influenced our thinking when talking about cases. We discussed our supervision model, what we needed individually from our supervisor and each other, and how we would honor all opinions within our team room. These conversations created a relationship built on our genuine interactions and support of one another.

In these teams, people may wonder about favoritism or the competitive nature inherent in some doctoral programs. However, our openness redirected us into the roles of supporters of one another. Each case belonged not to the co-therapists in the room but each member of our team as we worked together to brainstorm for our clients. Our supervisor modeled this behavior and we began to model it ourselves. We shared not only our ideas about cases but our anxieties in the room, local political climates, culture, and how to navigate it all. We were ourselves who just happened to also be therapists and supervisors. This made for many teaching moments, professional and personal growth, and profoundly simple yet empowering conversations with our clients and each other.

Graduating From Supervisee to Supervisor

Chrystal: Over a Fall semester in the clinic, Brittany and I were part of a therapy team that consisted of a group of four other training therapists in the master's program. As doctoral students, we were seen as co-supervisors by our supervisor, who encouraged us to consider ourselves in the same light. We had both completed our supervision requirements in the prior semester, which consisted of a 16-week long course in supervision. On this team, we were already thinking about how we would supervise certain scenarios and were encouraged by our supervisor to talk about these thoughts and share them with the team. Supervision is relational. As such, our team members' perspectives provided us with the exceptional opportunity to hear not only how another supervisor would respond to particular situations but how supervisees would like their supervisors to respond.

After building the confidence to share my thoughts on many past teams, I was comfortable talking to the team about my ideas, sharing when someone had a question, and engaging in occasional agreement to disagree. However, I had since graduated to a stage where I had to develop my confidence in answering questions as a supervisor. As a past supervisee, I had often held my supervisors' opinions in high regard. Sometimes, higher than those of other team members. In making the leap from supervisee to supervisor, I was very aware of the innate power differential between the two roles and understood how influential a supervisor's feedback can become to a trainee. The strengths-based approach helped guide my feedback, suggestions, and encouragement of autonomy and trusting my intuition in all the conversations I had with my fellow team members. I focused on always collaborating with my team, beginning first with encouraging individual growth, highlighting the suggestions made by the team, and creating a positive environment through modeling. As a supervisor, I now understood that it wasn't a team of six team members and one supervisor (as I had always thought about it) but rather a team of seven members, and it was this realization that I would share with my teams in the future.

Brittany: I found my comfort as a supervisee quickly because it was closely related to my experience as a college athlete. Live supervision mirrored the memories I had of playing center on the basketball court with the fans watching and my coach screaming on the sidelines to run a certain play. Of course, supervision was a less intense environment with fewer observers but higher stakes. I drew on my history of being present in the moment and trusting my next move, which was inherent on the court, to aid me inside and outside of the therapy room. However, I had never been a coach in my athletic career, so being a supervisor was not a natural transition.

I developed my supervisor identity by thinking about how I was one step removed from the "action" of therapy, much like my basketball coach was from having control of what the players did on the court. From here I began to understand my new role. My fear about having to know all the answers dissolved as I reminded myself of the team-based approach that I had been a part of for so many years. It was time for me to consider the players I had on my therapy team and support them in their goal of learning and providing effective client-centered care. I bounced back to my memories as a supervisee and began to think about the positive and negative experiences I had with my past supervisors. Upon this review, I incorporated what was helpful into my own supervision playbook. My past relationships as a supervisee as well as my therapist-client relationships shaped my supervision style. I adopted a model of supervision that was collaborative, curious, and strengths-based. Similarly, my therapeutic approach was client-centered, and I found that supervision worked best when it was supervisee-centered. Most importantly, my playbook became very helpful as long as it was written in pencil and ready to be adapted with each new team member and team.

Tips for Thinking-Outside-the-Box

When considering how to incorporate this outside-the-box perspective in our own supervision, we like to remember to always first encourage our supervisees to answer their own questions they bring to supervision or team discussions. Often, when consulting before a case or during a mid-session consultation break, supervisees have many questions for the team, which is always encouraged. Similarly, many questions are "saved" for the supervisor; sometimes, these questions are the ones that the supervisee is most concerned about. In my own (CF) experience, any question regarding ethics, legality, or a dialogistically tricky situation would be "saved" for my supervisor.

My (CF) best learning experiences as a supervisee were when I was encouraged to speak to the team about my thoughts on what I would do if my supervisor was not there. My own personal model of supervision is always to ask a supervisee their first thoughts when they ask a question then open the question to the team before sharing my thoughts. When sharing my thoughts, I like to promote this autonomy of thought by bridging ideas together, providing feedback on the ideas shared, and ultimately asking the supervisee to take what was offered and make a decision based on their relationship with the client and unique intuitive conceptualization of the case.

In many cases, ideas come up that therapists think they "can't" do; my first experience of this was in my (CF) first year in the master's program. I was curious about how intimacy was playing a role in influencing a couple's communication difficulties. I asked my supervisor how I could bring this up in session and was told that I could simply ask. However, the idea about directly asking clients about their sex lives seemed like a "can't do," so I immediately thought that I needed to approach it from a different way. Later in the program, we both (CF and BH) spoke openly of these types of lessons with our team members and focused on how much our program emphasized curiosity in our conversations with clients and with each other. Curiosity in the therapy room means, "just ask." In supervision, just ask. As a supervisor, just ask. Encouraging someone to share their own instinctive ideas builds confidence and sometimes, as in the case of Sara (described below), leads to unexpected positive outcomes. To think outside the box, we respectfully share all of our ideas and incorporate those ideas into suggestions and interventions to fit our clients.

"Just ask" is the perfect title of a supervision style that I (BH) would strive to achieve in my supervisory relationships. "Just ask" is a wonderful tool that tends to promote curiosity and growth. In my own experience as a supervisor, "just ask" expands beyond asking the initial question supervisees have in their heads. The question itself is derived from intuition and leads to greater clarity and conceptualization. I think it is important for my supervisees to ask the question, and also ask themselves where that question comes from, when that curiosity was spiked, how it will aid them in therapy, and what made them hesitant to ask the question. Further reflection on the supervisees' curiosities inspires critical thinking and purposeful therapeutic interventions.

Finally, just as our clients have goals, so do we in our journey to become licensed psychologists. Our interest in challenging ourselves guided our intention to think as co-supervisors. It encouraged us to put anxieties aside and to ask our team members for feedback on our considerations and suggestions as co-supervisors. This interest in challenging ourselves was contagious for the team. Talking about our overall professional goals for the semester and specific goals for each case promoted conversations and a collaboration among the team members. Although we always talk about these goals with supervisees, making it an ongoing conversation created action. We would ask each other, "how can you get a step closer to your goal while observing this session?" Or, "how can you get closer to your goal for this semester with this client?" Team members reminded us of our goals, encouraged us to continue to challenge ourselves, and asked us to remind them to challenge themselves, too!

Integrating Holistic Wellness

Under the supervision of Dr. Charlés, we worked with Sara (name changed), a 36-year-old single, Hispanic woman. Her intake form listed her goal for therapy as help with managing her bipolar disorder. At her first appointment, while the team was behind the mirror, waiting to start, our supervisor asked, "why are we waiting?" We answered that Sara was still eating her breakfast, an Egg McMuffin, and we wanted to give her the opportunity to finish. Dr. Charlés suggested that since we were eating our breakfast and the client, hers, we might consider eating breakfast together as a different approach to traditional joining? Always up for a challenge, we (Brittany and Chrystal, who were team members but also supervisors-in-training at the time), joined her for breakfast and started discussing the age-old adage of why breakfast is the most important meal of the day. During our conversation, we learned that Sara's goal for therapy was related more to overwhelming anxiety regarding her upcoming bariatric surgery. She spoke about the impending lifestyle change, explaining that she was desperately trying to avoid foods such as her Egg McMuffin because she needed to lose 10% of her body weight or would forfeit the surgery. She explained that she had been making every effort to change the way that she eats but seemed to meet obstacles at every turn. Embracing our strengths-based perspective, we decided to celebrate her last bite and began to plan for the future together.

Sara's ideal future was 100-pounds lighter, exercising four times per week, eating healthier, and having the energy to play with her nephew. Taking a solution-focused approach, we asked Sara when she had been able to successfully lose weight in the past. Her face brightened as she shared how she had previously lost 20 pounds two years previously by portioning and weighing her food coupled with daily exercise. We created a new plan utilizing her previous success and information she had learned from her current nutritionist, to help her move in the direction of her goal.

When incorporating anything from another discipline, we have to be conscious of competency. In no way did our fellow team members nor our supervisor ever suggest that we had more training than our client's nutritionist. However, that did not mean we couldn't take what she knew and promote her and our own learning. As supervisors-in-training, Dr. Charlés encouraged us to speak with the team about how we could navigate this conversation of health with our client while still being respectful of her other providers. As a team, we discussed the importance of our individual general knowledge. Moving toward a biopsychosocial model, our team became larger than what was in our clinic. Our team now included Sara's nutritionist, doctor, family, and friends who had any influence on the journey toward her goals.

Thinking about our new team, we started to have conversations about where and how we fit in. We were not experts in Sara's life. We were not experts in nutrition. We were not experts in medicine. However, we did have expertise in assessing motivation, problem-solving, and promoting change. Understanding our role, we used information from Sara's resources to propel her toward her goals. Together we discussed what made her desired changes important, barriers to her goals, and past successes with her mental, physical, social, and spiritual health. These included suggestions from Sara to problem solve reduction in daily carbohydrates, incorporating smaller portion sizes, and avoiding high caloric drinks. In conversations behind the mirror and in the therapy room, where BH and CF were the therapists, we outlined Sara's network of medical providers with her and facilitated conversations about assertive communication between Sara and each of her medical providers to clarify her needs and questions about her health. Sara was completely on board—so much that she asked to meet the rest of the therapy team behind the mirror. The team gladly came out to introduce themselves to Sara in the therapy room.

Throughout the semester, we worked with Sara. We also need to give a shout-out to the therapy team, who all met Sara at multiple points during our sessions. When we talk about the team with our clients, we let them know that we are all working together. The team is referenced often; sometimes during the session, we might ask out loud, "I wonder what the team is thinking about this?" The idea is not abstract for our clients and when we talk about it from a supervisory perspective, we encourage the team to think of each client as the team's client, not an individual therapist's client.

At the second session, during a mid-session consultation, a team member suggested a phone app to help Sara track her daily calorie intake and exercise. Dr. Charlés asked us how we would feel if our team member entered the session and helped Sara download the My Fitness Pal app. Sara welcomed the team member and excitedly learned how to use the app, encouraged by our collective belief in her ability to reach her goal. Each member of the team helped to brainstorm strategies to overcome the barriers Sara faced each day including low self-esteem, anxiety, the importance of food in her culture, and past unhealthy habits. With each of Sara's successes, the team felt more comfortable brainstorming together. Dr. Charlés continued to nurture this comfort by asking us to think not only of cookie-cutter interventions but how to model our interventions to fit our client and her current needs. We brainstormed using the whiteboard both inside the therapy room and within the team room, building on each other's ideas.

During Sara's sessions, she spoke anxiously about her appointments with her nutritionist, who made her feel uncomfortable. Due to her anxiety, Sara didn't ask her nutritionist her burning questions or discuss difficulties making dietary changes. The team reflected their encouragement, normalized sometimes anxiety-provoking medical interactions, and reinforced our belief in her ability to advocate for herself. In preparation for her next-day appointment with her nutritionist, we developed a list of Sara's burning questions and role-played the conversation until Sara was comfortable. Keeping in mind that the nutritionist was a part of our larger team, we offered to call the nutritionist in one of our sessions to facilitate the conversation. However, after role-playing, Sara stated that she felt comfortable enough to have the conversation on her own and embrace the challenge of practicing her assertiveness training.

Just before Thanksgiving, Sara spoke worriedly about her ability to eat moderately. The team discussed Sara's problem and came up with clever strategies including changing her plate size to mapping out the Thanksgiving table to facilitating an imaginary experience of Thanksgiving thereby increasing her confidence in herself. In session four, Sara spoke about her family and how they often encouraged an unhealthy lifestyle. Instead of strategizing here to circumvent this, our team considered how we might recruit the family members to support Sara.

In session five, Sara arrived excited to share her progress with us but also spoke about continued difficulty motivating herself to exercise. We decided then that if we ate breakfast with a client, we could exercise with her and began to incorporate physical activity (walking) into our sessions. Sara, initially apprehensive, gained confidence throughout that session, and by the end, led the therapists in a post-workout stretch. After six sessions, Sara had lost 15% of her body weight and underwent successful bariatric surgery. We watched as Sara began to break through barriers and build confidence to tackle both her mental and physical health. Throughout the semester, we used a multidisciplinary approach to help Sara reach her goals and improve depressed mood and decrease anxiety.

Reflections for Practice

Reflecting upon the supervision process throughout our work with Sara revealed minute details that built an environment for each team member to feel comfortable discussing their ideas. The encouragement of sharing first came from casual conversations that occurred before the discussion of anything related to psychology. Often, our team would get lost in discussing what they did on the weekend, favorite foods, or different activities. Conversations about non-threatening topics created a culture in which sharing was welcomed, expected, and enjoyed. We focused our energies on developing our supervisory confidence and collaboration as well as being part of Sara's treatment team.

To expand the boundaries of traditional mental health in supervision practice, we recommend beginning with incorporating biopsychosocial models to promote whole person care. This begins with asking questions about who and what matters to our clients. When discussing stressors and creating goals, collaborating with our clients to consider holistic health is imperative to long-lasting change. Thinking outside the box starts with conversations between supervisors and supervisees but should extend to creating interventions that fit our clients' lives. To do this, we want to limit a one-dimensional view of our clients' difficulties. In this way, mental health is not siloed care but part of total health, which reduces stigma and normalizes mental health as a routine part of health care. As demonstrated in the case of Sara, the focus was not confined to reducing anxiety symptoms but addressing anxiety as a barrier to overall health outcomes. Multiple avenues of change were explored through various expertise by individual team members to target behaviors that would promote change. However, none of this happens without supervisors' promoting a larger view of health and inspiring supervisees to think outside the box of traditional mental health.

4

IMMEDIATE, INTENSE CHANGES

Setting Up and Conducting Supervision Across Conflict-Affected Regions of Sri Lanka

Amalka Edirisinghe and Anagi Gunasekara

Background to Our Services

Man-made incidents of trauma in the history of Sri Lanka led to a 30-year-conflict and has left behind many survivors of trauma in the affected areas. Some of the main incidents include Sri Lanka's 30-year-long civil war between the Liberation Tigers of Tamil Eelam (LTTE) and the Sri Lankan Government Armed Forces, the Black July riots in 1983, and the insurgency of youth unrest in 1971. The latter was carried out by the Marxist Janatha Vimukthi Peramuna (JVP) of the People's Liberation Front. The youth revolt on April 5, 1971 that tried to topple the Sri Lankan Government lasted till June, 1971. The insurgents were able to capture and hold several towns and rural areas for several weeks until they were recaptured by the army forces. However, the same insurgency reoccurred in 1987/1989 and posed a serious threat to state power. Janatha Vimukthi Peramuna sought to suppress anyone who expressed a contrary viewpoint to theirs and resorted to violence against any person who opposed them. Between 1971 and 1987—the JVP insurgency—the Black July communal riots started as a protest against the death of 13 army personnel due to a land mine attack by the LTTE in the northern region of Sri Lanka. It was alleged that the government did not take appropriate actions to prevent the riots and as a result, the riots that started in the capital of Sri Lanka spread to the other parts of the country, damaging many lives and property. These incidents led to the 30-year conflict and have left behind many survivors of trauma in the affected areas. Those painful years of violence, trauma, insecurity, brutality, and deprivation have scarred the survivors' lives in an irreparable manner.

Family Rehabilitation Centre

As a response to the trauma created by the incidents, the Family Rehabilitation Centre (FRC) was established in August 1992 and currently acts in the capacity of a humanitarian, non-profit, non-governmental organization that provides effective and quality psychosocial support to trauma survivors. With a vision of "Communities and systems strengthened to effectively address and prevent trauma in Sri Lanka," FRC strives "to serve as one of the leading national organizations in rehabilitation of trauma survivors by engaging in counseling and holistic psychosocial services to trauma survivors, building capacity of relevant stakeholders to effectively address and prevent trauma in Sri Lanka."[1]

Within this broad framework, and working toward the vision, FRC works in three specific spheres in the psychosocial field by rehabilitating trauma survivors, preventing trauma, and building capacity for relevant stakeholders.

In order to serve survivors of trauma, FRC makes initial contact with district-level government agencies that support in the identification of the neediest villages. The FRC then sets up Grass Root Level Action Committees (GRALCs), which are comprised of the village leaders. These committees continue to support FRC in program implementation and in identifying community volunteers. Along with this support, FRC then conducts community awareness programs on various topics as relevant and screening clinics with the support of the medical officers and physiotherapists, along with FRC's counselors. With the identification of the needs of the clients, they are provided with basic medical and physiotherapeutic care and systematic office-based counseling.

The counseling takes place roughly over three months with 12 sessions; clients are also referred to other service providers based on their needs. An initial home visit is conducted to inquire about the client's background and three follow-up visits are conducted after terminating services. We use a Client Intake Form, which is a validated psychometric tool specially designed for our program, to assess the progress of the client. The counseling is done based on Judith Herman's model of Trauma Recovery (1997).

Clinical Supervision at FRC

All FRC counselors have a minimum educational qualification of a diploma in counseling and varying levels of professional experience. Prior to 2011, many of the counselors were provided with administrative supervision but the need for clinical supervision was apparent. Due to their varying backgrounds, counselors were using different types of psychometric tools and intervention methods when working with clients. Further, many of the counselors originate from the conflict-affected areas and hence some were survivors of trauma themselves. As a result, it was identified that clinical supervision was a need that should be provided for these counselors. A Clinical Psychologist (Edirisinghe), who was qualified with an M.Phil. in Clinical Psychology, was assigned to carry out this task. A schedule was set up with each counselor receiving clinical supervision weekly for about an hour via Skype or face-to-face meeting during a supervisory visit to the field. The supervision was conducted in the Sinhala and Tamil, and an interpreter/translator was utilized where necessary.

The authors bring with them their own values and beliefs into the supervision process. However, a consistent value upheld at FRC is that the counselor should be empowered to develop their skills through supervision, capacity building, self-reflection, and practice. Further, as FRC works with clients who have been through traumatic incidents, the sensitive nature of the work should be identified and all counselors are encouraged to hold high ethical standards during the engagement with clients.

During an initial capacity-building program for FRC counselors, Edirisinghee introduced clinical supervision for FRC, and the importance and benefits of it for the clients, counselors, and organization. Following these initial processes, Edirisinghee initiated the clinical supervision process. It became apparent that the counselors were of different developmental levels, and a developmental model was employed for the supervision.

During supervision, the psychologist's major role was to identify the counselors' skill levels and implement supervision in a manner that facilitated the counselors' development. All of the counselors were encouraged by the Ministry of Health to obtain minimum qualifications of a diploma in counseling from the NISD (National Institute of Social Development) in Sri Lanka. Edirisinghee highlighted the importance of this training through one encounter:

> There was one client who used to get angry quite often. The counselor and I have been speaking about this client for about three weeks but there was no progress. And when I asked the counselors what was planned to be done with the client according to the intervention plan, the counselors pointed out the plan to use empty chair technique to reduce the anger.

Edirisinghee took a step back and asked the counselors to explain the theoretical underpinnings of this technique and their experience and training in implementing this technique.

Similar to the scenario explained above, some counselors were using different techniques such as free association and dream interpretations, simply based on their theoretical knowledge without any experience in implementation. Edirisinghe was mainly trained in Cognitive Behavioral Therapy and felt more comfortable employing such an approach during the clinical work. Discussions regarding the evidence base of therapeutic techniques were conducted with clients to select the best treatment methods.

During the developmental stage of counseling, Edirisinghe also had to pay attention to developing the counselor's basic skills. For instance, in one situation, a counselor kept raising his concerns about a client who was a bomb blast victim being fidgety during the counseling sessions. This fidgety behavior was distracting the counselor and the process. However, at this point, the counselor had not considered the possibility of the client experiencing discomfort from sitting in one position for a long time after the injury was sustained. The counselor failed to recognize this issue and was not able to address it. Such points were raised during clinical supervision; the counselor and the client were able to make simple adjustments such as taking small breaks during the sessions and providing the client with a cushion to sit on. Empathy was also a basic skill that needed to be developed among some of the counselors, especially among counselors who were survivors of trauma themselves and tended to be less responsive to the client's stories. After such sessions, Edirisinghe had to address this by providing positive and constructive feedback on the counselor's behavior.

After about two years of employing the developmental model of clinical supervision, FRC was able to progress into employing a social model. During this stage, peer exchange and peer supervision were encouraged and counselors were asked to bring cases and discuss them at training programs. During group counseling, the counselors were encouraged to co-facilitate the groups and the peer supervision gave insight to the counselors with regard to the dynamics of a group.

Moving on from this model, Edirisinghe implemented a reflective model of clinical supervision. By this time, a few of the counselors were maintaining journals about the work they do and were appreciative of being able to reflect on the counseling that they were providing the clients. Edirisinghe was now exposed to a new angle of the work that was being done in the field. The cultural aspect and the role it plays in the lives of the clients as well as the counselors were brought to light. For instance, Edirisinghe was able to fully understand the way in which women soothe each other in certain communities by embarrassing each other. The relationships between Edirisinghe and the counselors also improved to a point where the counselors felt more comfortable and were able to discuss sensitive aspects of the work they do. For instance, one of the counselors discussed her difficulty in supporting a client who had anger issues which were displaced on her child. The counselor was not able to look past this injustice that was taking place, and this was further exacerbated by the counselor's own inability to conceive. This was distressing the counselor. This was addressed during the clinical supervision where the counselor was supported to work with her own emotions and to look beyond the anger displayed by the client. Further work with the client brought out the fact that this child was an unintended consequence of sexual abuse and as a result was precipitating anger. The discovery of this information supported Edirisinghe and the counselor to implement effective intervention. The supervision also supported the counselor to reflect on her learning, where she was able to understand that beating the child was wrong but to be more open to experiences of the clients.

The clinical supervision process of the post-conflict era was quite dynamic with the role and needs addressed by the authors constantly changing. Generally, the clinical supervision concentrated on the provision of support for the counselors who were helping clients with past traumas. However, on certain occasions, current trauma-arousing incidents arose in the clients' lives (such as clients' loved ones being abducted or clients' being followed by members of unidentified groups). In such instances, the support provided by Edirisinghe had to drastically change to provide a more hands-on, active support to the counselor.

Amidst the ongoing implementation of the reflective model of supervision, many changes took place in the country and at FRC. Sri Lanka transited from the post-conflict era to the developmental era which brought about a new set of challenges. Developments in the conflict-ridden areas led to an increased number of job opportunities, which was taken advantage of by the experienced and trained staff at FRC. With the development of the country, the opportunities for donor funding was reduced, leading to difficulties in sustaining the program. It became increasingly difficult to retain trained staff and continue serving the communities in the previously established manner.

Along with these changes, a new strategy by FRC enabled the possibility to provide services to clients beyond the conflict and FRC initiated work with gender-based violence as well. Several changes also took place with the in-house clinical supervisors at FRC, which led to inconsistencies with the clinical supervision process.

With the developments of the country and the changes in the government in 2015, Sri Lanka started looking into reconciling with the past atrocities to ensure nonrecurrence. The government initiated Transitional Justice Mechanisms, which brought along more funding opportunities to sustain donor-driven organizations such as the FRC. Rehabilitation was once again looked upon as an important aspect that needed to be addressed, which supported the sustainability of the work implemented by FRC. The FRC developed as an organization and recruited more clinical psychologists (Gunasekara), which made it possible to reestablish and streamline the clinical supervision process once again.

Experiences and Challenges in the Clinical Supervision Process

The progress of clinical supervision experienced many challenges. One of the major drawbacks that hindered the progress of the counselors was the introduction of the government recruitment scheme that many of the counselors applied for. As a result, FRC had to look into recruiting new staff, and the supervision process had to be repeated. This is a continuous challenge with the government's releasing of scheduled recruitment annually.

The clinical supervision was and is being challenged by continuous technological issues. Power shortages are common in certain regions, resulting in the usage of the telephone rather than Skype to conduct clinical supervision. Even when the electricity was available, supervision was disrupted by technical glitches of computers.

From the initial stages of the process, a statement that was constantly shared by the counselors was, "Miss, you are very young…duwa (daughter), you don't have a lot of experience in life. You haven't lived as long as us to experience these and therefore you don't understand some of these things." This was an additional challenge for the authors who had to prove their capabilities of supervision irrespective of their age. The authors had freshly graduated out of the M.Phil. in Clinical Psychology program and were well accustomed to receiving clinical supervision but had no formal training in providing it. This challenge included implementing clinical supervision with 14 counselors along with the other issues and made the psychologists feel like "fish out of water." Edirisinghe had to work on accepting herself and to maintain supervision with consistency.

The implementation of group counseling brought in a new set of challenges that needed to be addressed. Initially, Edirisinghe was unaware of certain cultural beliefs that were held to by the group members. For instance, caste played a major role during group counseling, with those of a higher caste refusing to take part in groups with members from lower/other castes. Edirisinghe had to address these issues during group, where the counselor was supported to help clients understand that all group members were facing similar issues, regardless of the castes they were from. Clients were also given the option of going back to individual counseling if uncomfortable with group counseling.

A further issue that came up during group counseling was related to the supervisor's lack of awareness of the post-conflict context and FRC's method of categorizing clients for groups. For instance, a group was formed to address the grief that parents were facing due to the death/loss of their children and this included a former combatant who had lost his child. Other group members had children who were forcefully recruited into the paramilitary group that the former combatant represented and had faced violent ends as a result. This resulted in conflict within the group and Edirisinghe had to support the counselor to make decisions such as removing the former combatant from the group and providing him with individual counseling.

The supervision process was further challenged by the dual roles that needed to be fulfilled by Edirisinghe. The position of the authors at FRC is also a position within the Senior Management Committee and as a result, they are required to participate and contribute toward administrative decisions. In certain instances, this created difficulties as Edirisinghe had to transit between the authoritative role of an administrator and a more empathic role of the clinical psychologist. Playing these dual roles was uncomfortable in certain situations such as when there was discrimination occurring among the staff members. These issues had to be addressed and administrative decisions regarding such staffing matters had to be made by and adhered to by Edirisinghe. During these processes, Edirisinghe had to continue the clinical supervision despite the ongoing human resource discussions. In such instances, the supervision was impacted with Edirisinghe's feeling guilty and some counselors even distancing themselves from her.

Further, FRC, despite being a psychosocial organization, implemented clinical supervision only 11 years after establishment. Clinical supervision was a new concept to FRC, and the organization was unaware of the philosophies and values of it. This information needed to be communicated to the top management at FRC, who were not from a psychological background and hence were unaware of clinical psychology and supervision and the importance of providing clinical supervision regularly. Time management for clinical supervision was/is a constant difficulty for Edirisinghe amidst the duties of a Senior Management Committee member and she had to continuously and consistently emphasize the importance of supervision with the management. Ground rules were established, such as not disturbing the supervisors during clinical supervision, and so forth.

The FRC currently obtains the support of senior clinical psychologists to facilitate and support the clinical supervision process with the counselors but many of these psychologists are unaware of difficulties in implementing certain techniques in the FRC working contexts. For instance, the counselors at FRC provide direct counseling for many survivors of domestic violence, which sometimes results in feelings of helplessness in the counselors and supervisor, when alternatives for the situation of the client cannot be sought due to financial constraints of the client as well as the cultural norms. Therefore, even if a client wants to leave the abusive situation, this does not become possible. When consulting such cases, many external clinical psychologists discuss the possibility of exploring options with clients but the applicability of these options are limited in the context.

Being an organization operated through restricted funding brings a further set of experiences into FRC, which implements many projects that fit within the mandate of violence-related trauma. Many of the clients that FRC provides counseling with have been through multiple layers of traumatic incidents and are experiencing low adaptation and high levels of distress as a result. However, the clinical presentations of the clients are in some instances not limited to traumatic presentations. For instance, some of the clients that approach FRC for counseling services have other psychological problems, such as substance misuse and addictions, sexual dysfunctions and problems, and in some instances more clinical presentations such as features of Obsessive Compulsive Disorder or learning disabilities. These presentations become a challenge at various levels because, in some instances, the counselors at FRC lack capacity in working with such presentations and in other instances, additional needed support in such cases is not accepted or supported by the donor organizations. In order to prevent injustice taking place for any of the clients in such situations, the supervisors work with the counselor in identifying other service providers in the districts that can provide the necessary services to these clients.

One of the greatest challenges related to providing clinical supervision at FRC is related to language restrictions and capabilities of the clinical team. Many of the conflict-affected areas of Sri Lanka are predominantly Tamil-speaking, which is a language in which neither author is fluent. As a result, clinical supervision takes place with the support of translators/ interpreters. During the initial stages of clinical supervision, the FRC's Quality and Learning Officer supported the process with translations. She is from a sociology background and her main tasks at FRC involve designing and implementing the monitoring and evaluation (M&E) processes at FRC. She had a very limited psychology background and was unclear about the exact role of a translator. In some instances, the clinical supervision was disrupted as a result of this. On one occasion, the supervisor was supporting the counselor to identify the information that needed to be captured during a home visit. However, in the follow-up session, it was observed that the counselors had captured more information apart from what was discussed during supervision. The psychologist observed that some of this information was irrelevant and further inquiries confirmed that this information was sought by the translator to capture M&E details. This was also evident to the supervisor when the psychologists' message was short but the translation was lengthy. Further investigation into this brought to light that the interpreter with her past experience was adding information beyond what was stated by the supervisor. This disruption was also taking place in the information provided by the counselor, with the translator adding her own perceptions and opinions beyond what was stated by the counselor. On some occasions, only a summary of what was explained by the counselor was translated to the supervisor, leaving out much essential clinical information. These issues had to be addressed prior to progressing with the clinical supervision and several steps were taken to ensure the nonrecurrence of miscommunication during translations. The interpreter was specifically advised to do direct translations and was also supported in her knowledge of psychology.

Shared below is an extract of the insights of the officer/manager, Niranjala Somasundram, from her involvement in the clinical supervision process.

It was an immense challenge to be a translator without prior experience in translating technical subjects. It is important to assign a translator with the subject knowledge. Moreover, the translator must be orientated on the fundamental principles of this type of work. The dual role that I played as a translator as well as Monitoring and Evaluation Officer with the same group of people impacted the clinical supervision sessions and created issues in terms of data collection and reporting.

The most difficult challenge was the translation of complex client information. Working with the clinical psychologist gave me an invaluable opportunity to reflect on the experience of translating supervision sessions. It allowed me to identify and address the language-related challenges and concerns I encountered. Language-related difficulties such as misunderstanding accent, colloquial expressions or slang, and failing to recognize vocabulary were the main challenges I experienced during the clinical supervision sessions. Translation of a word does not imply a full understanding of its meaning, which may vary depending on context. Challenges were also encountered in relation to the translation of interventions, technical psychological terms, and translating specific turns of speech. Word-by word translation was not always possible and required investing additional effort.

Even though we as a team encountered many difficulties, the challenges were addressed, and necessary steps were taken within the organization to ensure that the cases handled were done so successfully. During the initial stages, Skype was identified as a potential effective technology for supporting availability of high-quality supervision by distance and in cross-cultural environments.

Translation/interpretation of supervision became more efficient and accurate at FRC when a bilingual counselor was recruited for Colombo. Hence, she was from the start better able to interpret the communication during supervision. She had also lived a few years in the Northern Province and was better aware of the context. However, this counselor is a fresh graduate and this impacted the supervision. For instance, as discussed above, the supervisor was adapting different models of supervision. As a result, the approach taken for clinical supervision varied from case to case. In some instances, the Colombo counselor/interpreter, being unaware of the different approaches used, would try to duplicate the information shared by the supervisor and this needed to be addressed to ensure that the supervision could continue to be provided based on the skill levels of the counselors.

Shared below is an account of the reflection of the Colombo counselor, Nithila Theivendran.

Being involved in the clinical supervision as a translator/interpreter made me realize how crucial and challenging it is to translate exactly what is being communicated. During the initial sessions, with no prior experience in translating, I realized that just knowing the language was not enough and that it is vital to understand the subject context and how FRC works. Fortunately, during times when I was unaware of certain approaches, the clinical psychologist patiently explained it to me and ensured that I understood it before I translated/interpreted it.

Interpreting was quite challenging as I wasn't a proficient Tamil speaker and had difficulty in translating technical terms exactly. Sometimes, when the sentences or expressions used in English can lose meaning or there is no literal equivalent word to explain it in Tamil, the supervisor usually breaks it down into sentences which make it easier to translate/interpret. Another challenging factor during translation is the dialects within the districts. I learnt that they had different meanings for several emotions and terms. However, interacting with the other counselors, who were very patient and supportive while trying to explain contexts or terms that were unclear to me made it easier for me to translate to the supervisor.

Further, there were also times where I found it difficult to interpret/ translate what the supervisor would want to say in a particular tone. This is something that I am keen on working on so that the clinical supervision is not affected. Overall, as I haven't had much experience with working with clients, these sessions have and are contributing towards learning more about counselling and its challenges apart from the language itself.

Note

1 FRC defines a trauma survivor as a person who has a physical and/or psychological injury caused by violence and/or acute stress. Apart from providing services to trauma survivors, FRC also provides services to the Immediate family members of the trauma survivors.

Reference

Herman, J. (1997). *Trauma and recovery: The aftermath of violence—from domestic abuse to political terror.* New York, NY: Basic Books.

5

SEVEN CHAIRS UNDER A MANGO TREE

Stories of Peer Support and Supervision from Sri Lanka

Roshan Dhammapala and Mihiri Ferdinando

Introduction

It was early morning and Kanchana is on her way to the community counselors' monthly progress review meeting. This has long been a formality to collate data on client numbers and any other monthly programs they have conducted within their district. But these meetings have changed in the recent past. They now include a time slot, and occasionally an allocated space, to engage in reflective work using a peer support and supervision model. The model was introduced through a series of Train the Trainer workshops and put into practice in recent months. She looked forward to this morning's meetings as she had asked for an opportunity to discuss a challenging case with her peer group comprised of counselors working in the same service and district.

Kanchana has been working as a counselor in Sri Lanka's State Services; Women and Children's Welfare for the past six years. She recalls her early days in the role as a young 24-year-old graduate with a degree in Sociology and an enthusiasm to help people in her own community. She now recalls how unprepared she was for some of the complex issues that found their way to her.

> Like the 18-year-old girl sent to her by the Grama Niladari (village administrative leader) for "bad behavior" at home. She was living with her uncle and aunt because her mother was working in the Middle East as a domestic worker. Her father had left them a year after her mother went overseas. The girl had two older sisters who were married and lived far away. She had lost contact with her older brother. She had befriended a boy in one of her tuition classes, which had outraged her aunt and uncle, who expected her to be a "good and diligent student instead of wasting her mother's hard-earned

money." The girl was desperately unhappy, missed her family, and felt alone and unloved.

Kanchana spent a lot of time talking with the girl but eventually referred her to the Mental Health unit at the District hospital because she appeared to be depressed. Kanchana later learnt that the girl was treated for delusions and hallucinations. She often thinks about this girl and wonders if she could have done more for her at the time had she had the support to guide her understanding and practice. Her peer group may have been able to add some insights and encourage her to also work with the aunt and uncle. But, at the time, Kanchana was not confident enough to take them on.

> Then there was the couple in their 40s with two young children and problems in their marriage. Both were military officers who had spent many years posted out at different military bases during the war, seeing each other only on weekends. When the war concluded and they resumed their life together under the same roof after many years, their relationship began to unravel. When they came to see Kanchana, the husband had already moved out. The husband said he left home not because he was having an affair (as per his wife's accusations) but because he didn't want to keep arguing and fighting with his wife. He was still open to reconciliation, but for now, he appeared distant. Kanchana hadn't known how to bring them together. The wife would call her frequently when she was upset to seek her advice and she had felt that she was helping her. But now in hindsight, she realized that this had made her more dependent.

Mapping Needs and a Response

Although Sri Lanka acknowledges a high prevalence of suicide and substance abuse (Knipe et al., 2018; Samaraweera, Sumathipala, Siribaddana, Sivayogan, & Bhugra, 2010) there is a low priority given to the role of non-medical services and interventions in their capacity to promote positive mental health as a mitigating factor. In 2013, The Asia Foundation commissioned two Mapping Studies (Asia Foundation, 2015a, 2015b) as part of a partnership with two government ministries that employ counselors within their service stream for social welfare, and for women and children. The partnership sought to invest in capacities of human resources responsible for the provision of counseling and psychosocial support services through local government centers across the country in Sri Lanka. The studies revealed that the counselors relied on their line manager or administrative supervisor for both administrative as well as professional practice support. The line manager is predominantly a head of a local government area (e.g., a District or one of its "Divisions"). He or she would have broad experience in managing community and administrative issues but would not be a mental health professional. This would at times influence the expectations placed on the counselor, and the methods of intervention that would be recommended or reinforced. This chapter reflects on the introduction of a peer support and supervision mechanism which was introduced to community counselors as a source of both emotional and practice support for challenging issues they encountered in their practice.

A Model for Peer Supervision

In the absence of securing regular access to skilled clinical personnel to provide practice supervision across the districts, we thought of using existing relationships among colleagues and peers and attempt to create safe spaces for peer reflection and support. A supervision model developed by Lansen and Haans (2004) to deal with the emotional impact of trauma therapy on therapists and later adapted and trialed among psychosocial workers in Northern and Eastern Provinces of Sri Lanka by Francis and van der Veer (2011) was identified. It was subsequently modified and piloted amongst teachers providing counseling and psychosocial support within the Ministry of Education and found to hold relevance and value (Ministry of Education and GIZ, 2018).

Minor adaptations were made with permission from Francis and van der Veer (2011). The objectives and purpose of each step were elaborated upon and continue to evolve in response to the peer group's capacities and expectations. The model that was eventually used for peer support and supervision is outlined below:

Step 1. Presenting the key issues to conceptualize a case based on four sets of information

(a) history and background to the presenting problem
(b) details of the client's present situation
(c) responses and interventions that have been attempted (by the client/ counselor) and their outcomes
(d) challenges or dilemmas faced by the counselor in relation to supporting this client /working on the case

The objective of step 1 is to engage counselors in a simple case formulation and attempt to organize the information they had gathered through the client's story. This would help them to work out what bits of information they have and what pieces are missing or hidden, what strengths and problem-solving approaches the client has used and filtering out their own barriers and challenges separate from the client's problem.

Step 2. Gaining perspective

Each member of the peer group formulates one or two issues that they pose to the presenting counselor to clarify details for themselves about the case presented or to enable reflective work for the presenting counselor.

The objective of step 2 is to enable thoughtfully crafted questions based on good insight that can assist the counselor to reflect on their approach, perspective, inferences, and assumptions. The skill of crafting questions enables reflective work and requires a particular degree of intuition and maturity to facilitate discovery for another person, instead of simply telling them what you think or what they should do.

Steps 3 and 4. Fostering an empathic perspective of the client

Each member of the peer group attempts to step into the role of the client and relate to the client's emotional experience. Peers each share an emotion they could identify with and explain reasons for it. The presenting counselor then considers these possible perspectives and attempts to integrate them into their own observations about the client's emotional experience.

The objective of steps 3 and 4 is to enable counselors to gain insight from multiple and diverse perspectives and consider these in light of his/her own knowledge of the client. It is an effort to broaden their perspective and understand the client's experience better. This is particularly useful to offset blind spots and biases that could prevent counselors from understanding the emotional experience of their client(s) or from being locked into linear perspectives.

Steps 5 and 6. Fostering an awareness of one's own emotions as a counselor navigating the helping role

Each member of the peer group attempts to step into the shoes of the counselor presenting the case, acknowledge feelings they may encounter in relation to the client's situation and challenges within the case, attempt to acknowledge these emotions and their sources. The presenting counselor also shares the emotions he/she experienced working with the client.

Objective of steps 5 and 6: The reflections of the peer group could generate insight and create space and acceptance for the counselor's feelings in response to their work and client stories. It may also enable counselors to identify countertransference matters. Empathizing with the presenting counselor enables a more accurate and empathically tuned-in response to the challenge(s) that might be shared rather than providing advice that is misaligned.

Step 7. Acknowledging and validating strengths

Peers listen attentively as well as intuitively to the counselor's management and response to her or his challenging case during the initial case presentation.

The objective of step 7 is to enable counselors to identify and acknowledge the constructive actions, insights, and approaches adopted by the counselor. It provides an opportunity for counselors to affirm skills and knowledge and build the confidence of their peers. Ideally, a peer group should have about seven to eight members to yield a range of possible thoughts, options, and actions to consider (other than the ones the counselor has already tried). If, at the conclusion of the session, the peer group is unable to offer new insights to the counselor, he/she may conclude that the client/case requires a referral to a specialist or more experienced practitioner.

Step 8. Problem-solving and brainstorming

In the final step, each member of the peer group offers one action and its corresponding strategy that could address or mitigate the challenge(s) identified by the counselor and contribute toward forward movement, new insights, and collaborations.

Objective of step 8: Each member of the peer group proposes their suggestion by stating "one action I would take to move this case forward …." This prevents the peer groups' telling the presenting counselor what to do and leaves them with the option of making this decision by weighing the presented options.

The noteworthy contribution of this model is that it encourages both empathy and perspective taking by drawing on the diversity of the peer group systems to enrich reflective practice. Each member of the group attempts to connect with feelings and perspectives of both the helper and the help seeker. It also offers a safe space in which counselors can acknowledge their own vulnerability and fallibility in relation to their work, which has been cited as one of the most significant sources of relief. Francis and van der Veer (2011) explain the purpose of the model further:

> It is the experienced workers that gradually become more at ease, and more effective. This is because they learn from their own experience and the experiences of their colleagues. So, if a worker wants to become more effective, they will have to reflect on his/her own experiences and the experiences of their colleagues.
>
> *(p. 155)*

A Session in Practice

As Kanchana arrived at the local government center, it turned out that their usual meeting space—the common room—was booked out. Their Coordinator suggested they set up some chairs under the shade of a large mango tree growing outside the center. A couple of colleagues who had arrived early were sitting around a serving of milk rice and sambol neatly packed in a banana leaf. This was their usual morning ritual at work—sharing their home cooked breakfasts with each other; this is more than a meal: It's also a time of fellowship. As the usual rumpus of the day unfolded, a small group of community counselors could be seen sitting under a large tree, leaning in, attentively focused on a narrative by Kanchana.

Step 1: Key issues

A mother in her late 50s came to see me (Kanchana) for support and advice. The mother is seeking help on behalf of her married daughter (28). The problem according to the mother was that the couple had not consummated their relationship. The daughter had returned to her parent's home and told them she did not wish to return to her husband. Her daughter had complained that her husband regularly argued with her over trivial things, stayed out late with his friends, and did not seem to like spending time with her. The mother felt that her daughter was being impulsive and making a bad decision. Divorce in her community would tarnish the family's reputation and might also subject her daughter to further judgment by the community. The mother feels that both the daughter and son-in-law need someone to advise them. Kanchana's father had developed a problem with his sight while the children were still in school, so she had gone to work to support both of her children to complete their education. But she also wanted to "see them settled before she closed her eyes."[1] She appealed to Kanchana to speak to her daughter and encourage her to repair her marriage. "She will listen to you; she is about your age and I hope you will be able to influence her to save her marriage." Kanchana encouraged the mother to bring her daughter to see her and if possible her son-in-law, too.

The daughter, Nimasha, subsequently visited Kanchana. Nimasha confided in Kanchana that she thought her husband liked men. She had confronted him about it but he had dismissed her, saying she should not misunderstand his friendships. He had stated that he still wanted to stay married. Nimasha does not wish for her mother to know of this as she would be torn apart if she knew her son-in-law was in fact gay. It would be a great shame on them all. Kanchana suggested she take some time to list out the evidence for and against a divorce to assist her to weigh her decision.

Step 2: Gaining perspective

Having laid out the details of her client to her peer group, Kanchana noted and responded to questions from her peers. One question was particularly useful to her: "Is it clear to you what exactly this couple's difficulties are? It may be the husband's sexuality that is in question but it also may be other unspoken problems with intimacy."

The question made Kanchana realize that her sympathies toward Nimasha had influenced premature conclusions. She also wondered if Nimasha or her husband were able to have an open conversation about their intimacy needs given the culture in which they would have grown up.

Steps 3 and 4: Empathic perspectives

It was somewhat comforting for Kanchana to hear that several of her peers felt sorry for both Nimasha and her mother—just as she had done! (Step 5) But one of her male colleagues shifted her out of her comfort zone stating that he felt empathy for the couple rather than just one individual. He said if he was either the man or woman in this marriage, he would feel sad that neither of them had been able to get to know each other sufficiently before they had committed to a marriage. If the husband was, in fact, gay, then it would be very sad that he had to go to such extremes to deceive another person and live a lie to be socially accepted. Or, if he was not, he would feel sad that neither of them had been able to communicate with each other about any fears or barriers in relation to intimacy.

Steps 5 and 6: Fostering awareness of one's own emotions

Kanchana's colleagues' perspectives shifted Kanchana away from her somewhat negatively tainted assumptions about her client's husband to a more neutral position. A significant proportion of problems related to sex and intimacy were very rarely expressed directly in counseling sessions. Instead, they would manifest as aggression and conflict within the family unit or as separation and divorce. After listening to colleagues share similar observations in their practice during peer supervision sessions, Kanchana wondered if she had fully understood Nimasha and her husband's situation. She felt less reactive in response to Nimasha's distress. For this, she was grateful for the diversity within the group. She could now acknowledge feeling motivated by her sympathy for Nimasha and wanting to help her. They were of a similar age and social background. It was not too difficult to identify with her client.

It is not uncommon for helpers to be drawn into the world and emotions of their clients, especially due to over-identification or counter-transference. During the steps involving empathy and perspective-taking, counselors would frequently report feelings of sympathy toward their clients and a strong desire to help them. Sometimes a peer group may inadvertently endorse and fuel an emotional response to the client's problem. However, the true value of the peer group is the diversity of experiences, views, and personalities that the members bring to their group that help to offset insularity and biases and broaden perspectives.

Step 7: Acknowledging and validating strengths

Kanchana's peers acknowledged that she had done well to give Nimasha some time to objectively weigh her decision and suspend her personal views.

Step 8: Problem-solving

Kanchana's peers also shared several options that they could explore. One colleague shared a particularly useful consideration based on a referral from the courts to counsel a couple who were filing for divorce. During a separate session with the husband, he revealed with great difficulty that he was suffering from a sexual dysfunction but felt so much shame that he avoided all intimacy with his wife. Instead, he would frequently go out with his friends and return home intoxicated. This further aggravated his problem. His shame prevented him from consulting a doctor because he was uninformed of such health conditions. He felt it was due to personal weakness. This couple had eventually sought appropriate support and chose to remain married. The colleague shared that since then, she had prepared a simple leaflet about sexual problems with information for couples considering separation or conflict. It listed out symptoms related to common sexual dysfunctions and provided details for seeking support at the local hospital or through counseling. It also stated that many of these conditions could be treated. This had occasionally encouraged clients to open up to the counselor about such issues or seek help at the hospital.

Another colleague shared that if Nimasha were her client, she would further explore her evidence for believing her husband was gay. This may also shed light on Nimasha's own perceptions and knowledge of sex, sexuality, and intimacy. Providing accurate information may also equip her to evaluate her marital relationship more accurately and objectively.

Within-Group Dynamics

It is argued that the experience of well-being is also mediated through power. The extent of power and influence a person exerts over their environment and identity mediates their experience of well-being (PADHI, 2009). This bears relevance to the system within which counselors are employed. The large majority of counselors in services related to social welfare and women and children work under the designation of "Counseling Assistant" (CA). Approximately 400 people with widely different experience, qualifications, and skills are employed as CAs. This designation is currently under review. Although it may be assumed that non-hierarchical, "flat" structures are more conducive to a democratic peer-led reflective practice, human beings seek out distinction and differentiation in different ways. Age and years of experience often hold power. A Training-of-Trainers (TOT) model that installs a peer or coordinator to impart the skills may also hold more power. Creating a safe space has not always been successful. The TOT method of installing one skilled person to teach their peers this model may have also installed them with power in a system that sees few options for career advancement. This may have influenced the ethos, approach, and style of facilitating the peer-to-peer exchange as a leader and at times prevented them from being participants who could be vulnerable within the group.

Client Systems

Kanchana's case reflects a common social norm of (mostly female) family members' seeking support on behalf of their children, spouses, and other extended family members. Men are less receptive and responsive to choosing counseling as a problem-solving method although they are certainly not absent from counseling services. It could also be that the majority of counselors are women. Stigma, shame, judgment, misconceptions, and religious interpretations about the causes of illness and suffering influence people's help-seeking behavior (Samarasekare, Davies, & Siribaddana, 2012). When problems do involve significant others, it is common for the help seeker to ask the counselor or health professional to mediate by inviting the other person(s) for counseling. These invitations are more likely to yield a response from the reticent member than their own family member's appeal. This is possibly due to gender norms within family and social relationships, as well as the need of a family member to be seen as a "good person" in the eyes of the community or local authorities. In Sri Lanka, similar to other South Asian cultures, people tend to prefer a direct or prescribed problem-solving approach within counseling. It resembles family structures that are more often hierarchical than democratic (Yeo, 1993). The counselor's age and gender may, therefore, influence how they are perceived and how effective they could be at transacting certain types of issues: for example, young women and men working with older men or older couples; unmarried counselors addressing marital or intimate partner issues.

The Relationship Between Counselors and the Community

Counselors in Sri Lanka are predominantly women between the ages of 31 and 40 years who have joined the service as graduate recruits and worked in the service for three to seven years. When a counselor is a member of the community in which they work, it can be an advantage because they may intuitively understand local culture and context. But they may also struggle to go against established social norms and values. For example, homosexuality remains illegal according to laws introduced by the British during the colonial era. In some communities, a counselor is likely to face judgment from the client's family system or their professional networks if they are seen to be supportive of culturally contentious issues such as divorce, gender equality, gender orientation, and sexuality. Liberal views may be associated with questionable moral values.

At the end of the session, Kanchana remained uncertain about how she might navigate a joint session if her client's husband revealed that his sexual preferences were outside the norm. Although peer groups may counter certain doubts and biases, the larger community within which counselors must live and work also exerts its influence. Conformity to social and cultural norms and values are also expected from administrative systems. This conflicts with the counselor's training or preference to be a non-judgmental presence to their clients with difficult-to-talk-about stories.

Conclusion

There also are times when a peer group could not add any new perspectives to a challenging case. In such an event, counselors conclude that they may have reached the limits of their scope and competence and consider this as an indication to refer the client to a more experienced counselor or available specialist.

An unpublished, self-administered survey conducted by the Asia Foundation in 2017 indicated that counselors held an overwhelmingly positive view of the practice of peer supervision with 96–98% of the respondents rating the benefits to counselors (The Asia Foundation, unpublished). However, they also flagged the need for a confidential counseling service for themselves, preferably through external service providers. Although the model may not enable peers to explore personal barriers and stressors, the above feedback indicates that community counselors have found peer support supervision to be effective in addressing some of their practice needs.

Note

1 Sri Lanka parents often find suitable partners for their sons or daughters through marriage proposals. Some families may consider this a parent's duty—especially in relation to their daughters because it sometimes required the provision of a dowry or savings.

References

Francis, F. T., & van der Veer, G. (2011). Peer support supervision as a procedure for learning from practical experience in a mental health setting. *Intervention, 9*(2), 154 –158.

Knipe, D. W., Gunnell, D., Pearson, M., Jayamanne, S., Pieris, P., Priyadarshana, C., Weerasinghe, M., Hawton, K., Konradsen, F., Eddleston, M., & Metcalfe, C. (2018/May). Attempted suicide in Sri Lanka: An epidemiological study of household and community factors. *Journal of Affective Disorders, 232*, 177–184.

Lansen, J., & Haans, T. (2004). Clinical supervision for trauma therapists. In J. P. Wilson and B. Drozdek (Eds.), *Broken spirits: The treatment of traumatised asylum seekers, refugees, war and torture victims* (pp. 317–354). New York, NY: Brunner-Routledge.

Ministry of Education – GIZ (2018). *Psychosocial support skills: A training guide and handbook.* Colombo, Sri Lanka: Education for Social Cohesion Programme (Joint publication of Ministry of Education, Sri Lanka and Deutsche Gesellschaft für Internationale Zusammenarbeit – GIZ).

PADHI. (2009). *A tool, a guide, a framework: Detailing a psychosocial approach to development.* Colombo, Sri Lanka: Social Policy Analysis and Research Centre, University of Colombo.

Samarasekare, S., Davies., M. L. M., & Siribaddana, S. (2012). The stigma of mental illness in Sri Lanka: The perspectives of community mental health workers. *Stigma Research and Action, 2*(2), 93–99.

Samaraweera, S., Sumathipala, A., Siribaddana, S., Sivayogan, S., & Bhugra, D. (2010). Prevalence of suicidal ideation in Sri Lanka. *CRISIS, 31*(1), 30–35.

The Asia Foundation (unpublished). *Developing State counselling services in Sri Lanka. A comparative report on the 2013 and 2017 review studies conducted with counsellors of the Ministry of Social Services and the Ministry of Women and Child Affairs.* Colombo, Sri Lanka: The Asia Foundation.

The Asia Foundation (2015a). *Mapping study of the work and capacity of counselling assistants of the Ministry of Child Development and Women's Affairs*. Colombo, Sri Lanka: The Asia Foundation.

The Asia Foundation (2015b). *Mapping study of the work and capacity of counselling assistants of the Ministry of Social Services and counselling officers of the Ministry of Child Development and Women's Affairs*. Colombo, Sri Lanka: The Asia Foundation.

Yeo, A (1993). *Counselling: A problem-solving approach*. Singapore: Armour Publishing.

6

RESPONSIVE SUPERVISION

Playing with Risk-Taking and Hyperlinked Identities

Saliha Bava

Kitha[1] was placed for her internship at a leading family therapy center, let's call it The Center. Kitha identified herself as a black woman in her late 20s and I, an immigrant brown woman from India in my late 40s, was her practicum supervisor. The Center was regionally famous for its work addressing issues of sexism in our field of mental health and culture; however, its staff and clients were primarily white. The site supervisor, Lewis, a white woman in her mid-40s, was very sensitive to issues of diversity, having worked in several contexts including disability and the social service sector. She had extensive experience in the area of diversity and had been supervising for at least five years when the two of them crossed paths through Kitha's placement at The Center.

Initially, Kitha had been comfortable engaging Lewis in conversation about how the site was "very white," making it difficult for her to pursue her goal, which was to work with people of color. This goal emerged for her after she encountered the striking absence of people of color at the site. She began to wonder if she had chosen the wrong site, but over time, she spoke less about race, telling herself she would buckle down and make it work. This gave me pause but I saw it as a way of her going with the flow, that over the months, new ways of organizing her relationships were continuing to emerge for her.

About three months into the internship, Lewis contacted me. She said she was frustrated because, after giving Kitha ample opportunities to follow up with her and the clients, she continued to have to be the person reaching out to Kitha about follow-ups. She was concerned about Kitha's scheduling, communication, and other daily responsibilities of a therapy practice. We brainstormed some ways to address this, and I said I would follow up with Kitha. I also wondered how this set of issues was intersecting with the issue of color they had been discussing? Was there a relationship or some intersection?

In a follow-up conversation, I asked Kitha why she was not bringing her reflections on race up any longer with Lewis and Kitha's response was, "I don't think Lewis 'gets me'." I asked her, "What do you mean?"

Over the course of several conversations between Kitha, Lewis, and me, the talk of "color" was reframed as an issue of "diversity." One day, during their conversation, Lewis mentioned to Kitha, "You can learn how to work with diversity by working with people of other backgrounds," at which point Kitha said she felt shut down. It was the point at which she didn't feel understood.

Meanwhile, Lewis had also been making efforts to address the issue of race and color directly, offering to invite another experienced black therapist familiar to Kitha to help facilitate their conversation. Saying, "I don't think she would still get it," Kitha felt resigned and chose not to take Lewis up on her invitation. Lewis, unaware of Kitha's reason for her feelings, didn't think she could force the three-way meeting. Thus, over time, the two felt less connected and, although Kitha was tracking the lack of understanding, Lewis was tracking Kitha's lack of "professionalism" at the site.

The question raised by the above story is, "How can we be in dialogue with supervisees where the focus of socially just supervision is not only what are the expected practices, but also on *our critical-creative storying (analysis) of our interconnected lives?*" We can apply the analytical gaze as lived-sense making, an ongoing lived experience of what we are co-creating in language and action. How do we create a context for interconnectivity? How do we create stories of power *with* rather than stories of power over? I think the simple answer is, we must take the risk required to create alternate stories. The more challenging questions become, "how are we to take those risks in risk aversive contexts? How might we reflexively question the popular discourses of social justice[2] to open up space for alternate ideas and practices that are yet to emerge?"

Responsive Supervision: P.L.A.Y.-Oriented Pedagogical Stance

In my 28 years of practice, I have come to construct a P.L.A.Y.-oriented pedagogy in response to the above questions. P.L.A.Y. stands for: P for *presence*, an improvisational way of being spontaneously responsive; L for *listening* with curiosity; A for *attending* to the context, how we are relating with each other and to the emergent and; and Y for *yes, and*—a practice borrowed from improvisational theater that encourages one to receive another's response as an offer to build with, rather than to block (Bava, 2016b, 2017). In my supervisory practice, I have come to rely on play as a powerful tool for encouraging risk-taking, discovery, and agility in order to engage our complex, fast-changing world. A number of thinkers (Bain, 2004; Pink, 2006; Sicart, 2014; Thomas & Brown, 2011) in teaching and learning and cultural change contexts echo similar ideas. Play in supervision is central because such conversations spontaneously weave in and out of multiple discourses—those of the client, therapist, supervisors, and contexts—over the course of consultations. Staying curiously attentive to the context and the emergent is a way of being "relationally responsive" (Shotter, 2011). In this way, as supervisors, we are present to that which is emerging from within our ways of relating and understanding. Thus, supervision, an improvised activity, discursively constructs the identities of both the therapist and the supervisor even as we recursively construct clinical situations. So, how might we view our identities in supervision?

Hyperlinked Identities

In 1998, when I moved to Houston, TX for my doctoral internship, I was invited to a conversation on being a "minority" by a faculty member from Mexico who was interested in learning about trainees' experiences. As a doctoral intern, I agreed to participate, but remained troubled by the use of the term "minority." When the meeting started, I asked for the meaning of the word and wondered aloud if it still applied to me if I didn't use it as a way to identify myself. Did I belong in that group? Or was I to accept that "label" because I was now living in the U.S., meaning it is to be imposed on me? Through conversation, I came to understand that by "minorities," we were talking about "people of color," another label that didn't sit with me in my language. This was a very sticky moment of my experience as a trainee and I continue to revisit it as I continue to struggle with the term *people of color* as often applied. Whose language is this? Escobar stated that "people of color" is a provincial United States' term that "unconsciously reinforces prejudiced and distorted concepts to classify people" (p. 97). Use of such terms positions us to be referential to "white," which Escobar believes is the "masters' terminology." He clarifies that such struggles in language lies in:

> The power to name or to be named [which] is also a part of the class and ideological struggle....As in any politics, the power of decision is not to be located in language itself but in the people who use that language through their discourses.
>
> *(1991, p. 98)*

McNamee (2008) illustrated that language and discourse practices emerge from everyday activities of coordination with each other. And even though over time they may calcify as dominant discourses, they have the potential to shift because they are social practices. Escobar illustrated one such social practice in his call that "the codes and language of Power, which otherwise want to conquer my heart and yours, must be defetishized by a language and discourse of *liberation*" (1991, p. 98, italics added). Thus, language and discourses, produced socially and contextually, continuously shape our identities. Our identities, the stories/texts we perform, are contextualized and if we don't examine and play with our textual choices, we might be reproducing the very same oppressive discourses that we are fighting to change.

The relationship between context and identity (as text) and how we are responsive to this relationship is what I call *hyperlinked identity* (Bava, 2016a). Hyperlinking means linking from one textual space to another. Our identities, interconnected and interrelated, are interlinked to stories of self (texts) that emerge from the discursive processes that we are a part off (Bava, 2017; Combs & Freedman, 2016). Our supervisory/clinical identities are impacted, modified, and constructed in relationship to the larger web of our stories and conversations. It is this dynamic interconnectedness that shapes our identities to be *intertextual, fluid, plural, emergent* and *constitutive/performative* (Bava, 2016a; Combs & Freedman, 2016; Laird, 2000). Thus, supervision is a discursive space where our identities are centered and decentered within these shifting relational contexts. It is in our supervisory interactions and utterances we make up each other (Pearce, 2007), thereby introducing a performative quality to our identities of supervisor and therapist. Let's turn our attention to a supervision conversation where we see the centering and decentering of various hyperlinked identities and how I used a P.L.A.Y.-oriented stance as one way of being responsive.

Learning to Learn by Hyperlinking Identities

One evening, in practicum, Kate, a student from Southern Africa in her late 20s, was consulting on a contradiction she was feeling in relationship to a couple who were on the brink of a divorce. While listening to the clients speak, Kate said she found herself having the following internal conversation:

> "Oh, please don't get divorced."
> "That's not my position to say that. That's not how I should feel."
> "In fact, I can't be the one making that decision."

In conversation, I spontaneously responded to Kate, "Stay in the contradiction. Don't choose." I was inviting her into a *relational play* between the contradictions she was experiencing. Kate replied with evident concern, "But I have to choose between one and the other."

Being in play means to *engage with what is emerging while suspending our knowing; taking a risk; listening with curiosity.* I followed what was emerging for Kate, although I was unsure where the conversation would lead us. So, I reflected back and invited Kate to tell us more about the contradiction she was experiencing. Kate *hyperlinked* and went on to tell me about her parents, changing the context and her identity from a therapist to the daughter to her parents. She spoke of them as "very learned people." I listened with curiosity, unsure where the conversation would lead us.

Kate said, "They are diplomats who, at the same time, value the spirit world." Kate expressed puzzlement that her parents were so learned and yet, could believe in the spirit world as well. In my internal dialog (Anderson, 1997), I was also hyperlinking to my cultural heritage where we believe in the spirit world and back to the Western world where it might be pathologized or undervalued. And back to the present moment with Kate. The meaning I read into her struggle was that she was challenged by that contradiction. I shared with Kate that I saw it as a teaching/learning moment to foreground the notion of engaging "both/and" along with the accompanying "knot of contradiction" (Baxter & Montgomery, 1996) and sought her permission to proceed with it. Seeking permission was a way to attend to our relatedness (Anderson, 1997). *Learning how to hold the both/ and, the inherent contradiction, is learning how to engage uncertainty.* The dynamic interplay of the two elements is formless, and each individual's engagement with this interplay is unique. It cannot be taught, but only learned by the conditions we create for engagement with the dynamic interplay.

Then Kate quickly hyperlinked back to the couple's session and started to describe what happened and then hyperlinked to her internal dialog. I asked her, "So, what does it say about you, that you had a second voice that said, 'it's not my position to say if they should be divorced or not.'"

This conversational back and forth between her identity as a therapist and as the daughter to her parents, and their relationship to contradictions as storied by their spiritual practices is an example of crisscrossing stories, hyperlinked identities in motion. It is in these discursive moments that we continued to negotiate and perform our identities that allowed us to stay fluid and emergent. Both Kate and I moved through our contexts and identities, as we co-created our relationship and conversation (Anderson, 1997).

Playing with not only what she was learning but how she was learning to learn, was a *processual way of learning* for Kate. Learning that Kate revisited her clinical contradiction by hyperlinking to a contradiction in her personal life was both an emergent and uncertain process of what we were co-creating. But hyperlinking allowed for a playful way to stay curiously present to what emerged for Kate and to learn how it made sense of her clinical dilemma. It asks us to be in dialog about our everyday practices as sites of learning. It is a learning context that requires us to play, that is, risk the unknown and our vulnerabilities. However, research shows that risk-taking as play is not a popular cultural activity (Zinn, 2017).

Risk-Taking in Supervision

In the clinical world, risk-taking is narrowed to the potentially harmful behavioral view that requires some kind of harm-reduction approach. Instead, in supervision, how might risk-taking be viewed as "part of managing a number of everyday challenges in a reasonable way" or "how people negotiate and challenge structural and cultural conditions in everyday life" (Zinn, 2015, p. 103 as cited in Zinn, 2017)? Safety, the flip side of risk-taking, cannot be promised by supervisors from our position of authority because that recreates the positionality of power over (super-vision). Instead, engagement, the process of *staying curious* and in *mutual inquiry* (Anderson, 1997) furthers the relational activity of making safety. Taking the risk to explore what affects the supervisory relational space—such as our contextualized hyperlinked identities, positionalities, emerging relationality, and what is being co-created—is one example of how in risk-taking we create safety. We have no scripts, all we have is the play—*explicit attention to our process of trial and error, our relatedness to it* and *its attendant risk taking.*

Relating to Risk: Playing our Way Through

Nadeem, a beginning therapist (intern) asked me, "how much do I need to share?" on an assignment on cultural genograms (Hardy & Laszloffy, 1995). Nadeem's family migrated to the U.S. from Southeast Asia. "Enough to make sense of your story for others and enough to make you feel you are growing from sharing," I responded.

As I was packing up after class, Nadeem came to me after everyone had left and stated his uncertainty about sharing details about his life. This was the first class I had had with him and that evening was our first meeting, thus, I had no previous history with him. He stated that recently, in the cohort, he felt sharing his genogram in a previous course had caused his fellow students to withdraw from him. He stated that he talked about being a Muslim from Southeast Asia and how he was exploring his gender fluidity. He stated his peers' responses—rather, lack of response—left him feeling isolated. So, he was not sure he wanted to do a presentation of his cultural genogram to avoid further feelings of alienation.

In that moment, I had the choice of saying to Nadeem, "Say as little as you need to say to stay comfortable." Instead I chose to take a risk by asking him to further engage with his discomfort. I stayed present and asked him questions to understand what had happened. He spoke about three intersecting identities— religious, ethnic, and gender. He spoke about how he was reclaiming his Muslim identity as a gender non-conforming person who was negotiating and navigating his community and family, who performed their dominant ethnic discourses of gender and religious practices. Wow! I listened carefully. In my inner dialog, I wondered if he could guess that we shared some of these identities based on my name and skin color. I wondered to myself if that made a difference in approaching me with the high degree of vulnerability and courage he exhibited.

I listened with curiosity over the next half-hour as Nadeem interwove his hyperlinked identities of being a Southeast Asian Muslim, a liberal Muslim in NYC, gender non-conforming, a student with expectations, and a challenger of his family traditions, among others. I reflected back my understanding and with his permission I expanded that not only was he not responded to as he anticipated, but also that this was the first time in a "professional" space he was sharing two marginalized identities—his religious and gender narratives that, within the current U.S. context, let alone with his family, was a risky move. I wondered aloud how that complexity affected him. I also wondered if this was his way of "coming out" to his peers. We further reflected on how it intersected with his expectations that his peers would be progressive because "they were from NYC and in a therapy program." I asked him how the lack of an anticipated response combined with his going public and then encountering students not as progressive as himself, was creating a challenging learning/supervision context for him. Nadeem reflected back with a pondering look that he hadn't put it together that way. I invited him to carry this issue forward as part of his presentation with my support, if needed. That is, not do the presentation as if it is devoid of this relational context that he found himself in within the class. I offered to engage the class in an examination of the issues this raised. I asked him if our shared religious identities would be a source of help in class. To which he replied, "not really." I continued to listen with curiosity, learning more about the contexts and intersections that mattered to him. Later, I came to see it as activism: creating the space for our marginalized identities creates discomfort for others (and ourselves). Yet, at one level, all we are asking for is the right to live the lives we want to live. Activism is risky!

For Nadeem, the risk was to put more of his story out there. For me, the risk was that of an emergent process, with no guarantees and unforeseeable outcome. What was I hoping to co-create? I was performing what creativity consultant and artist Steve Chapman[3] calls playful with not-knowing (Anderson, 1997). I was discursively co-creating how to be in conversation about that which is discomforting. How do we see ourselves as not only performing from the spaces of our marginalized identities, but also as creating the change that we seek in this world? A both/and positionality. I asked Nadeem to reflect about it further, as I was going to as well. I also asked him to follow up again in preparation for his presentation, which would be a few weeks later. I invited him to meet with me individually. He reflected back that he saw that such parallel situations might arise in therapy and that he needed to learn how to engage. I saw him take a courageous step to play/experiment with a situation that was disconcerting and uncomfortable.

A week later, I invited Nadeem to follow up with me on our conversation. I thanked him for taking the risk. I also was feeling the risk of the play I was asking both of us to engage in within the supervision context of revealing our social identities and the relational process it would co-create in the team. As a supervisor, I have to consciously keep putting myself out there (a form of presence) just as I ask my students to do so. I have to co-create these conditions with them. There is no other safety than that which we tentatively co-create with each other. The conversation continues.

With Nadeem, as his conversational partner, I was keenly aware of how I might create a condition for learning that his discomfort was not his alone; rather, it was part of the collective where it belonged. Even as he realized that it was created within the context of a classroom presentation by how others perceived him, he was still feeling vulnerable—sick to his stomach. So, how do we tell our own stories as part of our current cultures' collective? How do we open space for learning and reflection on how our self-representations are locally co-created in the back and forth of our responsiveness?

As supervisors, such moments give us a pause and we either pass on them or at times attend to them. Lynn Fels (2013), a scholar of performative inquiry and pedagogy, speaks about such moments in teaching and learning as "tug at our sleeve," or "stop." The stop is *a moment of risk, a moment of opportunity*. A stop is a moment when we realize that there are multiple possibilities, that the script that we have committed to memory can be improvised, that other choices of action are available to us. A stop reveals our habits of engagement; a stop reminds us that we don't yet have all the answers. A stop invites us to reconsider our engagement with others. A stop is an invitation to reimagine who we are, and who we might be, in relationship with our environment, with those we love, and with those we teach. A stop is a reminder to let go of what we know or expect of others and embrace the uncertainty, surprise, and joy of learning (Fels, 2013 pp. 135–136).

Risk-taking in a supervisory relationship around our social, fluid, and emerging identities is like tugs on sleeves. A pause; a stop. It takes the form of curiosity, combined with cultural humbleness, which emerges from adopting a not-knowing position and embracing the emergent uncertainty (Anderson, 1997; Laird, 2000). It requires us to experiment and to do the trial-and-error work of co-creating the relational script that is unknown as we enter and engage in relationships (Bava & Greene, 2018). It is a form of suspending our knowing in favor of being surprised. It is a way of being with uncertainty and not rushing in to make sense of the other by labeling their experience from our position of knowing. It is a form of joint inquiry where we check in with each other to see if we are on track for our supervisee. *Risk-taking is play*.

Thus, risk-taking occurs in a number of different ways, from discursive practice for safety making, to self-disclosing, to acting on those moments in supervision that give us a pause. So, how might you attend to creating conditions in supervision (and teaching/learning) where you encourage the therapist's relationship to risk-taking?

Conclusion

Responsive supervision is when we take the risk to play and co-create new language with our supervisees, to play with our hyperlinked identities. The practice implications of responsive supervision are as follows:

1. We approach our supervisory conversations as meaning-making spaces where both the supervisees' and the supervisors' hyperlinked identities are co-created through dialog and the context of our relationships.
2. We imagine these identities as interlinked multiple texts and remain curious about how they are interlinked by attending not only to the identity narratives but also to the relationships among them.

3. We engage in joint inquiry *with* our supervisees' emerging narratives; actively noticing *with them* how the identity narratives are being made and remade through the conversations. We also attend to our creative process of relating and making meaning to promote collaboration (Anderson, 1997; Bava, 2017; McNamee, 2009).

4. We notice that our understanding of any one of these texts is dependent on our lived experiences, theories, and the stories of larger social systems that we bring to make sense of these texts. Simultaneously, we are coordinating *with* the supervisee's text and context.

5. Consequently, we need to hold our theories of supervisory practice lightly, as a map or guide, rather than as a certainty about social justice, identities, or our supervisees' lives. Because they also have their own maps by which they are making sense of their lives. Thus, the supervisees' and the supervisors' maps are among the many multiple texts from within which to find generative resources to design our lives.

Responsive supervision is a joint activity of play. It is a relational space for risk-taking and inventiveness. It is a performative context where are our hyperlinked identities are constituted and reconstituted in our relatedness. To close off in Escobar's (1991) words, supervision needs to become a space where:

> We must become *creators*, and cease to be subjected to the other's fantasies and myths. We must become *the dreamers* and cease to be the dreamed ones, because in fact transformation is a question not of "color" but of *vision* and *sensibility*, both how we *see* and *feel* the world. It is our (political, philosophical, ethical, aesthetic) vision/sensibility searching for its realization.
>
> *(p. 98)*

Notes

1 All examples are composites from supervision context.
2 An example of this is in Bava, Gutiérrez, & Molina (2018)
3 Read more at http://cansorcpionssmoke.com/about/

References

Anderson, H. (1997). *Conversation, language and possibility*. New York, NY: Basic Books.

Bain, K. (2004). *What the best college teachers do*. Cambridge, MA: Harvard University Press.

Bava, S. (2016a). Making of a spiritual/religious hyperlinked identity. In D. Bidwell (Ed.), *Spirituality, social construction and social processes: Essays and reflections* (pp.1–17). Chargin Falls, OH: Taos Institute Publication.

Bava, S. (2016b). *Play-oriented pedagogy: Liberating emergence and uncertainty in couples and family therapy training*. Unpublished manuscript.

Bava, S. (2017). Creativity in couple and family therapy. In J. L. Lebow, A. L. Chambers, & D. Breunlin (Eds.), *Encyclopedia of couple and family therapy*. New York, NY: Springer.

Bava, S., & Greene, M. (2018). *The Relational book for parenting.* New York, NY: ThinkPlayPartners.

Bava, S., Gutiérrez, R. C., & Molina, M. P. (2018). Collaborative-dialogic practices: A socially just orientation. In C. Audet & D. Paré (Eds.). *Social justice and counseling: Discourse in practice* (pp. 124–139). New York, NY: Routledge.

Baxter, L.A., & Montgomery, B. M. (1996). *Relating: Dialogues and dialectics.* New York, NY: Guilford.

Combs, G., & Freedman, J. (2016). Narrative therapy's relational understanding of identity. *Family Process, 55*(2), 211–224.

Escobar, E. (1991). Language, identity and liberation: A critique of the term and concept "people of color." *Yale Journal of Law and Liberation, 2*(1), 93–98.

Fels, L. (2013). The upside down picnic table: The wonder of learning though improvisational play. In K. Egan (Ed.), *Wonder-full education.* New York, NY: Taylor & Francis/Routledge.

Hardy, K., & Laszloffy, T. (1995). The cultural genogram: Key to training culturally competent family therapists. *Journal of Marital and Family Therapy, 21*(3), 227–237.

Laird, J. (2000). Theorizing culture. *Journal of Feminist Family Therapy, 11*(4), 99–114.

McNamee, S. (2008). Transformative dialogue-coordinating conflicting moralities. Retrieved October 4, 2018 from: https://mypages.unh.edu/sheilamcnamee/publications

McNamee, S. (2009). Postmodern psychotherapeutic ethics: Relational responsibility in practice. *Human Systems, 20*(1), 57–71.

Pearce, B. (2007). *Making social worlds: A communication perspective.* Malden, MA: Blackwell.

Pink, D. (2006). *A whole new mind: Why right-brainers will rule the future.* New York, NY: Penguin.

Shotter, J. (2011). The dance of rhetoric: Dialogic selves and spontaneously responsive expressions. In. C. Meyer & F. Girke (Eds.), *The rhetorical emergence of culture,* (pp. 35–51). New York, NY & London, UK: Berghahn Books.

Sicart, M. (2014). *Play matters.* Cambridge, MA: The MIT Press.

Thomas, D., & Brown, J. S. (2011). *A new culture of learning.* Createspace Independent Publishing Platform: Douglas Thomas and John Brown.

Zinn, J. O. (2017). The meaning of risk taking key concepts and dimensions. *Journal of Risk Research,* 1–15. DOI: 10.1080/13669877.2017.1351465

7

WHERE IS MY SUPERVISEE?

A Supervisor's Dilemma

Cindy Silitsky

I have the luxury in my small private practice, separate from my university responsibilities, to select whom I choose to take on as a supervisee. I enjoy conducting supervision and charge a reduced fee for my services because I recall far too well how challenging the cases are as a registered intern, how little money is being earned, and how long the path to licensure seems. I typically supervise only two or three people individually at any given time, and they are generally former students with whom I have developed strong relationships and whose clinical judgment I trust. They are in the beginning stages of their professional development, but they know what they don't know and are not afraid to ask.

However, a colleague at a neighboring university had contacted me and asked me if I would meet with a recent graduate who was looking for a supervisor. He described Sheree (a pseudonym) as a single mom who needed a reduced rate for supervision; he viewed her as smart and motivated. She was completing her paperwork to register with the state of Florida as an intern, which requires a commitment from an approved supervisor. She had obtained a new position as an independent contractor, providing home-based family therapy services for a community agency. I contacted her and we scheduled an initial meeting to see if we would be a good fit.

First Interactions

I was impressed with Sheree during our first meeting. She was able to articulate her theory of change and her beliefs about therapy. She worked from several postmodern models of therapy and used relational systemic terms to describe her views. I presented several hypothetical ethical dilemmas that could occur in family therapy and she answered them appropriately. I asked questions about diversity and populations that might challenge her; she described a lack of experience but expressed a willingness to learn. She was energetic, engaging, and likable; I could easily see how she would be able to join well with clients. After several years of interviewing students as the director of a family therapy program and with many years of clinical experience, I perceive myself to have fairly good judgment in assessing potential and there were no "red flags" that jumped out at me.

Sheree was in her late 20s, a single mother of a young daughter, and was excited about this new phase of her career and her first "real job" in the field. She expressed great appreciation at the reduced rate for supervision, as her place of employment was not able to offer this benefit. We established a signed contract with consistent weekly meetings every Friday at the same time. We ended the meeting by scheduling our first supervision session, which would begin in a few weeks after her employment start date. Although initially a bit reluctant to take on a supervisee I did not have prior experience with, my anxieties were greatly reduced after this meeting and I was looking forward to working with her over the next two years.

The Disappearance

I confirm with all clients and supervisees the day prior to scheduled appointments, a practice ingrained in me since graduate school. Some people respond to the confirmations, even if just to affirm their attendance, but it's not unusual for a message to go unresponded to and for the appointment to commence at the designated time regardless. On the day of our appointment, Sheree did not arrive. I was perplexed. I called her about 20 minutes past the appointment time and left a voicemail message reminding her that our first scheduled supervision was that day and time as we had agreed upon and I had confirmed the day prior, and to please contact me to reschedule.

A week went by. No response.

I left another message. No response.

My anxiety was mounting. What could have happened? Was she seeing these difficult cases that I was liable for without any guidance? How liable *was* I for them? Although it's my general understanding that the supervisor is ultimately responsible for a supervisee's work (Falender, Cornish, Goodyear, Hatcher, Kaslow, & Leventhal, 2004), I was not her on-site supervisor; I was serving as her state-approved qualified academic supervisor for licensure. It did not make sense. Most people would call or send an email to cancel an appointment or terminate our contract, simply out of etiquette. If it was financial difficulties, I had assured her of my flexibility on this, especially in the beginning when she was awaiting her first paycheck. If she had only wanted my signature for the state supervision form, she must have known that I only needed to inform the state that we had not been meeting for supervision and my name would be removed as her approved supervisor. This aspect of supervision is the part that is often the most challenging for me in the context of academia: the power dynamics within the supervisory relationship, in that I now felt more like an agent of social control, which is not my preferred style of supervision and why I prefer to conduct supervision outside of the constraints of academia.

How many times could I contact her before it turned into "stalking"? Why was I so anxious about this anyway? It is possible her place of employment offered supervision for her and she was reluctant to tell me? Perhaps she changed her mind about supervision with me and had a difficult time telling me this. Could she have lost her job and been too embarrassed to inform me? Wilson, Davies, & Weatherhead (2016), in a meta-synthesis of therapists' experiences of supervision, discuss how supervisees can find it difficult to voice concerns with a supervisor if they feel unsafe; was it possible that Sheree felt this way and I was insensitive to it? I found it difficult to believe my colleague would have referred a supervisee to me who was irresponsible or unethical, as I am known for having high expectations of students and supervisees. I was uncertain how to proceed.

I sent a letter to Sheree's address on file, asking her to please contact me to discuss the lack of communication. No response. I wondered if I should I keep our designated supervision slot open for her or schedule a client in that time? Should I contact her supervisor at her place of employment or would that be overstepping my boundaries as her academic supervisor?

I sent an email. No surprise: no response.

I consulted with a colleague. It had now been weeks without contact. He advised me to leave one last message with a clear firm deadline. Additionally, if I did not hear from her by a date in the next week, I would have no other option but to contact the state to let them know that she was in violation of the agreement that we had signed and that I would no longer be serving as her state-approved supervisor. He also advised me to document all of the previous attempts at contact with Sheree in her file, just in case there was any doubt about whether I had diligently attempted to maintain contact with her. I left that voice mail message, again feeling like an agent of social control and, quite frankly, rather frustrated with Sheree at that point. If she responded, I was not sure if we would be able to work together and maintain a positive relationship after such a tumultuous beginning.

The Reappearance

That last message provoked a response. The next day, I received a call from an unknown number and answered it to hear her voice. As best as I can recall, here is our conversation:

Sheree: Hi, Cindy, it's Sheree. I am so, so sorry that I have not returned your calls and that I missed our meetings.

Cindy: OK. … um, well, what's going on? Have you changed your mind about the supervision?

[Long silence]

Cindy: Sheree? Are you there?

Sheree: (in a quiet voice) I was walking between two cars in a parking lot, the week after we met. I might not have been paying enough attention ... there was an accident. I have been in the hospital. I have not been able to return home yet or go to work. I was not conscious for a while and nobody knew to call you or my job, which I think I lost because I did not show up for so long. I am so sorry.

Cindy: Wow ... that sounds awful ... are you ok now?
           [Long silence]

Sheree: (quietly): I won't be going home for a while. I must go to a rehab center and am trying to find someone to take care of my daughter while I am gone. I don't know when I will be able to start supervision now and that job is gone. I am sorry.

Cindy: That sounds serious. Your injuries must be severe. Whenever you are ready, of course, just let me know.

Sheree: (more quietly) They amputated both my legs above the knee.
           [Very long silence. What could I say? I felt so ... petty for calling her multiple times while she was in a hospital bed, dealing with such incomprehensible loss.]

Cindy: Sheree, I don't have words ... please just focus on improving ... and on your daughter.

Sheree: Again, I am so sorry for any inconvenience and if I wasted any of your time since you lost all those open appointments. I hope you will forgive me. I felt terrible when I heard your messages.

Sheree felt terrible? I felt terrible.

Cindy: Sheree, please, do not worry about that. Take care. You are not seeing clients right now, so let's just leave everything as is, and whenever you are ready, we can revisit it.

I was haunted by this call for months. I was uncertain if she would have the same career goals after sustaining such life-changing injuries. Even if she did, I felt confident that I had ruined any fledgling relationship that we had started to form and was doubtful that I would ever hear from Sheree again.

One Year Later: Our Work

Sheree contacted me approximately a year later. She explained that she was now using a wheelchair and had obtained a new position as a family therapist, very similar to her previous position. She wanted to know if we could schedule supervision. I was quite impressed that she was committed to her original plan and very surprised that she was still interested in my supervision. When I expressed my surprise to her, she was surprised at my surprise and asked why that would have changed.

My assumption as to why that could have changed goes back to the need to mention in my voicemail message the power I had over her in contacting the state to remove my name as her supervisor if she did not respond to my multiple attempts to contact her. For me, that felt like a shift in the collaborative type of relationship I typically employ with supervisees. I adhere strongly to the finding that "the most pivotal and crucial component of good supervision experiences is the quality of the supervisory relationship" (Worthen & McNeill, 1996, p. 29). What surprised me was Sheree's ability to perceive that we could potentially have a positive supervisory relationship after this interaction.

Our supervision began, but the work contained many unanticipated challenges related to the accident. I realized the many ways supervision would be affected in our first meeting. I had assumed that our office was wheelchair accessible, as we have wide front doors and accommodations for parking. However, our inner doors to the offices where I conduct supervision and therapy are much narrower and it was difficult to maneuver her wheelchair through them. I was able to do this with some finagling, but the bathroom doors were impossibly small and could not accommodate the wheelchair. We discussed in our first meeting what to do about this, as I had, to my shame, never even noticed this prior to that day. Our plan was that Sheree would use the bathroom prior to the hourly supervision meetings, but I also consulted the other offices in our shopping center until I located an office that had a larger bathroom facility. When I explained the situation to them, they kindly agreed that if Sheree needed to use their facilities during or after a supervision session, they would accommodate her.

I had not supervised someone prior to this time who utilized a wheelchair. Using a wheelchair presented many new supervisory concerns about therapy when conducting home visits with families. First was the issue of self-disclosure. How much was necessary and how much was she comfortable with? At what point in the process did it make the most sense to disclose? Many homes were not wheelchair accessible. Safety is always a concern when conducting home visits, and it presented even more of a concern for Sheree, as her physical condition rendered it more difficult to leave a threatening situation. The bathroom situation that we encountered in our office is one that was also problematic in some clients' homes.

Part of our new supervision routine was to integrate an assessment of the home's condition when doing an intake with the family, prior to taking the case. We formulated a brief, basic self-disclosure statement that Sheree would make during an intake about the fact that she used a wheelchair and posed questions to the family about the home's ability to accommodate it. If the home could not, we would devise plans to work around it, such as meeting the family in their outside yard or in a private location such as a park; we would create bathroom and safety plans as well. If the home could not accommodate her needs, if the changes would be too arduous for the family to complete (such as a lack of transportation), if Sheree felt unsafe in a home, we would discuss it with her on-site supervisor and make plans for some cases to be transferred to a different therapist. We also explored various ways to address questions by curious clients about her injuries.

Our supervisory work also differed in content. For example, there was a case Sheree was struggling with in which a single mother was diagnosed with a terminal illness and had not disclosed her diagnosis to her two children. The mom was not open to discussing her illness in therapy and Sheree was uncomfortable discussing it if the mother did not want to. The therapy was, at best, superficial and focused on the children's behavioral problems. The children appeared to have some knowledge of the health issues the mother was struggling with, but it was a topic that everyone avoided discussing. I challenged Sheree about why she was hesitant to discuss the "elephant in the room." Given the severity of the diagnosis, the fact that this single mother had few resources, and the children would be moved into foster care if there were no other plans made for their care, it felt urgent to discuss the practical matters of what would happen to the children upon her death and to not squander the opportunity therapy would give this family to say goodbye to the mother and have important conversations prior to her death. Sheree explained that she did not feel competent to work with this case and discuss these topics because she "had no experience with loss." I was stunned. I told Sheree that it seemed to me that she had much more experience with loss than most people her age, considering the huge loss of her legs, her mobility, her previous identity. Sheree had not viewed her accident as "loss" and we had a very intense discussion about this topic. Sheree then connected her reticence to both culture and her own experiences in the hospital with her daughter when she thought she might die from her injuries. She felt "too close" to this case and worried that she might "break down" if she engaged in these topics with the family. We discussed at length what "breaking down" might look like, what that would mean, what the cost of avoiding "breaking down" would be to this family. Sheree worked with this family under close supervision and helped them make these emotional and difficult decisions in an open collaborative way.

Broader Ethical Questions

Fortunately, in Sheree's situation, she had not been seeing clients when tragedy struck. However, the question lingered in my mind: What if she had been seeing clients? If clients were unable to reach her as she lay incapacitated in a hospital and they were in crisis, what would happen to them? If there were no procedures in place to notify the agency or me, obviously clients would not have been notified and Sheree would have missed scheduled sessions. It's likely that a client might attempt to contact the organization if they had been unable to reach Sheree, but how long might that process take? Sheree was hired as an independent contractor and it's notoriously difficult for clients to contact staff at these under-resourced organizations. Our clients are often in severe crisis and experiencing trauma, whether it be in relation to domestic violence, substance use, suicidal ideation, and so forth. If a client could not reach Sheree while in this state and had a history of being abandoned by those they entrusted, it is not difficult to imagine that they could also believe that Sheree was neglecting them. If clients made choices during that time of incapacitation, whether it be days, weeks, or longer, what is the therapist's ethical and legal responsibility? What are the effects on their relationships with those clients if they do return? What is the supervisor's ethical and legal responsibility? What are the effects on the supervisor/supervisee relationship if the supervisor is held responsible for client actions during that period?

Mental health professions cover this concern broadly in the American Association for Marriage and Family Therapy (AAMFT), the American Counseling Association (ACA), the National Association of Social Workers (NASW), and the American Psychological Association (APA) codes of ethics. The first is in relation to not abandoning clients.

> 1.11 Non-Abandonment. Marriage and family therapists do not abandon or neglect clients in treatment without making reasonable arrangements for the continuation of treatment.
>
> *(AAMFT, 2015)*

> A.12. Abandonment and Client Neglect. Counselors do not abandon or neglect clients in counseling. Counselors assist in making appropriate arrangements for the continuation of treatment, when necessary, during interruptions such as vacations, illness, and following termination.
>
> *(ACA, 2014)*

The second is in relation to anticipated or unanticipated events that may affect clinical practice.

> 2.6 Preparation for Practice Changes. In preparation for moving a practice, closing a practice, or death, marriage and family therapists arrange for the storage, transfer, or disposal of client records in conformance with applicable laws and in ways that maintain confidentiality and safeguard the welfare of clients.
>
> *(AAMFT, 2015)*

> B.6.i. Reasonable Precautions. Counselors take reasonable precautions to protect client confidentiality in the event of the counselor's termination of practice, incapacity, or death and appoint a records custodian when identified as appropriate.
>
> *(ACA, 2014)*

> 3.12. Interruption of Psychological Services. Unless otherwise covered by contract, psychologists make reasonable efforts to plan for facilitating

services in the event that psychological services are interrupted by factors such as the psychologist's illness, death, unavailability, relocation, or retirement or by the client's/patient's relocation or financial limitations (see also 6.02c regarding transfer of records).

(APA, 2017)

1.07 (t) Social workers should take reasonable precautions to protect client confidentiality in the event of the social worker's termination of practice, incapacitation, or death.

(NASW, 2017)

1.15 Interruption of Services. Social workers should make reasonable efforts to ensure continuity of services in the event that services are interrupted by factors such as unavailability, disruptions in electronic communication, relocation, illness, mental or physical ability, or death.

(NASW, 2017)

It is reasonable to assume that most therapists and supervisors make plans to protect client continuity of care, transfer of client records, and other best practices when a life change is anticipated such as a pregnancy, retirement, relocation, or planned surgery. It is less clear how many therapists and supervisors have plans in place for unanticipated events. Sheree was in her late 20s at the time of this event; statistically, the odds of this type of incident occurring were low. The Codes of Ethics are broad enough to leave the details of how this process is enacted up to individual therapists, supervisors, agencies, and employers. Many practices have informal policies and coverage for unplanned events.

However, it's unclear why our profession has not formalized procedures and policies. Lawyers in the state of Florida, for example, must appoint a person to be responsible for client records in the event of their incapacitation; this person must be listed and verified each time the lawyer renews their license to practice in the state (personal communication, Jacqueline Schneider, P.A., June 2, 2017). As every state requires licensure renewals, this could easily be implemented and create accountability to protect our clients, therapists, and supervisees.

The Appearance.

When creating this chapter, I was struck by the idea of Sheree's disappearing and then reappearing, which is defined as "becoming visible, into sight," and then "vanishing from sight, under suspicious circumstances." However, an alternate definition for appearance is "to give the impression or appearance of being," "to look as though" (Dictionary.com). My supervision experience with Sheree fits this definition exactly: her disappearance gave the impression of being something else, more sinister or unreliable, to look as though it was one thing when it was another.

It is difficult to summarize the lessons learned from our relationship, as there are many. Since this experience, I have worked harder at giving students and supervisees the benefit of the doubt when they miss class or an appointment before jumping to a conclusion. I am much more aware of the physical limitations of my clinical office setting. I have explored my anxiety and level of trust in accepting new supervisees. I have great admiration for Sheree's resiliency, and I believe that was evident in our work together.

I believe I judged myself and my actions over her disappearance more harshly than Sheree did; my initial attempts at establishing a relationship with her and empathy in our phone call were somehow stronger than my actions while attempting to contact her. I do not think I will have another supervisee disappear, as I now ask new supervisees to provide an emergency contact number (similar to my policy with new clients) and ask for authorization to contact this person if they miss supervision appointments or I am unable to reach them. I have, thankfully, never had to utilize this policy.

Sheree and I worked together to complete her required supervision for the state of Florida. Although it took longer than two years, requirements were successfully completed.

Today, Sheree is a licensed marriage and family therapist in the state of Florida.

References

AAMFT. (2015). *American Association for Marriage and Family Therapy: Code of ethics.* Retrieved from http://www.aamft.org/iMIS15/AAMFT/ content/legal_ethics/ code_of_ethics. aspx

ACA. (2014). *American Counseling Association: Code of ethics.* Retrieved from http://www. counseling.org/about-us/about-aca

APA. (2017). *American Psychological Association: Code of ethics.* Retrieved from: http://www. apa.org/code-of-Ethics

Dictionary.com. Retrieved from http://www.dictionary.com/disappear

Falender, C. A., Cornish. J. A. E., Goodyear, R., Hatcher, R., Kaslow, N. J., & Leventhal, G. (2004). Defining competencies in psychology supervision. A consensus statement. *Journal of Clinical Psychology, 60*(7), 771–785.

NASW. (2017). *National Association of Social Workers: Code of ethics.* Retrieved from https:// www.socialworkers.org/About/Ethics/Code-of-Ethics/Code-of-Ethics-English

Wilson, H. M. N., Davies, J. S., & Weatherhead, S. (2016). Trainee therapists' experiences of supervision during training: A meta-synthesis. *Clinical Psychology and Psychotherapy, 23*(4), 340–351.

Worthen, V., & McNeill, B.W. (1996). A phenomenological investigation of "good" supervision events. *Journal of Counseling Psychology, 43*(1), 25–31.

8

TENDER IS THE HEART

Supervising High Impact Emotions During Sex Therapy

Paula Leech

Introduction: Another Car Ride

I can't recall how old I was, but my gut is telling me ten. It was dark out and we had taken a drive together to talk. This was not unusual; drives were not only a means to get from one place to the next in our family but also something to pass the time and a way to have meaningful, often hard conversations while watching the world go by to the 90s greatest hits. We were sitting at a drive-through window waiting for our food. The content of tonight's drive wasn't creating thoughts so much, just feelings: just heavy, blurry, stomach-twisting feelings. Confused, maybe? Sad … probably? Not sure. Definitely dazed, likely knowing intuitively that this would be something that would take my entire life to process. That what was just disclosed to me was monumental, bigger than anything really, and was going to forever change my relationship with my mom, the way I looked at the world, and how I interacted with the subject of sex. Having no clue whatsoever of how this would live in me and take on a critical role in the therapy, and subsequently supervision, I do professionally. In the meantime, Taco Bell, and our drive home, and 90s hits.

Operation: Therapy Superstar

I never knew I wanted to be a supervisor, to train budding therapists. It took a long time to really begin to know what I should do at all. I never felt particularly smart according to the textbook definition. Looking back, I was more than miserable at math, not terribly clever, and just plain lousy at memorizing facts. I cheated like crazy in science, history, and yes, math in order to survive school with a decent GPA. After trying on a few majors in college, I began taking some classes concerning child development, relationships, and family therapy and suddenly unearthed a proficiency. I distinctly remember sitting in a massive, 500-person auditorium with the professor explaining family systems with a mobile like those found dangling above an infant's crib. He pushed one of the hanging geometric shapes, let the mobile and all of its parts spin, then explained that families are much the same. Change in one piece excites change in all of the other pieces; the system itself shifts. This seemed so novel, and yet explained so much. I feverishly wrote down every word of his explanation and subsequently the rest of his lecture, and left with a kick in my step and a new major. I was going to become a marriage and family therapist.

Having completed the prerequisites to take a course in human sexuality, I chose carefully. It felt not only exciting but also important that I enroll. Sexuality was a completely normal, even positive subject and topic of discussion in my house; not too small, and not too big. My mother made sure to arm me from a young age with all the information she could. There wasn't just one conversation, but many, often under the covers of her and my father's bed, looking at books, studying the pictures while I feigned disinterest. She worked to shine a light on the aspects of sex and sexuality that make it fun, intimate, empowering, and sacred, and yet was practical about discussing safety, boundaries, and consent. She was purposeful in how she relayed this information; serious when called for and playful the rest of the time. She was knowledgeable, real, accessible, and yet appropriate with the content she shared and the advice she gave. She was still very much a parent, and this is what made her an exceptional one.

My home provided one distinct culture and atmosphere around sexuality, met by an entirely different ideology in the outside world. What was open was hidden with seemingly rigid rules and often deeply shrouded in shame. This odd collision seemed to fuel a fascination with the idea of sex and a deep desire to understand it in a greater way. The very first day of my very first class in Human Sexual Behavior 101, another piece of the puzzle fell into place. My fascination with relationships was inextricably tied to my fascination with sexuality. The notion of leaving the study of sexuality out of the work with relationships felt backward, even neglectful. A sexual dynamic or level of intimacy is present and part of our romantic relationships whether we are acting on this component or not; it is often nuanced, seemingly hidden, but very real and very there. Sexuality arguably holds a critical place in what makes us human; sex therapy, therefore, seemed the logical add-on to my professional goals in studying how we humans "do" connection and relationship. I knew my mother would agree.

Supervision: A New Beginning

Supervised internship became a topic of discussion, an abstract idea, and an intimidating last hurdle in the pursuit of a master's degree during the final year of my graduate school studies.

My supervisor Stephen and I frequently saw couples as co-therapists, granting me access to his very diverse caseload. Co-therapy was a significant part of my supervision experience, accounting for about half of the cases I would ultimately see. One of these couples came in struggling to reconcile a significant desire discrepancy between them. Like most couples together for any significant amount of time, they had found themselves bored with their go-to sexual script. The male partner (we'll call him Frank, cisgender, heterosexual) yearned for his wife's touch (we'll call her Amanda, cisgender, heterosexual) and missed their long-since-absent sexual relationship tremendously. Amanda, on the other hand, was quick to proclaim her total lack of desire and her struggle to find any motivation to try to reclaim or rediscover it. Yet she understood that this was unfair to her partner given her desire to remain monogamous, and therefore was willing to work toward locating those motivations in order to enjoy physical connection with Frank and herself once again.

Flash forward: a great deal of therapy had been done to get to the point where they were both ready to explore different positions and discuss their desires within the context of true, embodied consent. As a supervisee, I was eager to "fix things quickly" for this couple, without regard for the emotional readiness of each partner, the role of pacing in therapy, or consideration for the arc of therapy as a whole. Supervision with them would challenge me to tune in and allow progress to unfold according to different criteria, including the strength of the connection of the couple, their engagement in the therapeutic process, the level of trust in the relationship with Stephen and me as their clinicians, as well as their reactions (both verbal and non) to prescribed or suggested steps. We were all ready for what came next.

The night prior, Amanda had shocked Frank by asking to experiment with some manual stimulation. I sat eagerly next to Stephen, withholding my enthusiasm because of my still very present performance anxiety, anticipating their reactions to what seemed like a significant step forward as Amanda had yet to initiate any ideas in this way. Sex therapy supervisees, out of their own discomfort, will often collect incredibly brief descriptions of both the couple's feelings and the series of events leading up to and during their sexual play. My inclination at that point was the same. Yet in order to (a) identify any barriers to intimacy or aspects of the experience that might contribute to the presenting problem, and (b) locate and build upon what worked, the therapist must zoom way in. Clients are frequently warned of the seemingly voyeuristic nature of the work.

Stephen did just that and the questions necessarily became increasingly detailed and explicit. Questions about thoughts and emotion that emerged were layered between questions around behavior. Talking about bodies, sexuality, and sexual functioning requires that the clinician use specific, explicit language, and often that we prescribe specific, explicit behaviors to be explored at home. I had yet to experience this kind of discussion in my caseload. Abstract concepts and ideas, such as "intimacy" and "tenderness" and "desire" had been commonplace; breaking them down into tangible, actionable components had yet to emerge, or perhaps had been avoided on my part out of intimidation. Approaching the most intimate details of people's private lives requires a skilled hand, as the therapist is both modeling a process of communication and introducing a critical tone to an area of life often undiscussed and therefore, infamously challenging for clients to breach. To be able to witness this being done by my supervisor felt extremely critical to my learning at that point, another aspect of supervision that cannot be taught via text.

As proper terminology began to emerge from the conversation, words such as "vulva," "scrotum," "ejaculate," and "cunnilingus" were introduced by Stephen, and treated like any other words you might use to describe everyday, routine behavior. They may have felt everyday and commonplace for him, but as he put language to what had previously been referred to in my life as "private parts," I felt my face heat up. I could certainly discuss sex comfortably, but it became clear very quickly that this was context-dependent. It is one thing to chat with lifelong friends about their sexual adventures and mishaps while driving to class versus approaching near-strangers about their innermost private lives while attempting to treat the information with respect and utmost professionalism. I was caught off guard by this realization, and I could feel myself squirming in my chair. When discussing the utility of lubricant, Stephen raised two fingers up in the air in order to present a visual of the kind of manual penetration they might explore in order to reach more stimulating areas inside of the vagina. With that, I began fighting back the intense, nagging urge to smile, or worse, laugh! The fourteen-year-old inside of me was in hysterics at the awkward foreignness of it all, while my adult-self tried desperately to get this under control. With all of this stirring inside of me, I wondered how I was presenting. How do you "look" when discussing other people's "private parts"? What do you do with your face?

Out of Somewhere

Perhaps because of the fact that every second of my supervision seemed full of intense, challenging, fascinating, and anxiety-producing moments, most of the time I was quite simply exhausted. I spoke with Stephen one evening about feeling as though my brain was literally swollen within my head, unable to take in another word. I traveled home in a daze each night, nestled inside a sort of quiet vacancy. My boyfriend would be forewarned: I have nothing to give to tonight's conversation so please keep it simple.

One day, I walked into internship feeling lighter, enthusiastic about my similarly light caseload. Only a few couples to work with, a supervision meeting, and then home. Perhaps I would have enough brain space left over to allow for at least a glimmer of meaningful interaction with my incredibly patient boyfriend. To be able to step outside of my therapist-mind-under-construction and connect to a more familiar part of myself again felt like really good self-care, another vital component of the making of a good therapist that I had been severely neglecting.

After completing my time with my couples, I got myself comfortable in my usual chair in Stephen's office, ready to review our cases alongside the list of challenges and areas of improvement from the week. I knew I was ready for whatever he had for me; my mood could buffer even the most "constructive" of criticism.

Stephen: Hi Paula, have a seat.

I could immediately sense from his tone that something had happened.

Stephen: We have a situation we have to address immediately. Last night, Amanda's boyfriend raped her. I don't have all of the details just yet, but her mom called me this morning and I've spoken with Amanda briefly just now. She is not doing well.

Amanda was in her early 20s, a cisgender, heterosexual female who was part of a large family Stephen and I had been seeing for several months. All of the relationships within the family were complicated and strained, so spending time focusing on any one relationship proved challenging. What we did know, however, was that the boyfriend involved had behaved in aggressive ways toward Amanda in the past. Their relationship was volatile, but until then only emotionally, culminating in screaming matches and calls to the police.

Stephen: We are going to need to report him. Have you had to do that before?

That last question did not resonate; I was several seconds behind. As soon as he mentioned "rape," the shift was instant. There was no containment, no fighting back any kind of urge or emotion because it surged to the surface before I could even recognize what was happening. My entire being felt it. My body shook, my rational brain in full-on paralysis as the tears fell. Suddenly I had no control, no ability to manage myself, there was no "me" anymore, no thoughts. I was my reaction. This had never happened. I was purposeful in what I would show others, meticulous in how I would allow myself to "appear" to the world. There were no exceptions, this was a complete break in my very practiced script.

Stephen sat by my side, kindly, patiently waiting it out with me. That was all there was to do, just allow the emotion to run its course. I was inaccessible, unreachable even if he had attempted, and as a skilled and focused supervisor, he must have known this. The surge eventually began to subside, bringing me back to reality. I looked around, looked at Stephen, and found my old self again.

Me: I'm so, so sorry. I have no clue where that came from! That has never happened to me before. I must be extra exhausted...or something. Oh my goodness, I'm sorry.

Stephen: This is absolutely ok. You're human, and it's about time! I had yet to
see any emotion from you in this work, and if you're really present
and invested in your clients, this becomes an eventual inevitability.
Something to consider, however, is what it is about this client, and/
or about this incident in particular that inspired the magnitude of the
reaction you just had. We have done some challenging work together,
and have encountered truly upsetting experiences, yet there was a
definitive something that gripped you just now. What was it and what
was it connected to? Let's just sit with this for a second. Take your time.

Supervision up until this point had consisted primarily of discussion of cases, therapeutic strategy, theory, and of areas of growth technique-wise. Often in that order.
This was the first time I had really been asked to delve into "self-of-therapist"
work in this capacity. He looked at me as if to suggest that this, too, was an eventual
inevitability. I was being challenged to continue to be vulnerable, to really dig in
when what I longed for was to regain my composure, brush past the experience
like it had never happened, and continue with our routine: to become invulner-
able as a reaction and a means of coping with my embarrassment, and to step back
into the supervisee version of myself that he had known just a few minutes prior.
Yet even greater than this desire was the sense of trust in the room, the feeling of
being supported and encouraged toward the experience unfolding inside of me
as a means of growth both professionally and personally. I suddenly heard myself
telling a story, my mother's story, without making the conscious decision to do so.

I told of the teenage boys who lived next door to her home. Of their mother
who welcomed mine in for food and comfort during days of boredom after
school. I described how those boys eventually sexually violated my mother, who
was no older than four when it began, on most days over the course of several
years. I combed through the difficulty that followed: eating disorders, anxiety
and panic, hospitalizations, and running away. Without room or time to choose
language, it poured out of me carrying with it what I now know to be decades
worth of undigested grief for my mother, for that little girl who had to continue
to walk past those boys for years after, and for her forever-shattered sense of safety
and peace within herself, her family, and the world.

Stephen continued to bring compassion and curiosity to our exchange. He
was gentle and strategic about the timing of his inquiries, careful not to interfere
with my process. His usually rather directive approach to supervision had vanished
in favor of something much more subtle and empathic, making himself known
just enough to keep me tethered to the present moment. I was in supervision
and my emotional experience, connected enough to one as an anchor in order
to freely navigate the other. This process unfolded in a matter of minutes, and in
that brief time, supervision became my secure base through which I could delve
even deeper into myself, the work of therapy, and the complicated and intimate
relationships born from both.

I walked out of our meeting changed, ready to be a different version of myself in therapy. I longed to have the kind of powerful exchange that had just transpired between supervisor and me with my clients, knowing that the ability to do so required that I abandon my script, my mask, and my defenses. There were many unknowns hanging in the air: What would this look like? How can I speak so profoundly to my clients from a place beyond words, as Stephen had done? How might a therapist strategically use her own emotional experience to encourage expression from their clients? In the months that followed, these questions would be explored at length with Stephen and via cases. On that night, however, I drove home with a new appreciation for this incredible work, for the importance of supervision, and for my mother.... This was a drive unlike any other.

Growing-up in Supervision

Post-licensure, I did not seek out sexual trauma cases, but they arrived, one after the next until they comprised the majority of my caseload. As if by design, this work continued to show me how to be a therapist by showing me myself, my family, and the imprint left by my mother's trauma. Supervision of my cases continued on a regular basis. As I allowed more of myself to be revealed in our meetings, I became more skilled at strategically using what was "mine" in the therapy room. This was counter to a great deal of my thinking around what it meant to be a therapist while I was in graduate school. Although many models of systemic therapy emphasize the position of the therapist as that of collaborator, as curious co-pilot rather than expert, I found myself attached to the stereotype of therapist as a neutral, non-alliance-forming, emotionally disengaged expert. Put to practice, this was not a stance I could productively adopt. When sitting with a client, too often, parts in need of grieving revealed themselves, parts in need of anger or self-compassion came forth, and I had to give them permission to express themselves by connecting with those feelings myself. I learned that I must be willing to tap into a degree of the emotions my clients have worked to avoid or have locked away in order to come closer to connection, to really work through the emotions and inspiring change.

We must bring emotions into the room. Supervision lets us practice facing and becoming intimately familiar with our own emotional experiences, our own ghosts so that we are steady enough emotionally to do this work with clients. Supervision gave me a context whereupon I could develop a strong voice as therapist in order to do so. Through the deliberate breaking down of my movements in sessions, often reviewed via video recordings, I got to know myself intimately in this role. I was able to step back from myself, critically examine this new person in interaction with others from a systemic lens, and deliberately construct the blueprint of my therapist self in a way that felt authentic and synchronous with the other aspects of who I was at the time.

Through Stephen's eyes over time, this was reinforced. A reflected sense of self with regards to my role as therapist, including my own personal style and perspective, became influenced-by rather than trying-to-be Michael White, Virginia Satir, Masters and Johnson, or any of the other family and sex therapy greats. The evolution of my supervision was such that over time, rather than Stephen's being my anchor, keeping me grounded as I navigated the universe of other people's lives, I became my own anchor, able to hold onto myself, my perspective, and my role in the midst of massive complexity emotionally, psychically, and mentally. In this way, supervision ultimately did mirror the stages of human development from infancy to adolescence to adulthood. From complete openness and wide-eyed fascination in infancy; to the development of a sense of autonomy, therapist identity, and often proud push-back from the feedback given in adolescence; to the ability to appreciate the learning that has happened, but also the depth of the lifelong learning that is still to come as part of this work in adulthood.

From this "adult" place, supervision helped me to externalize and conceptualize the emotion that came up around sexual trauma as that little girl version of my mother. I began to carry her picture with me as a means of inspiration and courage. If the work of therapy required that I make space for and allow big emotion to come to fruition in the room, I knew I needed to be brave enough to permit enough of mine to surface in order to inspire it in my clients. She became a source of strength, as if holding me by the hand as client and therapist attempted to dismantle often lifelong-practiced methods for shutting away pain, fear, and memory. To be able to tell my clients I was sorry for what happened to them and to be able to really mean it would require a challenging balance of strategy, timing, emotional attunement, and personal resonation. As therapists, we have to reach those deep, dark places—the hidden, wounded children that live in all of our clients— and really connect with them. We have to communicate through and with emotion and let it manifest through our eyes, our posture, our tone, our pacing, and our words. Through supervision, I learned that it's not enough to do therapy and subsequently talk about cases from a solely rational place. We are emotional beings, affected and affecting. This is in the room with us. Supervision shines a light on how we can use it to bring about deeper, more intimate moments and therefore more meaningful change. We are physically, mentally, emotionally, and spiritually in conversation; trying to stay within one terrain hinders contact with the others. Too much information gets lost at too great a cost.

Stepping into Big Shoes

After completing my time with Stephen, I went on to have another incredible sex therapy supervisor, Ricky, who would help me to prepare to become a supervisor of sex therapy myself. Supervision became a topic of discussion, an abstract idea, and an intimidating last hurdle in the pursuit of a master's degree during the final year of my graduate school studies. I made this decision to pursue supervision as a supervisor after reviewing many clinical decisions I had made that were profoundly shaped by my supervision experience. Looking back, I have come to understand the role of the supervisor as comprised of many components: honing of the supervisee's technical skill when it comes to the implementation of theory and therapeutic strategy, assessing areas of clinical strength and growth, assisting the development of a clinical orientation/therapeutic voice, and supporting the supervisee in navigating the licensure process. One component that I didn't expect was the illuminating of and curiosity around the emotional reactions of the therapist that surface during and/or because of the work. Both of my supervisors knew that it was not their job to provide therapy to supervisees, yet the end result was incredibly therapeutic. They were supporting me in becoming more myself in order to become the best therapist I could be. They both instinctively knew that in order to be the latter, I must have access to all of my inner resources. Therapists must be open enough in heart and mind to receive or make contact with what is being revealed both overtly and covertly.

This openness is foundational to our lives as therapists and supervisors. To connect with ourselves, our past, our families of origin, our trauma, our wounds, and our hearts allows us a degree of familiarity with the resilience and courage needed to really venture in and take the necessary risks with our clients. Supervision helped me find within myself a critical resource: my mother—my grief, my love, my compassion, my playfulness, and my source of strength. I have been touched by her trauma, but because of her determination to protect me from its intergenerational impact, because she set out to raise me as sex positive as she knew how, I am able to call on its imprint as a gift and tool rather than a roadblock or obstacle. I endeavor to help my supervisees discover the similarly locked away yet ever-present and influential parts in themselves. I hope to help them understand the magnitude of the work that we do and the adventure that they've undertaken for themselves. I expect to walk with my supervisees through the developmental phases as a parent would: learning, listening, and shadowing my example in the early days; pushing me away and trying on different styles as they begin to construct their voices in the middle; and then filtering in the feedback that resonates with their more established sense of therapist self in the end.

Supervision shows us that there is no map to this work, no "one size fits all" to hold on to when our minds get caught up and our studies fail us. This is scary, but there is another form of wisdom available and it makes itself known in a smile, a shift in tone, the making or breaking of eye contact, the long pause in the midst of a plethora of words, or in a full-on breakdown. Supervision prepares us for what we might encounter when we dare to allow our curiosity to lead when these shifts occur, when the body and subconscious speak, by revealing to us our hidden stories. I encourage my supervisees to take a breath, come into the room and go there; with themselves, with me, and with their clients. In doing so we learn the most profound lessons possible about what it means to be ourselves, to be therapists, and to be human. I never knew I wanted to be a supervisor, I was led there from a place beyond words.

9

SUPERVISION IN SCHOOLS

Learning to Hear Many Voices

Anne Rambo, Brittany Henry, Alexandra E. Alfaro, and Elizabeth M. Jarquin

For over a decade, Rambo has been supervising graduate interns in public schools in Broward County, the sixth largest publicly funded school system in the United States. For the past five years, she and the master's and doctoral students working with her have provided the counseling for the PROMISE program, a school-based diversion program designed to interrupt the school-to-prison pipeline (www.browardprevention.org). Henry, Alfaro, and Jarquin all worked in the program as master's interns and then moved on to supervisory roles within PROMISE as they became doctoral students. Henry has now graduated and completed a research project in South Africa, taking the supervision ideas developed in PROMISE to a different country and a different task: supervision and training of teachers rather than beginning therapists (Henry, 2018). This chapter focuses on supervision in this school-based work in the United States and in South Africa.

Introduction

In both the United States and South Africa, clinical work in schools requires an awareness of the individual voices of the children, the voices of each member of the family system, and the voices of each individual teacher and school official, a sort of collective voice of the school system, as well as various voices within the community. In the United States, the collective voice of the school system gives us information about resources legally mandated through the Individuals with Disabilities in Education Act and any state regulations. Those in the system also need to attend to the meaning of acronyms such as RTI (response to intervention), ESE (Exceptional Student Education), and IEP (Individualized Educational

Plan)—these acronyms come into play as we listen in on ongoing conversations between those advocating for the rights of students with special needs and their parents, and those advocating for the rights of school officials to set limits. Kim, Kelly, and Franklin (2017) note that school-based therapists in the United States must attend to the language of rights and entitlements.

In South Africa, the conversation is less about legal rights and entitlements, and more about tradition coming into conflict with change (Henry, 2018). Those working with the school system in South Africa do well to be aware of the ongoing debate between the government's stated desire to outlaw corporal punishment and the prevailing cultural preference for such punishment still honored by many in schools in rural communities. Tradition is also honored in music and ceremony. Henry (2018) notes that each training session opens with all the teachers present singing familiar songs, thus bringing in on their own the voices of tradition.

Political and social issues speak loudly in schools as well. In both the United States and South Africa, long histories of racism and segregation cast a shadow over the educational system, and, in the United States in particular, current battles over immigration and deportation are fought daily in the public schools (Jarquin, Alfaro, & Rambo, 2018). As Anderson (2016) reminds us, "Each encounter, relationship, and conversation is part of past, present, and future ones. Each dialog entails a multiplicity of voices of those present and not present" (p. 3). For us, school-based supervision involves honoring that multiplicity of voices.

We have found four practices to be of particular utility in teaching beginning therapists—and ourselves—to hear and honor the many voices. These are: the use of the ROPE guide to spark conversation: role-plays of multiple perspectives based on Harlene Anderson's "As If" exercise (Anderson & Burney, 1996); live supervision, which involves the client as part of the supervision/co-vision team; and live supervision that focuses on what the supervisee is doing well. These supervision approaches help us help beginning therapists and teachers shift to a more systemic, non-blaming, and resource-oriented perspective. But our work is also about gaining access to resources for clients, and we embrace that social justice responsibility as well (McDowell, Knudson-Martin, & Bermudez, 2017). A fifth practice is the sharing of resources between all of us on the therapy team and our clients in a lively back and forth process. We see this as another way of bringing in additional voices.

The ROPE Guide

ROPE in the United States

The PROMISE program was established within a large, urban school district in the United States to provide an alternative to the suspension and possible arrest of students. Although the district is very diverse in both eco-nomic and cultural terms, there were a disproportionate number of students of color being suspended and a high percentage of these students were also arrested (www.browardprevention.org). This led Broward county to have the highest rate of schoolhouse arrests in Florida (www.browardprevention.org). The PROMISE program exists to provide an alternative to arrest or futile repeated suspensions. Students sent to the PROMISE program learn study and behavior skills in the classroom. They meet individually at least once with a graduate intern[1] from our program. In this initial meeting, the intern establishes goals with the student and changes the student would like to make. Subsequently, the intern has a session with the student's parent, parents, or guardian, and writes a recommendation to the student's school that outlines useful changes school officials could make based on the student's goals and other information.

The suspended students we see are initially understandably wary of yet another adult asking questions. It is easy for them to hear a question about goals as a "trick question"—something that should be met with jeering, silence, or with what the adults usually seem to want to hear: "My goal is to have a better attitude just like they said—can I get off from being suspended now?" Even experienced solution-focused therapists struggle with initial goal setting when the client is mandated or reluctant (Osborn, 2011). Our graduate interns are not so experienced, and we wanted to help them with a bridge to hearing their student client's as yet unexpressed wishes and dreams.

In response, we came up with the ROPE guide to conversation. The graduate intern is prompted by the guide to ask the student to talk about times the student felt happy, proud, was enjoying himself, felt most like himself, or whatever topics seemed to work to turn up positive experiences. This generates a more relaxed and enjoyable conversation. Students typically become quite animated, talking about happy times in their lives—often far away from their current predicaments!

Once the student has shared three or four such happy times, the graduate intern is prompted to wonder aloud what all those times have in common. The answer may be concrete: for example, they all involve working on cars or interacting with animals, or they may be more process oriented: for example, times the student felt needed and valued by others. This becomes part of an ongoing collaborative conversation.

Ultimately, this initial conversation can easily become a bridge to goals—what could everyone do more of so that the student could experience more of those happy times? What would need to change around the student? Is there anything the student himself or herself could do differently to create a likelihood of more of those times? This conversation becomes a bridge to a plan, aspects of which can then be shared with parents and school officials.

We have put the conversational guide in worksheet form, as we encourage students to take the guide home and use it to think further or even to journal. It looks like this:

> **ROPE** to pull yourself up to where you want to be:
>
> 1. **R** ecall two to four times when you were proud of yourself and happy with who you were.
> 2. **O** rganize those memories to see what they have in common.
> 3. **P** resent and Future: How can you do more of that now? How could you do more of that in the future?
> 4. **E** xpand on this: Tell others about it.

EXAMPLE:

> 1. I remember when I helped rescue a stray cat, and I remember my dog who loves me, and I remember being proud that I did well in my biology class.
> 2. All those memories have to do with animals and living things.
> 3. I could do volunteer work with the Humane Society; I could look for a part-time job at a pet store; I could pursue becoming a veterinarian or a vet tech; I could look at colleges which offer these programs.
> 4. I would like to tell my parents about my plans and join a club at school.

We have found ROPE to be an effective intervention helping graduate interns and students create together a more collaborative, positive conversation.

ROPE in South Africa

Having noted the positive results of the ROPE guide in her work with PROMISE, Henry (2018) decided to use it as a central tool in her supervision/consultation sessions with South African teachers. Her trainings were targeted to three distinct regions within South Africa and a fourth was geared toward the Epworth Children's Home, a residential school. The first training targeted teachers from the only officially recognized solution-focused private school in Johannesburg, the School of Merit. The School of Merit serves primarily middle to upper-middle-class families from a range of ethnic/cultural backgrounds.

The second training targeted teachers primarily from Pongola and its surrounding areas. Pongola is a rural, primarily Zulu-occupied region of South Africa that generally falls within a moderate to low socioeconomic status bracket.

The third training included teachers from the urban region of Durban. Durban's teachers are primarily employed in moderate to low socioeconomic government schools similar to the educational settings in Pongola. However, Durban's culture is not as homogenous as Pongola's primarily Zulu population and is identified as a mix between Zulu, Afrikaner, and Indian cultures, creating another unique set of experiences and challenges for its educators, distinct from School of Merit and Pongola.

The fourth training was with the Epworth Children's Home staff and affiliated educators. This training was also held in Gauteng province. The Epworth staff faced a different challenge than the other demographics in that a sizable portion of the population they serve are orphaned by AIDS or are carriers of the virus themselves (Henry, 2018).

In the trainings, teachers were shown the ROPE conversational guide and encouraged to use it with their students to better understand students' goals. Teachers in all four regions reported positive experiences trying out ROPE and indicated they planned to use it in classrooms and individually with students. Interestingly, teachers in all four regions also found it a culturally congruent tool that was a sufficient fit with their traditions. At the Pongola site, it was also identified as offering a viable possible alternative to conversations leading to corporal punishment (Henry, 2018).

The "As If" Perspective

The "As If" Perspective in the United States

Harlene Anderson has developed a supervision activity in which different members of the supervision group listen from different perspectives, which she calls the "As If" exercise (Anderson & Rambo, 1988; Anderson & Burney, 1996). At PROMISE, we have enthusiastically embraced this idea, listening out loud from different perspectives, often with humor and (slight) exaggeration, to sensitize graduate interns to ideas about multiple perspectives.

Part of our work at PROMISE involves writing recommendations to the school that suspended a particular student, suggesting what school officials could do differently to prevent further difficulties. This is an intervention that needs to be made with tact and sensitivity to maximize the chances the school officials will be willing to actually see the student in a more positive light and to implement changes.

Accordingly, one of our regular supervision activities is "assistant principal time," in which an intern is asked to read aloud his or her recommendation letter while one of our team listens from the perspective of the assistant principal or other school official who is likely to read that document first. A recent such conversation went like this:

Intern (reading aloud): Johnny is very bright. He wants to join the chess club but has not been allowed to do so.

Rambo (role-playing assistant principal): Why do these counselors think Johnny is bright? He is failing most of his classes! And I don't care what clubs he wants to join. The little creep set off a stink bomb in the boy's restroom and he should be punished for it.

Intern (trying again with a revised version of the same recommendation): We notice despite poor grades in many subjects, Johnny has an A in his most challenging classes: calculus and advanced literature. Johnny himself has noticed he is less likely to get into trouble when he is busy and occupied. At present he is not in any activities outside of school hours, though he plays chess in the park with friends. We notice X School has a highly regarded chess club.

Rambo (again role playing the same assistant principal): Oh, okay, keep him busy, good idea. Let's put him in something so we can keep an eye on him after school. I know: chess club!

We practice these role-plays until all are satisfied the recommendations represent the best hopes of both the school official who will receive the document and the student who wants a particular change.

Another part of our intervention is to call the parent or guardian of the student and report on our conversation with the student, enlisting the parent's support for the student's goals, and also offering longer-term family counseling if desired. Here again, listening from an "As If" perspective has been very useful. Although some of our interns are younger and not themselves parents, we have a significant percentage of interns who have children, and some who have already raised their families. Interns who are also parents enjoy the opportunity to take the parent's perspective in this exercise and share what that feels like. Here is a recent example:

First intern (not a parent): Hi, my name is Suzie, and I am a family counselor with the PROMISE program. I am calling to let you know about my conversation with Johnny today. He was mentioning he feels like no one in the family really supports his desire to be a musician.

Second intern (a parent and enacting the perspective of Johnny's parent): Okay, that feels like a stab to my heart. So now my kid is complaining about me all over town as well as dropping out of school to be some kind of wanna-bee rock star—things could not get worse. I am hanging up the phone now.

First intern (trying again): Hi, my name is Suzie, and I am a family counselor with the PROMISE program. I was calling today to let you know I talked with Johnny and I was so impressed with your efforts to support his goals. He mentioned you had attended his school band concert last Saturday.

Second intern: Really? He told you about that? I didn't know he even noticed I was there. Well, he's a good kid and I try to do what I can. Could we arrange some family counseling to talk more about this?

We have found listening from multiple perspectives very useful in increasing both the sensitivity and efficacy of our interns.

The "As If" Perspective in South Africa

Henry (2018) embedded a shift in perspective directly into her training exercise by asking teachers to first try the ROPE conversational guide on their colleagues. Thus, every teacher got to experience how it felt to be asked about his or her happiest times and guided to talk more about them. Teachers remarked on how pleasant this was and could extrapolate to how this might then feel to students.

Live Supervision as Co-Vision

In the United States, in the PROMISE program, we have the opportunity to walk around and directly observe interns as they work with students. We can sit down with an intern and a student together and join in on all or part of the conversation. This is unique to the United States' setting and is possible because all our intern/student conversations are held in one very large room (the cafeteria) with each intern/student pair sitting away from others to achieve privacy. Although this at first did not seem ideal and came about due to school concerns about space and about possible abuse allegations if interns and students were alone together, the arrangement has turned out to be positive. Somewhat to our surprise, students do not seem at all inhibited by the setting and it is very helpful to be able to directly observe every session.

When we sit with interns and students, rather than taking over the session or trying to tell the intern what to do, we try to provide a collaborative perspective that includes both the intern's and the student's voices. Here are two examples:

> Henry recalls sitting with a student and intern who were discussing the student's past suicide attempts. The student stated he would not attempt suicide again due to his faith. The intern kept asking about ties to family, friends, or other human resources and the student kept insisting he put his trust in God alone. Sitting with them both, Henry asked the student to explain more about what his faith looked like and how the intern could be sure he had enough of it. The resulting conversation led to an agreement that the student would check in weekly with his youth minister, participate in church-related activities, and utilize the human as well as the spiritual resources of the church should the need arise.
>
> Alfaro recalls sitting with a student and intern who were also initially at cross purposes. The student described herself as "nonbinary," stating she still preferred the female pronoun and did not consider herself a man, but also did not consider herself a woman. The intern wanted to talk about resources for LGBT youth, and the student was becoming annoyed. Alfaro asked the student to explain more to both the intern and herself about the full implications of being nonbinary and what support would be helpful with that.

These examples illustrate working together with the client to provide supervision or what might be called co-vision.

Supervision as Resource-Focused Practice

When all of the interns are working well with all of the students, as supervisors, we stealthily observe and write down what is going well. Later, after the sessions are done for the day, we surprise the interns with an individual assessment of what each intern was doing uniquely well. We try to be as specific as possible, and we share our commendations in front of the whole group. One intern might be commended for introducing humor at a tense moment, providing an example; another might hear that she joined well with a student who was initially reluctant to engage; still a third might find us noticing her use of language which was a fit for the student. The interns eagerly receive these comments and often join in to praise a colleague they have just heard praised. We make sure to commend each person for something unique to increase cooperation rather than competition and to include everyone. We notice this practice has several useful effects. Interns do tend to do more of whatever they were doing that got commended—they increase that behavior. In addition, interns who have heard us be positive about their skills and have experienced being positive about the skills of colleagues tend to be more adept at noticing skills and resources of student clients. Finally, the practice promotes a positive, collaborative team where all members are supportively engaged with each other as well as with our clients.

Applications to South Africa

Although a similar live supervision set up was not possible in the South African setting, Henry did encourage teachers to commend each other on how well they were doing at trying out the ROPE exercise (Henry, 2018). She also made it a point to praise each individual's efforts. This increased enthusiasm for the task and for trying out the ROPE guide later on (Henry, 2018).

Sharing Resources

Sharing Resources in the United States

In the United States, the public school system is complex and enormous, with federal, state, and local resources. In addition, each community generates unique resources, and within a large urban area such as South Florida, there are multiple communities. Difficulties our student clients face are seldom primarily due to a lack of existing resources; the difficulties come about because of differential access to resources and unshared information about resources, which tends to perpetuate inequity (Watson, 2012). We push back against inequity by creating a network of shared resources. We keep a loose-leaf binder with information on all the available school programs including private school vouchers, magnet schools, charter schools, and so on. In addition, every time we hear about a resource that might be interesting to one or more of our student clients, we bring it in. Faculty and doctoral supervisors contribute resources, but so do interns and increasingly so do student clients.

Each time we add a new resource, we publicize it to all the interns, including telling the story of how the resource came about. At times the story itself is a resource. For example, one of our resources is an alternative school program started by a business owner who saw a need for trained mechanics (www.yatc.org). Youth can be accepted into the program despite failing grades, difficulties with reading, and a history of arrests or probation; all that matters is their mechanical ability and willingness to learn. A follow-up study of the program's success determined that 20 years after graduation, 92% of the program's graduates were gainfully employed as mechanics and doing well (www.yatc.org). The program itself has been useful to several of our student clients. But probably even more have been warmed by the story, realizing that success in high school is not the same as success in life and that there might be areas of life in which they could succeed despite academic difficulties and legal troubles.

Our student clients have gotten into the spirit of our collective endeavor and have contributed resources about which we knew nothing. Thanks to our student clients, we now know there are 30 universities nationwide that offer significant scholarships to students with video game skills (www.scholarships.com/financial-aid/college-scholarships/sports-scholarships/esports-scholarships-scholarships-for-gamers/). It was a tenth-grade student who let us know about the app which lets high school students earn college scholarship money for each A they make and each club they join (www.raise.me). And it was our student clients, not us, who were the first to know that rap mogul Jay-Z had set aside scholarship funds specifically for C students (www.shawncartersf.com).

We give interns credit for time spent in the community researching resources, and they have brought information about many valuable resources including free therapy services, alternative schools, mentor programs, and so on. We operate on the assumption that if the need is there, the resource is there—if we don't know about it, we just haven't found it yet. Alfaro responded to several student clients who wanted free art classes by diligently searching all over the county until she found a free photography class that students could join with only a cell phone as camera.

Sadly, due to political changes in the United States, we are increasingly seeing student clients facing the deportation of themselves or their families in life-threatening situations (Jarquin et al., 2018). Given this situation, we are also compiling resources for students with these needs. In this situation, there can be a tragic lack of resources, but increasing access to what resources there are is at least one thing we can do. Jarquin and Alfaro both have been active in the community around immigration issues, and have helped us compile resources including legal rights if ICE knocks at your door (www.aclu.org/know-your-rights/what-do-if-imm igration-agents-ice-are-your-door), names and phone numbers of agencies that support asylum seekers and refugees, and ways to obtain pro bono legal help (www. splcenter.org/our-issues/immigrant-justice/southeast-immigrant-freedom- initiative-en). Our "big book" of resources has been life-saving and we are com- mitted to sharing and publicizing every resource we can find.

Sharing Resources in South Africa

In South Africa, the school system to date is less enormous and resources have remained more locally based. Henry (2018) noted that music was a resource often used both by children and teachers; beginning to sing a traditional song seemed to unite the classroom or training meeting in community. Singing, getting up to take a walk outside and then coming back, taking a few days off from school, and other exercises of individual choice by children are more likely to be tolerated in South Africa than in the United States, giving individual students access to a wider range of personal resources. Much remains to be done to explore resources within South Africa as a whole and equalize access to them.

Conclusion

We took a minute to reflect on the programs in which we supervise. In the United States, over the four years that PROMISE has been in existence, the program has consistently reduced school recidivism rates by 90% (Mendel, 2018).[2] Our interns saw over 4,000 suspended students during this time period (Mendel, 2018). Not only did the approximately 25 masters-level interns per year we have supervised survive that workload, for the most part, they report a highly positive experience, and all have gone on to graduate and work in the field. In South Africa, follow-up indicates that the ROPE guide is still in use by teachers three years later (personal communication, Jacqui von Cziffra-Bergs, July 30, 2018), and Henry has been asked to return to Africa to provide more training. We think something is working well with our collaborations with schools in both countries.

When we ask our student clients what is working about what we do, over and over we hear, "you are the first people who really listened to me." Collaborative therapy has been described as "ordinary, everyday conversations about hopes and concerns" (Levin & Bava, 2012, p. 139); solution-focused therapy has been described as "listening in the present with an ear towards the future" (Duffy, 2012, p. 143). Both are good descriptions of what we do in therapy and in supervi- sion: listen intensely to all voices, expectantly listening for hopeful future clues. In particular, with the interns and teachers we supervise, we listen intensely to what they are already doing well, calling their attention to the multiplicity of voices all around them, and hoping to engage them in increasingly productive conversations as time goes on. And we share all the resources we can find with them and with our clients, as we hope they will in turn share with us.

Notes

1 Although our graduate interns are technically students as well, we will refer to our K-12 student clients as students, and our master's level graduate interns as graduate interns or interns to avoid confusion.
2 Recidivism is here defined as being suspended again in the same school year, for any offense, and the outcome relates to middle and high school students in K-12 public or charter schools.

References

Anderson, H. (2016). Listening, hearing and speaking: Brief thoughts on the relationship to dialogue. *Psychological Opinions, 7*, 10–14.

Anderson, H., & Burney, J. P. (1996). Collaborative inquiry: A postmodern approach to organizational consultation. *Human Systems: The Journal of Systemic Consultation and Management, 7*(2–3),171–188.

Anderson, H., & Rambo, A. (1988). An experiment in systemic family therapy training: A trainer and trainee perspective. *Journal of Strategic and Systemic Therapies, 7*(1), 54–70.

Duffy, M. (2012). Solution focused brief therapy: Listening in the present with an ear towards the future. In A. Lock & T. Strong (Eds.), *Discursive perspectives in therapeutic practice* (pp. 143–162). New York, NY: Oxford University Press.

Henry, B. (2018). Exploring the impact of solution-focused ROPE tool trainings on South African private and public-school educators in Kwa Zulu Natal and Guateng provinces. Fort Lauderdale, FL: Nova Southeastern University. (Unpublished dissertation).

Jarquin, E., Alfaro, A., & Rambo, A. (in press). Intervening in larger systems. *Journal of Systemic Therapies, 37*(1), 36–46.

Kim, J., Kelly, M., & Franklin, C. (2017). *Solution focused brief therapy in schools: A 360-degree view of the research, practice, and principles.* New York, NY: Oxford Press.

Levin, S., & Bava, S. (2012). Collaborative therapy: Performing reflective and dialogical relationships. In A. Lock & T. Strong (Eds.). *Discursive perspectives in therapeutic practice* (pp. 126–142). New York, NY: Oxford University Press.

McDowell, T., Knudson-Martin, C., & Bermudez, M. (2017). *Socioculturally attuned family therapy: Guidelines for equitable theory and practice.* New York, NY: Routledge.

Mendel, D. (2018). An evaluation of the efficacy of the PROMISE program in Broward County. Fort Lauderdale, FL: Nova Southeastern University. (Unpublished dissertation).

Osborn, C. (2011). Solution-focused strategies with involuntary clients: Practical applications for the school and clinical setting. *The Journal of Humanistic Counseling, 37*(3), 169–181.

Watson, M. (2012). Psychoeducation in family therapy. In A. Rambo, C. West, A. Schooley, & T. Boyd (Eds.), *Family therapy review: Contrasting contemporary models* (pp. 203–206). New York, NY: Routledge.

10

EVALUATING SINGLE-SESSION/ WALK-IN TRAINING WITH THE *LEEDS ALLIANCE IN SUPERVISION SCALE*

April Trejo and Monte Bobele

In this chapter, we present the findings of a preliminary study of graduate student supervisees' experiences in learning single-session/walk-in therapy (SS/WI). We are building on the considerable body of literature that addresses training therapists in this approach (Bedggood, 2018; Harper Jaques, 2018; Hoyt, 1991; Rycroft, 2018). Single-session therapy arose out of the clinical experiences and research efforts of the creative team of psychologists at Kaiser-Permanente in California in the late 1980s (Rosenbaum, Hoyt, & Talmon,1990; Talmon, M. 1990). Single-session therapy has been defined as "one face-to-face meeting between a therapist and patient with no previous or subsequent sessions within one year" (Hoyt, Bobele, Slive, Young, & Talmon, 2018, p. 4). Put another way, "SST is therapy that the therapist expects, from the beginning, to potentially comprise a single visit. The therapist acts as if the first session will be the last" (Hoyt et al., 2018 p. 4).

Training Setting

The Community Counseling Service (CCS) began at Our Lady of the Lake University (OLLU) in the 1970s as a site to provide training to practicum students in the Graduate Psychology and Marriage and Family Therapy programs. In the early 1980s, the clinic was relocated to share space with the communications disorders department. This was a serendipitous move because the speech and hearing clinic was equipped with one-way mirror suites that were heavily used during the daytime hours by the speech therapists but were free in the evening when the counseling students needed practice. At that time, the CCS was open one night a week and about two or three clients were seen for free in the live-supervision format. Over the years, the CCS has expanded significantly. Presently, it is located a couple of miles from the main university campus and is open about 12 hours a day Monday to Thursday with shorter schedules on Friday and Saturday. There are three rooms that are regularly scheduled for therapy and are equipped with video cameras to record the sessions and transmit the sessions to nearby observation rooms.

Description of CCS Training

The training model used at the CCS has remained consistent for the last 30 years. The model is familiar to many professionals who have trained in family therapy, less familiar to those with conventional psychology training.

> The CCS is a community-based service that trains counseling psychology master's and doctoral students. We employ a team approach with six therapists and a supervisor on a treatment team. Typically, the supervisor and six team members participate in the session from an observation room connected via closed circuit TV, while two of the team members interview the client. The observing team members occasionally make suggestions by telephone during the course of the session. More typically, the team meets together toward the end of the session to compare observations and plan interventions. Nearly 50% of OLLU's graduate students are Hispanic and this diversity is reflected on the CCS treatment teams.
>
> (Bobele, Lopez Scamardo, & Solórzano, 2008, p 78)

Most of the clients seen in the clinic are self-referred or referred by community agencies, friends, the court system, the University, or other schools. The clinic serves an Hispanic area of the city with the majority of residents being Mexican-American.

For the most part, the supervision for students learning the SS/WI approach is the same as that described above, with the important exception that students learn to make each session count. They learn to approach each case as if it were the last opportunity to help the client in front of them. Many beginning therapists feel demoralized when they begin seeing clients because they frequently don't return. They doubted their career choices, their ability to establish a therapeutic alliance, and experienced an overall blow to their self-confidence. We know from years of experience that about half of initial appointments in any setting result in no-shows or cancellations of subsequent appointments. When we introduced the practice of single-session therapy, with no expectation of subsequent appointment, supervisees' confidence soared. Ironically, students began to wonder, when clients did come back, what they could have done to have been more helpful in the previous appointment. We embarked on the study reported here to assess, more systematically, doctoral student trainees' experiences in learning to apply SS/WI for the first time.

A "Culture of Feedback"

The Community Counseling Service has employed the *Partnership for Change Management System* (PCOMS) for many years as a required part of the classroom and practicum training experiences (Duncan, 2010). The students first encounter feedback-informed therapy in classes before starting their clinical practica. Feedback-informed therapy is a practice that capitalizes on measuring therapeutic outcomes based on clients' evaluations of their own progress.

Our "culture of feedback" involves the consistent use of the *Outcome Rating Scale* (ORS) and the *Session Rating Scale* (SRS; Duncan & Miller, 2008) in sessions, case conceptualizations, and research. Trainees at the CCS support the culture of feedback by attending to the importance of clients' reported outcomes and perception of therapeutic alliance. Clients rate the progress of therapy at the start of each session. This feedback guides decision making about termination, aids in goal-setting, and choice of therapist.

Several instruments have been developed to measure supervisory competence and the supervisor-supervisee relationship. One such instrument is the *Leeds Alliance in Supervision Scale* (LASS; Payne, Smith, Tuchfeld, & Suprina, 2013; Wainwright, 2010), a brief instrument that isolates the common factors among supervisory constructs typically measured on longer instruments including Approach, Relationship, and Meeting Supervisee Needs. The LASS is administered to supervisees following each supervision session like the SRS. We utilized the LASS throughout the semester with a cohort of first-year counseling psychology doctoral students during their first practicum experience. Using the LASS created opportunities for the students to isomorphically experience the culture of feedback. Furthermore, the LASS allowed us, supervisor and doctoral student co-supervisors, to reassess our approach when needed, and created an opportunity to have intermittent check-ins with the students. In his article on postmodern supervision, Ungar (2006) reasoned that there is "still merit to the argument that the supervisor succeeds only to the extent that good practice is modeled through the process of the supervision" (p. 59).

The collated results of the LASS throughout the semester indicated that, overall, our approach was viewed as helpful, that we established good working alliances with the students, and met their needs consistently throughout the semester (see Figure 10.1). On some occasions, supervisees asked us to adjust our approaches to be more concise and structured during the brief consultation breaks to allow more time for post-session briefings. Our LASS scores immediately improved as we implemented such feedback. The use of session-by-session measures of the supervision alliance allowed us to make the most of each supervision opportunity and customize sessions according to students' needs. This session-by-session feedback coincided with the necessary practices for SSW we set out to teach and model.

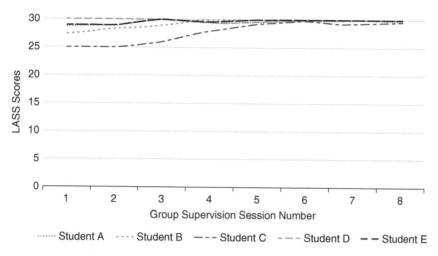

FIGURE 10.1 LASS SSWI First Year Doctoral Students.

We solicited more expansive views from each of the first-year supervisees at the end of their initial semester learning and practicing single-session/walk-in therapy:

Prompt Question 1:

What was it like to learn about walk-in therapy while expecting to practice it as well?

The Responses

"Exciting. We had to think fast, and it requires rapid decision making in less than an hour. Kind of like the E.R. (emergency room)."

"Reassuring." "It took away a stereotype I had about therapy." "It was legitimate work in 30 to 40 minutes without this processing over a long term."

"It was a good framework to keep a session on track and we had to be mindful… to stay on track. We had [to work] towards an attainable goal."

"Really eye-opening." "It made me think about the client perspective to be brave enough to go into a place and seek help immediately." "I think we changed clients' minds about what therapy is."

"Reassuring." "For me, it was also reassuring to be able to provide services when people are at their worst. They may be reconsidering not coming in at all, but a walk-in service takes that excuse away." "Also, I think it breaks a stigma about the 'long-termness' of therapy."

"Cost-effective for the client." "It makes me think of a spa, you can go get a massage to get a strain out." "It's cost effective to get what is needed quickly."

As supervisors, we were curious to discover if introducing walk-in and single-session work with these students trickled into their work outside of this setting. Many students begin to experience a paradigmatic shift in their perception of therapy and how people change when exposed to novel ideas.

Prompt Question 2:

"Did it [training in walk-in/single-session services] have an effect on your work in other practicum teams?

Responses

> "I like to think that most can be single sessions." "It reinforced what I felt before which is that people didn't really need this for long term."
> "I did a single session on another team, it just took normalizing what the client was going through."
> "That was the mindset for every session, but clients didn't always agree."
> "On Spanish-speaking teams, it was harder to break the stigma that people assume they are going to be coming a lot. I questioned on those teams if we should be trying to break that stigma?"
> "It was harder on different [Spanish] teams." "Some families have different elements that are harder to tease out."

Student Perspectives

The ideas that emerged from the post-semester interviews with the SS/WI students were revealing. Much of the feedback reinforced what has been written in other SS/WI supervision literature (Bedggood, 2018; Harper Jaques, 2018; Hoyt, 1991; O'Donovan, Clough, & Petch, 2017; Rycroft, 2018) including that working in a walk-in setting can be fulfilling, exciting, and increases accessibility. Furthermore, the students identified the unique skills SS/WI settings required that differed from typical by-appointment settings. Brief therapy requires structure, attentiveness, and a "think on your feet" improv-like ability to plan and execute the therapeutic performance. Furthermore, the therapists working on Spanish-speaking teams grappled with the extension of the SS/WI mindset and recommended supervision and training in SS/WI from Spanish-speaking supervisors. In addition to these familiar themes, a new topic emerged: How does the SS/WI mindset extend beyond training and across settings?

The Enduring SS/WI Mindset

Interestingly enough, although most of the supervisees experienced the semester as eye-opening, reassuring, and even exciting, they had difficulty cultivating the same sense of competency on teams with supervision that was not SS/WI focused. In fact, over the years, we have found that beginning therapists' confidence is shaken when many of their clients do not return after the first visit. In the SS/WI training, students begin to experience success, and ironically, begin to wonder how they could have been more helpful in the first session when their clients come back. This reflects the importance of the supervisors' influence in promoting confidence in a student's ability and willingness to take risks and experiment with novel ideas like SS/WI. This experience also suggests that supervision that is theoretically isomorphic with the student's own practice of therapy is helpful in their carrying out of the work. However, supervision is rarely, if ever, provided for a walk-in or in one solitary visit. How can supervision in SS/WI services extend beyond the supervised setting and endure throughout the student's clinical work?

The SS/WI literature suggests that the adoption of an SS/WI "mindset" is helpful for students to adapt to the possibility that therapeutic change can occur in a single session. Campbell (2012) suggested that experience and skill are agreed-upon characteristic prerequisites. When considering a developmental framework of supervision, new therapists in training typically need supervisors to operate in a teaching and supportive role. As students progress, and each does so according to her or his own ability and preferences, they begin to form their own opinions about therapy separate from their teachers and supervisors. The SS/WI mindset, therefore, may not be a skill or competency that can be expected in the beginning stages of therapy and supervision. Beginning student therapists may find themselves focusing on the basic skills of therapy such as listening, learning session structure, and orienting to the team and clinic. This divided attention may make it difficult for some supervisees to integrate more complex therapeutic ideas conducted in a single session or to balance being in the present along with the tentativeness required for walk-in work.

When assessing students' potential and interest in working in SS/WI settings, maintaining a developmental perspective may be helpful to consider providing new supervisees when introducing SS/WI to them. It is also important that supervisors reserve judgment that supervisees "don't have what it takes" or "are too stubborn" for SS/WI. Taking a patient and feedback-informed stance with each student may foster better outcomes for inspiring supervisees to practice this creative approach. Furthermore, some supervisees may originally be enthusiastic for SS/WI work but have trouble practicing the work outside of a sheltered SS/WI setting as our students informed us with their feedback.

It may also be possible that supervisees who are able to develop confidence in their SS/WI work may be more likely to be able to reproduce the work outside of SS/WI specific supervision settings. It may be difficult for supervisees to replicate focus and directedness without having had the opportunity to successfully facilitate or observe a single session or a walk-in session.

Conclusion

Single-session/Walk-in therapy is an innovative service delivery model. Training supervisees is a complicated endeavor, made even more complicated by the overlay of SS/WI therapy. Serving clients at their moment of need on a walk-in basis is a new idea for most doctoral students who have received extensive exposure to the by-appointment model in popular culture, most textbooks, and most other supervision experiences. Indeed, it is often a challenge to persuade other professionals to consider offering walk-in services as a way of opening the door for clients who might be otherwise intimidated by the lengthy and complicated hurdles.

References

Bedggood, J. (2018). The first time: Teaching skills that prepare interns and new therapists for walk-in counseling. In M. F. Hoyt, M. Bobele, A. Slive, J. Young, & M. Talmon (Eds.), *Single-session therapy by walk-in or appointment* (pp. 327–333). New York, NY: Routledge.

Bobele, M., Lopez, S. S. G., Scamardo, M., & Solórzano, B. (2008). Single-session/walk-in therapy with Mexican-American clients. *Journal of Systemic Therapies, 27*, 75–89.

Campbell, A. (2012). Single-session approaches to therapy: Time to review. *Australian & New Zealand Journal of Family Therapy, 33*(1), 15–26.

Duncan, B. L. (2010). *The heart and soul of change: Delivering what works in therapy.* Washington, D.C.: American Psychological Association.

Duncan, B. L., & Miller, S. (2008). "When I'm good, I'm very good, but when I'm bad I'm better": A new mantra for psychotherapists. *Psychotherapy in Australia, 15*(1), 62–71.

Harper Jaques, S. (2018). Supervision and the single-session therapist: Learnings from ten years of practice. In M. F. Hoyt, M. Bobele, A. Slive, J. Young, & M. Talmon (Eds.), *Single-session therapy by walk-in or appointment* (pp. 334–346). New York, NY: Routledge.

Hoyt, M. F. (1991). Teaching and learning short-term psychotherapy. In C. S. Austad & W. H. Berman (Eds.), *Psychotherapy in managed health care: The optimal use of time & resources.* (pp. 98–107). Washington, DC: American Psychological Association.

Hoyt, M. F., Bobele, M., Slive, A., Young, J., & Talmon, M. (2018). *Single-session therapy by walk-in or appointment: Administrative, clinical, and supervisory aspects of one-at-a-time services.* New York, NY: Routledge.

O'Donovan, A., Clough, B., & Petch, J. (2017). Is supervisor training effective? A pilot investigation of clinical supervisor training program. *Australian Psychologist, 52*(2), 149–154.

Payne, J. H., Smith, S. D., Tuchfeld, B., & Suprina, J. S. (2013). Relationship development between racially matched and non-matched counselor supervisors and practicum supervisees: preliminary findings. *Practitioner Scholar: Journal of Counseling & Professional Psychology, 2*(1), 108–118. Retrieved from https://ezproxy.ollusa.edu/login?url=https://search.ebscohost.com/login.aspx?direct=true&db=a9h&AN=92621828&site=ehost-live

Rosenbaum, R., Hoyt, M. F., & Talmon, M. (1990). The challenge of single-session therapies: creating pivotal moments. In R. A. Wells & V. J. Giannetti (Eds.), *Handbook of the brief psychotherapies* (pp. 165–189). New York, NY: Plenum Press.

Rycroft, P. (2018). Capturing the moment in supervision. In M. F. Hoyt, M. Bobele, A. Slive, J. Young, & M. Talmon (Eds.), *Single-session therapy by walk-in or appointment* (pp. 347–365). New York, NY: Routledge.

Talmon, M. (1990). *Single session therapy: Maximizing the effect of the first (and often only) therapeutic encounter*. San Francisco, CA: Jossey-Bass.

Ungar, M. (2006). Practicing as a postmodern supervisor. *Journal of Marital & Family Therapy, 32*(1), 59–71.

Wainwright, N. A. (2010). *The development of the Leeds Alliance in Supervision Scale (LASS): A brief sessional measure of the supervisory alliance* (Doctoral thesis, University of Leeds, Leeds, England).

11

WHERE DO I EVEN BEGIN?

Muriel Singer

Out **beyond ideas** of rightdoing and wrongdoing, there is a field.
I'll meet you there.

Rumi (emphasis added)

As supervisors, we have to be prepared to manage the multiple layers of different families and systems and to tease out, "Where is the opportunity here?" We have to be prepared for a range of presenting cases and to calibrate the supervision to be attuned to both the supervisee and the presenting case. The goal is for supervisees to progressively trust themselves and their abilities to develop their own creative ideas and options.

During our initial supervision session, Lori had told me about her impressions when she first met with Janelle and her 16-year-old daughter, Danielle. The mom, Janelle, presented with symptoms of depression and her daughter Danielle had presented with a history of oppositional behaviors. When Danielle and her mother first came to see Lori, they were barely speaking. Danielle's mother, Janelle, was of Haitian descent and had been divorced from Danielle's father for many years. In her early 40s, Janelle walked into the session with her head held high. She was immaculately-dressed and she looked at her daughter's sloppy appearance in torn jeans and an oversized shirt with disgust. The mother and daughter sat in chairs on opposite sides of the room and when Lori inquired about what had brought them in to see her, Janelle began by complaining bitterly about Danielle and defending herself. She said Danielle's grandparents would be shocked at how disrespectful she is. "I would never dare speak to my mother the way that Danielle talks to me!" Janelle said that she and her daughter used to be very close and did everything together. "We were two peas in a pod. Now, she's not doing any of her chores and she talks back to me when I ask her to do simple things like clean her room."

Lori asked her what she usually did in response to her daughter's "disobedience." Janelle said that it usually led to a huge argument involving name-calling and many threats being hurled on both sides.

When we met for supervision, I had asked Lori if she felt any compassion toward this mother. She confessed that she disliked Janelle and thought her strict, authoritarian parenting style was pushing her daughter away and blamed her for ruining their relationship. I suggested that Lori might find a way to reconnect to herself and the relational field as a way to help them figure out how they might recover some of the warmth and affection of their earlier relationship. Perhaps Lori could introduce the idea that demanding respect and compliance might matter less than the importance of preserving their relationship. I encouraged Lori to examine her own assumptions about Janelle and to empathize with Janelle's struggles as a single mom trying to do her best to bring up her daughter by herself and to do the right thing. We discussed how challenging it must be for her to see an alternative to her deeply ingrained parenting style and to change the legacy of parenting in her family to make it more mutually respectful and more intimate.

In their next sessions, Lori greeted Janelle warmly and told her that she could imagine how hard it must be for her to relate to her daughter empathically when she was behaving so disrespectfully. She told Janelle that even though Danielle thought she was too tough and demanding, the complementary truth was that she was also a loving and protective mother. It is always useful to acknowledge the positive, loving intentions underlying a parent's punitive approach. Lori suggested that Danielle was probably wrestling with dual identities herself as both a rebellious teen who wanted her independence and a girl who craved her mother's love and approval.

During this supervision hour, Lori walked in, beaming with pride. Her clients were behaving like different people than the ones who first came to see her two months earlier, and they were very grateful for her help. When Lori met with Janelle and Danielle for their final session, they were both smiling broadly and walked into the therapy room arm in arm. This is the magic of the therapeutic relationship and the just desserts of good therapy.

With Lori's reconnection to her own center and reconnecting Janelle and Danielle to their complementary truths that had seemed incompatible, Lori was able to model a more compassionate approach to their disengagement. Lori had made a difference in this family's life and she was savoring the fruits of this well-deserved victory. Things were bumpy at first with a few setbacks, but Lori remained steady and encouraging through the ups and downs, managing to straddle that fragile balance of remaining connected to both mother and daughter while simultaneously challenging them to do better. I praised Lori's skills and success.

One of the major functions of both a supervisor and therapist lies in maintaining a connection to one's own center while also tapping into the guidance and intelligence of the bigger relational field. In this circular supervision cycle, the most important connection a therapist and supervisor has is to himself or herself. This is generally referred to as a self-of-therapist orientation, meaning the willingness to participate in a process that requires introspective work on issues in one's own life that have an impact on the process of therapy and supervision in both positive and negative ways (Timm & Blow, 1999). A basic premise of this style of supervision is that multiple truths and identities exist simultaneously. In *The Courage to Love,* Steven Gilligan (1997) writes,

> A basic premise of this relational knowing is that multiple truths exist simultaneously. When the relational connection between these truths is lost, bad things tend to happen.... For example, say the person holds the idea, "Life sucks" how do you respond to such a statement? Do you agree or disagree? I would propose that such a statement is true and as true as the opposite truth that "Life is also incredibly beautiful." It is precisely the sustained disconnection of one truth from its complement when a problem defined identity appears.
>
> *(p. 42)*

In supervision, I assume that in addition to the problem-defined self, each supervisee also has a competency-based self, so a major task in therapy and supervision is to access the competent and resourceful parts of the self and to sponsor and support them. I begin by first validating the position the client or supervisee has identified with (e.g., "I have no idea how to help this client") and then activating and holding the complementary truth ("when I get quiet and centered, some good ideas come to me") and finding a way of holding both at the same time. As such, conversations that touch the wounds and failures as well as the competencies and resources of a person create the possibility of holding and validating both simultaneously. The basic issue is not that problems occur, but that when they do, a person generally forgets the rest of her or his life. The skill in supervision lies in remaining authentically connected to ourselves and to remind our supervisees to stay connected to their clients and themselves, and to notice and track when they have lost connection so they can bring themselves back to being fully present. This practice of relational connection includes deep listening and a willingness to touch each presenting identity and complementary truth with love and acceptance.

My own decision to teach marriage and family therapy was based on my passion for systems thinking and my desire to pass on those ideas. I was enthralled by Gregory Bateson's *Steps to an Ecology of Mind* (Bateson, 1972). Even though I could only understand about 30% of Bateson's writing, that 30% was so rich and brilliant I thought I had found the holy grail or code through which I could more fully understand my own way of perceiving the world. I was even more captivated by Brad Keeney's (1983) *Aesthetics of Change.* They rocked my world, giving me the language to describe things I intuitively knew but now had the language for.

According to Keeney, family therapy was built on an appreciation of difference and context, and respect for multiple realities. The merit of such an approach can be illustrated through the systemic concept of double description, the ability to hear different ideas from separate sources within a system and to consider each to be valid and useful despite discrepancies and oppositions. As one remains receptive to several views, a more complete picture comes into focus than would have emerged from just one understanding (Keeney, 1983). We actively seek to gather multiple perspectives as they emerge, dissolve, and reshape themselves in the crucible of relationships. I wanted to keep that passion for systemic ideas alive and thriving, and pass the torch to the next generation of family therapists.

As the coordinator of an MFT program at Kean University, each week I have the opportunity to provide supervision and mentoring to students. It's a Monday morning and the students file into my office one or two at a time to meet with me for their weekly hour of clinical supervision. They're beginning their second year of a master's program in Marriage and Family Therapy and have just begun their internship training at various agencies throughout N.J. They're excited and very enthusiastic about being able to practice their craft and to apply the ideas and techniques that they've studied in several family therapy theory and technique classes. They have read about cybernetics of cybernetics, repetitive cycles of interaction, and negative and positive feedback loops. Their intentions are totally honorable, and they really want to do good work, seeing their careers as family therapists as a calling, sometimes born of their own suffering and painful family histories.

Shaina comes in for supervision after Lori, and she is not feeling as pleased with herself. She has a 52-year-old male client who is unemployed and living with his disabled mother. The client reminds her of her uncle Joe whom she detests, and she dreads seeing the client again. "What a loser! He hasn't worked in three years and expects his mother to support him. When I try to talk to him, he only argues for his limitations!" She wants to know if she should refer him to another therapist. She asks, "How can I treat him when I find him so annoying? I don't even like being in the same room with him." I remember one of my supervisors telling me that therapy cannot really begin until you find a way to like your client. I agree and have always been guided by that caveat. Likewise, I feel myself judging Shaina for her quick dismissal of this client and her absence of any compassion. This was a red flag that it was time for me to tune into myself and my own reactions as a way to mentor Shaina to tune into herself and her client. Without that connection, we tend to be reactive rather than responsive.

There is a clear connection between Shaina's reaction to her client and her own family history. I ask Shaina if we might explore the strengths and the resources she could bring to this case? How might her family history make her well suited for this client? What understanding might she have that another therapist might not?

Shaina and I use our supervision time to search for redeeming qualities in her client and to see his other identities besides "loser." Shaina conceded that her ne'er-do-well client must feel like a failure, but did she believe that he's capable of growth and change? By the end of our supervision meeting, Shaina had decided to keep her appointment with the client and to use it as an opportunity to also examine her own reactivity and to learn about how she could check in with herself during a session to ensure that she remains present, attentive, and receptive.

After Shaina, Abi comes in for supervision. Abi is working at an agency doing home-based work with disadvantaged, court-referred youth. The agency was funded through a grant to provide Multisystemic Family Therapy. "During the 1980s, various models appeared that deliberately included therapist interventions aimed at family-school, family-church, family-peer group, and family-agency relationships" (Hanna, 2007, p. 45). As part of this trend, Henggeler, Schoenwald, Borduin, Roland, and Cunningham (1998) developed a multisystemic approach to child and adolescent problems. The home-based approach positions the therapist to significantly reduce crime and substance abuse. And, according to a review of multiple studies, the results have been impressive in that 70–80% of inner-city families were successfully engaged and completed the treatment protocol (Cunningham & Henggeler, 1999). The authors suggested that their success came from paying attention to the obstacles to engagement. The process is supposed to begin by linking the goals of the larger system with the individualized goals of the family. The goals of the court might be to prevent repeated crime and rearrest and increase school attendance. The family might want the youth to come home at a reasonable hour at night or to stop smoking weed. After centuries of trust being broken in these communities, this mandated, manualized treatment program falls short.

Abi usually had at the most, four to six months to work with these families. She felt she was flitting about from one crisis to another in quick succession and never had a chance to actually do family therapy. Her clients were frequently suspended from school or they just didn't go to school at all. They were in and out of juvenile court for criminal activity and were often placed in residential treatment facilities for months at a time. She described one of her clients, a 14-year-old African American young man named Henry who was living with his 70-year-old grandmother in a crime-ridden neighborhood in Brooklyn. His father was incarcerated for life for murder and his mother was battling drug addiction. Abi said the boy had not been to school all year although the school had not alerted her or the family. Henry had already acquired a long rap sheet with multiple encounters with police and the juvenile justice system. He'd been charged with a long list of offenses ranging from assault to possession of marijuana with intent to sell. He had been arrested several times for stealing cell phones and placed in a group home for three months. He had just returned home and seemed to be doing better when he was rearrested for stealing sneakers.

Abi looked distraught as she described the family to me and I was also feeling her distress. She said that she did not even know where to begin. The intensity of my own reaction to Henry's troubles and Abi's frustration took me by surprise.

I had heard these kinds of stories before. I think it was in observing and feeling the depth of Abi's discouragement and disappointment with herself, her job, and her prospects for her future as a clinician that got to me. She was losing her faith in Henry and herself, losing faith in family therapy, and I was feeling my own uncertainty. My heart sank. If I felt hopeless, and my supervisee felt hopeless, what chance was there of helping the client?

I had often used these gridlocks as opportunities to encourage supervisees to experiment and try out fresh techniques and models for size. "You're young and you have your whole career in front of you. Have some fun. Write letters to your clients in between sessions and tell them how surprised you are that things aren't much worse. Bring your yoga mat to the next session and do some yoga with him!" Somehow this brand of supervision seemed to be missing the mark. I sensed that there were broader, bigger issues at play here that we were ignoring and not attending to.

Many of Henry's problems centered on social issues that seemed beyond the reach of psychological solutions that made up our standard treatment protocols. Is the narrow, pathologizing focus of the therapy field too limited in its ability to address broader social issues that are so embedded in these clients' daily lives? Our difficulty in meeting kids like Henry's needs are not just because of greater "pathology" or "resistance." There's an overfocus on what's wrong with these kids on every level. Boys like Henry are characterized as bad and not as hurting or traumatized while more and more punishment is heaped upon them. How could we expect Henry to invest or believe in a system that didn't invest or believe in him? It seems clear that these kids do not need more harshness in their lives. If anything, they need more softness and more mercy. Additional school suspensions, incarceration, foster care and placements, and medication have not been the remedy. How do these kids internalize these ongoing messages of how bad they are? There's been an erosion of community and belonging on every level for them. They have been disconnected from the primary family, disconnected from school, and disconnected from themselves.

At that moment, I decided to take an aerial view of things and to engage in a totally different conversation with Abi. I decided to begin with a quick review of common factors research. This research has established that highest on the list of strong predictors of a successful outcome in therapy are the strengths and the resources of the client (Orlinsky, Grawe, & Parks, 1994). Second highest on the list of good outcome predictors is the quality of the therapeutic relationship. Therapy is much more likely to be successful when the client is engaged and the therapy is congruent with the client's goals for treatment (Duncan, 1997). We are trained to conceptualize problems on multiple levels—familial, societal, and intrapsychic—with sensitivity to the cultural and family context as current symptom-maintainers. However, Abi was spending all her time doing crisis management. She had a sense of failing her client and working with a model that was insufficient. The problem being offered to her was to single-handedly fix Henry without any support from either the school or the family. I asked Abi about where in this problem-laden, multilayered system could she make a difference and effect change? Could we hold Henry's behavior up to the light and look at it from all angles? Instead of just paying attention to his crimes, could we give voice to the untold stories of complete emotional and financial insecurity that have plagued his life? Might we consider the notion that Henry's behavior might actually be ineffective solution-attempts? Surely his criminal behavior had some survival value in his community and had been a way for him to win respect and status within his kinship group. All these questions were meant to disrupt Abi's and my own certainty about what was going on with Henry and to widen our therapeutic lens.

Henry's multiple losses throughout his life, including both of his parents, had been unacknowledged and ungrieved. If Abi was going to understand why Henry was doing the things he was doing, she would have to think beyond models and techniques and be willing to speak about this long string of losses, including hope, that Henry had experienced. I asked Abi to think about what the story is that Henry has been telling himself about himself. It's easy to get trapped in the tyranny of that powerful story. It's such a tight script with very little wiggle room. There were many layers to his story and we used supervision to pursue this line of inquiry. How could Abi listen in a way that validated the difficulty of Henry's circumstances, but also open a more empowering story that highlights his ingenuity and his resilience? Could Abi help Henry expand his life story and see himself as a warrior or a superhero in his drama that honors both his struggles and his resourcefulness (Hardy & Laszloffy, 2005)? Could Abi ask questions that open up this alternative story while still recognizing the central role that toughness played in his life?

We discussed how Henry might take responsibility for his life and his choices while giving legitimacy and language to the wider landscape of unfairness that had shaped his life. In expanding his story, could Henry begin to consider some important identity questions such as, "Who am I?" "What do I believe in? "What do I stand for?" Did he believe that he had lost the freedom to define himself, to declare who he is and who he wants to become? When we see someone through the lens of their circumstances, we're not seeing the person.

Abi and I were both feeling a bit more hopeful, although she was not sure if she had established enough trust with Henry and his family to initiate these difficult conversations. As we talked, this new line of inquiry made sense to Abi and she became more animated and hopeful about her work.

Abi recognized that she had to be able to see something redeemable in Henry to make a difference and to begin restoring his dignity. No one was encouraging Henry. I asked Abi if she believed that his life was already locked in? Could she disrupt that path that has been in motion for a long time, perhaps generations? Could she let him know that his life mattered, that he was valued, and his life is important? Could she make eye contact with him and tell him that she sees him?

I was challenging Abi to go deeper and to do the same with Henry. This does not mean making excuses for him but widening her gaze to accommodate the many burdens he has to carry. My goal was to help Abi believe in herself and her capacity to open up these conversations with this family. I encouraged her to provide a space where Henry could let his guard down and not have to worry about being disrespected or judged.

As therapists and supervisors, we want to leverage resilience and resources in ourselves and those we work with. Instead of only determining what's broken, can we look at the whole ecology? We are not just providing supervision or therapy, we are helping one another embrace each other's full humanity and opening space to become different kinds of human beings who support the highest potential in each other. Kids like Henry do not have language to articulate their unnamed pain that's also linked to humiliation and shame. They hold their unspoken shame close to them because it's so painful to expose it. Can Abi help Henry expand his notions of masculinity beyond physical aggression and invulnerability? Otherwise, that wide gap between his external swagger and his internal sorrow could be lethal. Violence often occurs because these kids don't know what else to do with their suffering.

There's power in properly naming something. It's hard to heal from conditions that have no name. Without being properly named, they do not exist in a human being (Gilligan, 1997). Proper naming involves seeing an experience, touching it with human presence, holding it in trust for the person, and giving it blessing. Without this base of love and respect, the named experience has no human value (Gilligan, 1997).

Abi and I discussed a plan to begin speaking about Henry's many losses, gently holding them and then moving forward with him in a progressive way. The basic idea is that problems persist when a person gets locked into a devalued, neglected identity, and solutions emerge when communication accesses other identities that include a person's competencies and resources. The therapist is always curious about who the client is in addition to the presenting problem-laden identity, and in holding an orientation to complementary, multiple truths simultaneously. These neglected parts of a person need our recognition and blessing so we can facilitate relational connection between them and become curious about how each has a place and contributes to a bigger, more complete picture. As long as trauma has no hospitable home to land, it can remain in a vegetative state.

I want my supervisees to cultivate a felt sense of themselves and their clients and to hold their clients' suffering in spacious, heartfelt awareness. Once connected to the relational field, we may become curious about various identity-related questions such as, "Who are you?" and "Who else are you?" and to note both the clients' and our own responses. The holding of these two responses together is what allows a therapeutic conversation to take place, especially when there are differences.

A basic principle of healing is that it is possible to accept and transform painful experiences. If we believe that negative experiences cannot be transformed, we turn away from them and relate to them with anger, malice, and violence. We want to encourage supervisees to find ways to be open to and be with each aspect of their clients' experiences. A need for a solid container is crucial, especially with clients with very chaotic backgrounds like Henry's. We each have to do our own internal work first and foremost and to be centered ourselves in order to build relational trust that can hold space from a place of being present and responsive. We want to open attention, develop receptivity and curiosity, and enter a relational field with the supervisee and the client. Once connected to the relational field, the supervisor may contemplate questions such as "What experience or identity is not being acknowledged?" If a part of themselves is being devalued or neglected, we begin to gently and slowly challenge that. What happens when a case does not work out and success does not occur? Success does not happen all the time; however, we all need those celebratory moments.

Every therapist and supervisor should be doing their own work to develop a state of centering, grounding, and openness to whatever arises and meeting it with curiosity and commitment to discover how it might become the basis for change and discovery. We can start by observing our own agitation or reactions as they arise around certain experiences in therapy and supervision. We can try little experiments of cultivating an open heart and acceptance of negative reactions in order to find ways to exercise curiosity in our practice.

The principle of sponsorship in supervision is the process by which we connect with, touch, bless, provide place, and support a living presence to assume human value. Without sponsorship, an experience will have no name, no voice, and no human value. Sponsorship in supervision is an act of compassion whereby the gift of life is honored by welcoming and holding unintegrated identities through the skills of deep listening, acceptance, proper naming, blessing, boundary setting, and skill building (Gilligan, 1997). Perhaps the true value of our work lies in our capacity to restore dignity and goodness in ourselves and others. The compassion we cultivate for ourselves directly transmits itself to others.

Bateson (1972) proposed that news of a difference, that is, information (p. 272), is a necessary component of all problem-solving and this is best generated by contrasting two or more descriptions of the same sequence of events. In therapy and supervision, we're challenged to be open to new information and different points of view and share responsibility for learning something new from the conversation. Meanings are constantly being negotiated within the communicative contexts in which they take place. With each word, we are scanning for differences and connections; the therapeutic conversation requires both to be effective. If I'm going to be helpful, I have to be willing to be authentic and broadcast expanded, newsworthy stories that both honor the tears our clients carry and also hold the possibility of redemption. When Abi pushed herself to have a conversation with Henry about his two selves, one who was full of hope, ingenuity, and excitement, and the other fearful and angry, his whole demeanor changed, and he smiled broadly, which surprised her. Most people can remember someone in their lives who really saw them as special and unique. These blessings from special people are crucial acts in the awakening of each person to herself and to the world (Gilligan, 1997). The opposite of blessings is a curse, which is prominent in most traumatic events. By pushing through her own fears, Abi was able to tell Henry that she "saw him" and to offer her blessings to him. She was jubilant in our next supervision meeting, having restored her faith in herself, her clinical skills, and in Henry.

References

Bateson, G. (1972). *Steps to an ecology of mind*. New York, NY: Ballantine Books.

Cunningham, P. B., & Henggler, S. (1999). Engaging multiproblem families in treatment: Lessons learned throughout the development of multisystemic therapy. *Family Process*, *38*(3), 265–281.

Duncan, B. (1997). Stepping of the throne. *Family Therapy Networker*, *21*(4), 22–33.

Gilligan, S. (1997). *The courage to love*. New York, NY: Norton.

Hanna, S. M. (2007). *The practice of family therapy: Key elements across models*. Belmont, CA: Brooks/Cole.

Hardy, K., & Laszloffy, T. (2005). *Teens who hurt: Clinical interventions for breaking the cycle of adolescent violence*. New York, NY: Guilford.

Henggeler, S. W., Schoenwald, S. K., Borduin, C. M., Roland, M. D., & Cunningham, P. B. (1998). *Multisystemic treatment of antisocial behavior in children and adolescents*. New York, NY: Guilford Press.

Keeney, B. (1983). *Aesthetics of change*. New York, NY: Guilford.

Orlinsky, D., Grawe, K., & Parks, B. (1994). Process and outcome in psychotherapy: Noch einmal. In A. E. Bergin & S. L. Garfield (Eds.), *Handbook of psychotherapy and behavior change* (3rd ed; pp. 270–369). New York, NY: John Wiley.

Timm, T.M., & Blow, A. (January, 1999). Self of the therapist work: A balance between removing restraints and identifying resources, *Contemporary Family Therapy*, *21*(3), 331–351.

12

LISTENING TO WOUNDED SOULS AND SILENT VOICES

Self-Supervision in My Work with Family Members of Missing Persons in Kosovo

Fatmire Shala-Kastrati

Introduction

Kosovo is a geographically small country located in the Western Balkans, a land-locked entity with a landmass of 10,887 square kilometers. It is a geographical basin, situated at an altitude of about 500 meters, surrounded by mountains, and divided by a central north/south ridge into two subregions of roughly equal size and population. Kosovo is now a partially recognized independent country in the Balkans that has experienced an immensely difficult history, especially in the 20th century. It is bordered by Serbia, Montenegro, Albania, and Macedonia, and it is roughly a third larger than the state of Delaware in the United States. Sandwiched between Albania and Serbia, Kosovo has struggled with its ethnic breakup.

A few years before becoming an independent country, Kosovo went through a war, internationally known more as an armed conflict that began in February 1998. The war took place between the forces of the Federal Republic of Yugoslavia (at that time, the Confederation of Serbia and Montenegro) and the Kosovo Liberation Army (KLA), with NATO (North Atlantic Treaty Organization—a coalition of countries dedicated to helping each other protect their sovereignty and borders) aids beginning in March 1999. During the 78-day air strike, particularly during March 1999, the Serbian army and paramilitary troops forced nearly one million Albanians to leave their homes; 650,000 fled to Albania and hundreds of thousands to Macedonia. During the period of almost two years from late February 1998 until mid-June 1999, around 15,000 people were killed and around 5,206 people were reported missing in Kosovo.

After the war, people of Kosovo attempted to restore their lives by trying to rebuild their destroyed houses and businesses, and going through their painful losses at the same time. The most sensitive group was the family members of missing persons who couldn't restore their lives or rebuild their houses. They lost their beloved ones and they did not know anything about their fate. Families started to search for their loved ones in every way on their own and also through different governmental and non-governmental organizations. Family members were always searching and, at the same time, carrying the pain, psychological and emotional burnings in their bodies and spirits so that they were not thinking about themselves because they had no time for this!

Besides all the losses, the issue of missing persons became one of the most pressing in Kosovo, so, as a result of this, in June, 2002, the newly established Office of Missing Persons and Forensics (OMPF; now the Institute of Forensic Medicine: IFM) under the United Nations Mission in Kosovo within the Department of Justice became the sole authority mandated to determine the whereabouts of missing persons, identify their mortal remains, and return them to their families.

The OMPF, in order to work more closely with family members of Missing Persons, and with a purpose to know more about the family members' experiences, developed the Memory Project in February 2005 and created a public record of the experiences of the families of the missing.

More than half of the missing persons had been located and their mortal remains identified by the end of 2018, while 1,652 are listed as still missing by the International Committee of the Red Cross and IFM as of October 2018.

Family Members of Missing Persons and the Memory Project

While working with the issue of the missing persons in the Institute of Forensic Medicine, the members of our team became more focused on the most tangible aspects of the problem. We tried to identify as many persons as possible and return them to their families, keeping the numbers of missing persons manageable, attempting to reduce the problem to something statistically insignificant.

Although this work was important, we came to the conclusion that there is much more to be done for the families of the missing persons. Since the damage they were subject to is literally irreparable, and restoration is always by definition incomplete, another answer was needed. Among other goals, the IFM Memory Project was designed to show family members of missing persons that they are not alone. Through different psychosocial initiatives, the Memory Project tried to support family members of missing persons in Kosovo.

The first initiative used theater to explore the painful issues the families of missing persons faced and was compiled into the publication, *Voices* (Office of Missing Persons and Forensics [OMPF], 2005b). The second initiative used an oral histories method, where video-recorded interviews were conducted with the families of the missing in order to build an historical archive. The publication, *"Hear What We Are Saying"-The Families Speak*, provides sample interviews where most (80%) were carried out by me (Shala-Kastrati) as a Psychosocial Support Officer for the OMPF (2005a).

The Memory Project was the first building block in a more complex structure that aimed to allow experience to unite rather than to divide people, enable the families of missing persons to share their stories with others and, most importantly, give the victims ownership of their own experience, and let them write their own stories.

Clarifying the fate of the missing is a long and sensitive process and it is of special importance for the families affected. In this chapter, I describe my personal experience during my years working with the family members of missing persons, providing some examples, and describing my self-supervision experience during my work.

I have an M.A. in Clinical Psychology and, since 2005, I work as a Psychosocial Support officer in the IFM under Ministry of Justice in Pristina/Kosovo.

Working with Family Members of Missing Persons

It was the summer of 2005 when I started a new journey in Kosovo. I started to work as a Psychosocial Support Officer in the Institute of Forensic Medicine-IFM. Even though at that time I had heard about the missing persons in Kosovo by various sources, I lacked the knowledge of the issue in general and especially didn't know about the pain, ambiguous loss (Boss, 1999), and many difficulties that family members of missing persons were going through. This was my first job after I graduated in my basic studies while I was doing a master's degree at the Department of Psychology at Pristina University.

Working for more than 13 years with family members of missing persons in the IFM was an exceptional experience and, at the same time, interesting and not an easy one. Even though everything was new to me—the building, the office, people, obligations, responsibilities, and, finally, the work itself—I accepted a position to work on the Memory Project where the main task of the project was to interview the family members of missing persons and to listen to their painful stories.

Everything was new to me, including the psychosocial aspect of the missing persons issue itself and their family members so that I had to start from the very beginning. My first task was to work on the procedures and formulating questions for the interview process. I began together with two other colleagues: one from Britain who was a UN volunteer with a Neuroscience education background, and a Canadian who was a Social Anthropologist. We worked together on every single detail of the procedures and the process itself, at the same time contacting and organizing meetings with the leaders of family associations of missing persons in different municipalities throughout the area based on completed questionnaires and organized interviews.

After completing this process, the Memory Project started and, as an interviewer, I gently guided the conversation with the family members of missing persons back in time to memories of loved ones. Having no specific professional training on how the interview should be done, I just followed my inner guide, bearing in mind that I, myself, had experienced the war even though I didn't have any losses in my close family.

In general, at the beginning of the interview, the family members of missing persons were asked to describe their beloved ones, to tell us about significant family events they had together and that they remembered well, and about the role their beloved ones played in family and society. On the canvas of such past experiences, a verbal portrait emerged as the family members of missing persons replied to the questions. The opening tone of the interview can be characterized as paying homage. The interview proceeded forward in time to the fateful moment of separation where sometimes family members directly witnessed the loved ones being taken, other times having been informed through others or a phone call.

During an interview, one father of a missing son commented, "I was holding his hand tightly but the soldier was trying to separate us with his automatic gun. My son was pale, like what the old people say: if you try to cut his skin there would be no blood. He probably knew what would happen to him, but the only choice was to go with him and not to be here today." That moment of knowledge of the separation is typically followed by a frenetic period of search. The last part of the oral history interviews addresses the situation of today and some of the issues facing the families of the missing. For some, the remains of their loved ones have been returned and the grieving process is allowed to begin. For other families, the fate of their beloved ones still remains unknown even after more than 19 years.

A pool of knowledge elicited firsthand from the spirits of the family members of missing persons is preserved in digital format and has been made searchable and researchable. We hope this pool will open new doors to understanding and assist in gaining deeper insight into the lives of the families of the missing persons in Kosovo.

Loss can be a specific moment, but the trauma of not knowing is a lived experience that does not end, it is an ambiguous loss (Boss, 1999) where gaining the meaning is even more difficult than in ordinary loss because the grief itself remains unresolved.

Self-Supervision During the Work with Family Members of Missing Persons

An introduction to self-supervision should give us the possibility to understand the meaning and the content of the issue and understanding why we have the need for self-supervision as a consequence of lack of institutionally-organized professional supervision in my workplace and almost in all institutions in Kosovo. Self-supervision is the ability of a person to understand individual capabilities, evaluate their skills and abilities, to gauge individual qualities, and to organize this information in order to aptly adapt to any situation, particularly the work environment. Self-supervision is otherwise known as internal supervision. A very essential aspect of self-supervision is being able to self-reflect on one's own work. Self-reflection involves two basic components: self-observation and self-assessment. The process of self-reflection requires asking oneself effective questions as provided by Borders and Leddick (1987).

Working with different family members of missing persons and listening to their painful stories required a lot of effort to keep my emotions in control and, at the same time, to support, empathize, counsel, and understand the family members. I recall a meeting with a mother, Ferdonije, and many other mothers and family members of missing persons from different places all around Kosovo. During the war in Kosovo, Ferdonije lost her husband, her four sons, and many other relatives who were listed as missing persons. After the war, she searched for them in different ways through institutions, organizations, and by herself. About seven years after the war, she was informed that two of her sons had been found dead in mass graves in Serbia, identified through DNA analyses, and could be released to her for reburial. However, she is still waiting for news about her husband and two other sons who are still missing. She lives alone in her house that she turned into a museum in order to remember her family members.

While listening to their stories, I heard elements that repeated themselves everywhere I had been: "children," "old people," "women," "walking," "searching," and so forth, the same things that I saw during my own war journey going from one place to another. Family members of missing persons called my attention through many elements they said out loud during the interviews we did together: "where they have gone, are they cold when it rains, do they have shelter, are they hungry, do they have something to eat?!"

While I, as psychosocial support officer, was listening, these questions and many others touched my feelings and emotions: I wondered whether it was ok to express my feelings, was it helpful or harmful for the family members? These are sensitive moments, and I don't want to let them feel more hurt with my own distress. Bearing in mind that the interviews were non-standardized and were not designed as therapeutic sessions or counseling as I was formally educated for, I was a bit confused about what to do and how to proceed.

These many questions about my uncertainty for how to act and not to hurt the family members left me with a need to find ways to help and support them and brought about my immediate need for supervision, support, and professional advice. However, in relation to this, our institution did not have such resources and there were no possibilities for obtaining them. Being in this situation, I needed supervision in order to take care of myself and at the same time be careful with the family members of missing persons to support them and not harm them unconsciously. I tried to find ways and talk with other professionals to overcome this obstacle. One way was to talk to my friends who had the same education in clinical psychology. There were a few of my friends, as Clinical Psychologists, with whom I met regularly and discussed my difficulties with the interview process, and also expressed my feelings about the stories of family members of missing persons.

Considering the fact that all of us were young in our profession and working in different settings made it a bit difficult to help each other. However, it was helpful for me to have an ear to listen to me about how I felt, how emotional the stories were, and to support me in continuing my interview process with family members of missing persons. We managed to meet in different places: in my dormitory room, in a cafe bar, and anywhere else we found to talk! It was not easy to set the same time since everyone had obligations but we met as often as we could.

Besides all this, every day I faced new things and I found myself in different situations, in moments that I had to react in "proper" ways. I thought that it was necessary to find ways to help myself by doing some kind of self-supervision as I was going through the interviews which were emotional, psychologically burdensome, and touched me so often. I continued to search on the internet for the best possible ways to manage my emotions during the interviews, trying to find the techniques for how to manage the difficult moments.

To make it more understandable, I will try to explain through some examples of stories from family members of missing persons whom I met and interviewed to whose painful stories I listened. During an interview, I was listening to an 80-year-old father who was telling a story of his only son who went missing during the war. The old father had searched for his 20-year-old son in many ways through different national and international organizations, but he had no news. The old father hoped that his son was somewhere alive; he also believed one person who was an extortionist who told him that his son was alive, but he should pay a lot of money in order to make it possible to see his son. Hoping that his son was alive, the old father decided to pay the money and since he didn't have that large amount of money, he sold his house and everything he had. After going through all these obstacles and pain after six years of searching and being betrayed by the extortionist, the old father received the news that the mortal remains of his dead son had been found in one of the mass graves in Serbia. They were identified by DNA analysis and would be handed over by IFM so he could rebury the mortal remains of his son.

While the old father was telling the story, he was very emotional and he started crying, which for me was normal, but for him uncomfortable, knowing culturally, men do not cry because this is seen as a weakness. I asked myself how he could keep his tears and bear all that pain and wounded spirit for his only son. I was emotional and crying, too, showing empathy toward him and motivating him to express himself and to feel it. I was uncertain whether it was ok to show my emotions and, at the same time, many thoughts crossed my mind: am I helping him; he is old—can his heart bear all this heavy pain; what if he collapses or faints; I was not sure ... uffff, not easy! I turned to myself in this thinking process, and in that moment, I was trying to feel and think at the same time: he was so old and maybe there was no one to talk and listen to him, and, at the same time, was burning inside to talk and say as much as he could. So, I was there to listen and give him room to express himself and experience a kind of catharsis of emotions and psychological load.

At the end of the interview with the old father, it was like he confirmed my thoughts by admitting that he had such a huge need to talk and express his emotions and was feeling very much relieved. I was relieved too and this motivated me to continue with other interviews.

The process of interviews continued with other family members of missing persons and each of the interviews was unique and required skill and knowledge. This was often confusing to me since I had not been trained for this kind of work.

In another case, that of Ferdonije who was mentioned earlier, having prior general information for her family members who went missing, I was uncertain about where to begin the interview. I found myself asking: Was I ready to listen to her story? Could I manage the interview, which I expected to be full of emotions and painful moments? In the moment, I thought, it won't be easy but I will give her the opportunity to talk and express her feelings, let her talk as much as she wants and maybe this will help her to experience a kind of emotional catharsis. If she is living with this terrible loss and awful experience, I should find courage, use all my knowledge, and do it. We did the interview, and afterward she was tired, almost exhausted, but very relieved as she admitted. And what about me? I was totally lost in my emotions. I couldn't bear my tears, and in my head, many questions were rising, requiring answers, but who was I to address them to?

I needed more supervision and consultation, again talking to my friends and my superior for the techniques and methods for overcoming my insecure moments, which were the possibilities to act differently, to express my empathy, to support in silence, or to stop the interview in a moment if I was feeling so bad and emotional that I couldn't continue? My friends encouraged me to continue and talk openly with the persons I interviewed, share the whole process with them. Perhaps after the interview, we could discuss how they felt about my sharing and their perception of me, whether I was helpful or if they needed some other kind of support or method to rely on.

It was the feedback I received from family members of missing persons after the interviews that made me so often sit in my office and talk to myself, reflect on the stories I had heard, the expressed emotions and psychological reactions of family members of missing persons. I analyzed whether I reacted properly in sensitive moments of interviews, whether I should have reacted differently in some other possible similar cases, and whether I needed to search for other, better techniques that would help me to be even more professional and helpful since I felt I was not helping enough. I continued to ask myself also for the emotional aspect of whether it was ok to show them how I felt, whether that was helpful to them, and, at the same time, thinking how to preserve my psychological well-being and not burn myself out. All this brought me to a self-supervision process in the absence of much-needed, institutionally organized supervision, and not always a good chance to call or meet friends and professionals to discuss in the moments needed.

Finally, even though proper supervision was not available, I tried to find the best possible ways to help and support family members of missing persons, and, with the support of my superior and my valuable friends, we did a great job. Even now the family members I interviewed appreciate what we have done for them, and this is the best motivation for me to continue working with the family members of missing persons in Kosovo.

Now, after more than 13 years of working with family members of missing persons in Kosovo, the families and I have together built rapport and trust with each other, and they still ask for meetings to discuss their difficulties openly. At the same time, together, we try to process their emotions and find meaning in their stories by developing capabilities to enhance their effectiveness in their daily lives. I am more and more confident in my work since this support is helpful for them and they trust my experience and cooperation.

General Brief Information

- As of October 2018 around 1,652 persons are still listed as missing in Kosovo.
- To date, 5,206 persons were reported missing as a result of the war 1998–1999 and related events in Kosovo.

References

Borders, D. L., & Leddick, G. R. (1987). *Handbook of Counseling Supervision*. Alexandria, VA: Association for Counselor Education and Supervision.

Boss, P. (1999). *Ambiguous loss: Learning to live with unresolved grief*. Oxford, MA: Harvard College.

Office of Missing Persons and Forensics (2005a). "Hear what we are saying": The families speak: An oral history initiative with the families of the missing. *OMPF Transitional Justice Series* (2nd ed.). Podues Press: Pristina, Kosov.

Office of Missing Persons and Forensics (2005b). Voices: an interactive theatre initiative addressing the issue of the missing persons in Kosovo. *OMPF Transitional Justice Series*. Podues Press: Pristina, Kosov.

13

CHALLENGES IN SUPERVISION IN FAMILY-ORIENTED APPROACHES IN PRISHTINA, KOSOVA

Meta-Talk, Peer Support, and Co-Supervision as Partial Solutions

Adelina Ahmeti Pronaj and Vjollca Berisha Avdiu

Based on the experience of the authors, most of the supervision on clinical work of mental health professionals is received through various project initiatives brought mainly by foreign providers. The first author is a child psychiatrist, whilst the second author is a specialist-clinical psychologist, both newly trained in family therapy, living and working in clinical settings in Prishtina. We both provide family-oriented consultations. When working together, we discuss cases with one another, offer support to each other in our work, and peer–supervise one another. In this paper, we will discuss our peer support model we developed as a result of the gaps in supervision and consultation for family therapy.

Some of Adelina Ahmeti's (AA's) and Vjollca Berisha's (VB's) Experiences with Receiving Supervision

For many cases we have seen, most of the supervision we have been provided was from mental health professionals, and more specifically from family therapists from foreign countries in terms of the projects/trainings they and we were part of. Supervision was also provided to us by local mentors/supervisors who were engaged in various projects over the years.

What follows are some (not all) examples of supervision that AA and VB received in the more recent years.

After VB finished her formal education at the University and was employed in a clinical setting in the first years of her employment as a psychologist, she received supervision related to her clinical cases mainly from her University visiting professor, both via technological means, such as Skype, and through individual meetings. VB is endlessly grateful to Professor Moshe Landsman, who always demonstrated willingness, energy, and enthusiasm to supervise and help his former student to become a professional in her work, but also helped other mental health professionals of Kosova.

Of course, both AA and VB could also always turn to their chief when this was needed related to their work, but also would discuss cases with their peer-colleagues, such as psychiatrist-specialists.

VB received supervision as one of the 20 trainees/residents in a postgraduate training in Clinical Psychology and Psychotherapy program, which was a collaboration project of Kosovarian, Swiss, and Dutch institutions. It was funded by the Government of Switzerland through the Swiss Cooperation Office in Kosovo, headed by the Clinical Psychologist Committee residing under the Residency Board of the Ministry of Kosovo and its implementation in Kosovo was facilitated by the Kosovo Health Foundation. This project also trained ten mental health professionals (psychiatrists and psychologists) to be supervisors, from some of which VB had supervision whilst the training was ongoing.

VB also had an opportunity to receive supervision from a local trainer and international trainers during several modules on trauma-therapy provided by the Psycho-Social Centre for Trauma Therapy, Diakonie Kosovo, a Mitrovica-based non-governmental organization. Both AA and VB were provided with mentoring by the trainers in the DIRFloortime Training they attended on helping children with special needs and their families.

Both AA and VB received supervision as trainees in a family therapy training program. Once the training was over, most of the supervision they received was from the international trainers/family therapists on a voluntary basis after contacting them and asking them for supervision on a case. However, as far as the supervision specifically on family therapy in Kosovo is concerned, the clinical settings where AA and VB work do not provide them with supervision on a regular basis, in a structured way. They both understand the importance of supervision to professionals in their work with clients, and this gives them a feeling of frustration for not having supervision on a regular basis.

Introduction to Our Peer Support Model

As co-authors, we, Adelina and Vjollca, typically see a minimum of five cases per day, for five days a week. We have completed the training in our respective degrees (Adelina is a Specialist in Child Psychiatry; Vjollca is a Specialist in Clinical Psychology), and we work in clinical systems of Pristina, Kosova. Once we finished our training, the official mentoring and supervision also came to its end. However, every once in a while, we find ourselves asking each other's professional opinions related to various cases but also expressing our concerns to each other when, in some way, we feel overwhelmed by them. Mental health workers often discuss cases with their colleagues and occasionally phone each other to consult on the more perplexing cases. We noticed that often we seem to be drawn to talking to each other about what is happening in our cases. Usually, this happens either over our breaks – breakfast time, or at the end of our work schedule, after seeing cases. If we added up this "informal" time together, per month, we realize it essentially adds up to the time we might have previously spent in supervision.

Sometimes we previously agree on the time we will meet in one of our offices to discuss a case. Or we might decide to meet in the restaurant right next to our workplace, which is usually attended by medical staff and which is surrounded by beautiful pear trees and fresh air. At other times, we start to discuss cases spontaneously, instantly sharing with one another about the case we had just seen, at our workplace.

How We Organize Our Peer Supervision Meetings

As colleagues, usually we meet in one of the offices where we work, after seeing patients, and start to discuss the case. We try to do a case formulation, discuss various therapeutic strategies that we think would be the most successful. As peer supervisors, we think and talk about the pros and cons of a certain therapeutic strategy. We offer each other literature, what we got from trainings, as well as use Google Scholar as a source of academic papers that help us prepare for the case as best as possible. We also find it helpful to share previous therapeutic experiences with each other (e.g., what appeared as successful and what did not, what specific therapeutic technique was helpful in similar cases).

Additional Benefits of Peer Support/Supervision

There are situations that are not case-specific; rather, they affect all cases. That is, when you need to instantly consult with the literature about a certain case, and the internet network happens not to function. In front of you there is an adolescent with an illness that is very sensitive to treatment, and at the same time, you have a mother who is very worried about her daughter's fate and is constantly crying. Only direct supervision would be a solution, or if we can say, a little bit of salvation in the fading of sorrow of a faded mother over the burden and fear about her daughter's health.

In such a case, if there is some hesitation from the therapist's side to work with the case, the peer-supervisor helps to make the therapist understand what makes it so difficult. The peer-supervisor helps with sharing her ideas on how to help family members talk more openly and how to deal with strong emotions that will arise in the session. Perhaps thinking and talking about what can happen in the session is already helpful. Sharing experiences from therapies with other clients (always respecting confidentiality) with similar problems can also be helpful.

As peer professionals, we meet again at the end of the day and discuss the case, firstly related to the trauma the child went through. We discuss the symptoms the child is presenting and intervention. In this case, we discuss what kind of effect this traumatic event can have on the child's future life, from the cultural point of view. Moreover, we try to jointly find the best solution for the case not only in the sense of offering professional mental health services, but we also seek collaboration with the institutions that need to be involved, for example, social work center, court, and so forth.

Vignettes of Challenging Cases and Supervision

What follows are some cases we have found particularly challenging, and in which we found our peer supervision model very useful to work with the family.

In cases with complex problems and unsatisfactory prognoses, such as in a case where a child has experienced the loss of an entire family, or in a case where a family lost a child after the war ended, supervision is definitely needed. For example, the B. family came back from a foreign country where they took refuge when escaping from war. After the war ended, they came back to Kosova and lost their child in a tragic death – a car accident. Ironically, they survived the war and experienced a tragic loss after the war ended. The identifying patient in this family is a new child they have and which his parents constantly compare with the one they lost after the war. The child is expressing various symptoms that warn that something is wrong and needs to be dealt with in the family. We realize that the problem is much more complex than it initially seems. It goes beyond the symptoms the child expresses. There is huge trauma that parents went through and never seem to have gotten over. Obviously, a lot of work needs to be done here, and peer support/supervision helps us decide how to best approach this family.

We often have to figure out how to approach cases when there is trauma inside the family, in the nuclear circle, starting from the war period when, for example, the parent (father) was forced to give up on his own life (to die) to rescue the mother of his children and the children. At this point, the supervision would be ideal in relation to therapist-client and family relationship. And in this case, the client is the mother, who is the head of a family with growing children. In this case, the supervision would be a key point that would lead the therapist to support the family in dealing with trauma and this way, hopefully prevent transmission of traumatic adverse effects of high intensity from one generation to another.

Another case example is a tragic loss of a sibling, which is again an example of the impact of a traumatic event on the family system. The traumatized family member didn't get treated until his child started to show symptoms and became an identifying patient who drew attention that something needed to be changed in the family. However, the question arose from the therapists on how to motivate the parent for the treatment when he did not seem ready yet to deal with his own trauma? Moreover, the parent did not yet understand the relationship between his own trauma and his child's current symptoms. At this point, supervision is the greatest hope for the therapist to achieve success in family therapy with this family.

What to do in situations when, on the one hand, a mother is asking help for her teenage son, and on the other hand, the father is a consumer of narcotic substances? With whom to start and how much can we succeed in treatment with clients who live in an environment where every day is threatening to them? What would the purpose of supervision be here? In such a case, we as peer-therapists would discuss the case and assess the level of risk to the family members. We would suggest contacting social services, if necessary. As professionals, we would broaden our knowledge related to narcotics and its effects. In this case, Adelina would be more helpful to Vjollca, because as a psychiatrist she would help V. (a psychologist) better understand the effects of narcotics.

Another case example would be a child with developmental problems, and who is the only hope for the better future of the family. The child's mother is going through a life-threatening illness and is under chemotherapy, therefore has no chance to have other children. In such a sensitive case, it would be great to have support from a supervisor to the therapist in relation to where to start from with intervention, what would be the major aims of therapy, and at least a little bit of help to alleviate the suffering of this family that has almost no hope for a better quality of their life in future.

How much support would supervision provide in the cases in which we have a loss of a father during the war, and on the other hand we have a young man in his twenties who has to deal with pain caused by his father's death, and consequences in the context he lives in? His father died as a soldier to protect his country, whilst for his son it is extremely difficult to ever mention his father's name. He even says, "it makes me nervous." The question is how to first make his mother aware that the family should talk openly about her husband's death and that this is a part of the intervention and treatment of the young man?!

How to deal with a case in which a teenager is a marijuana abuser and addresses his parents in the following way: "I will never quit since it pleases me." "You did this to me." "My father has harassed us a lot, he has abused us, both, us children and the mother, physically and now he tells me to behave well." However, the father has experienced two wars in the Balkan area. No doubt that the father has elements of PTSD. How to act then with a family with such a trauma? Where to start the intervention?! Our case consultation as peers recognizes the philosophical and practical parts of this question.

Another case example is a court case of a child that was abused in a village in his neighborhood, firstly by his friends and then by an old man. How to work with the child and his family, considering that tradition and honor are of high value to Albanian families? In this case, peer supervision is essential, more specifically with a colleague coming from the same culture.

The first author also dealt with a family in which the mother has a fatal illness but also has a job with a lot of responsibility. The father also has a very sensitive job. These two parents experienced loss in their history: both of them lost their fathers at the age of three. Now the parents are seeking help for their children, especially for their son who is labeled as hyperactive, problematic, both at home and at school. The major problem is that the father does not know how to approach his son as he has no experience or a model on approaching his father. We recognize that there are several issues to deal with in this case.

In a case where there is sudden killing as part of retaliation in the families, one of the things the therapist (Adelina) noticed was that the event was not discussed in the family yet the children carried a burden of the consequences of the accumulated trauma on their shoulders and expressed them in various unwanted forms. So, this is an additional case example where a severe traumatic event has changed the entire family system. How to work in a context with so many traumas?!

Apart from cases with trauma in their core, we also work with many children who have developmental problems and work with their families. When the first author works with a child with developmental difficulties, she very often needs to better understand the child's individual profile. The second author then assesses a child who has developmental problems and this way, as a team, they can better help the child. An example would be a little girl who had difficulties to adjust in the class in the first grade, once she entered school. Parents were worried whether the teacher would be able to understand the child's difficulties. The author did a thorough assessment of the child and wrote a report based on it, advocating for the child's welfare. Her parents were extremely relieved once the report was accepted by the teacher and she changed her attitude toward the child. This further helped the child adapt in the class.

Another case example is of an eight-year-old boy who grew up with his uncle and uncle's wife because his father died and his mother left him. The boy had concentration problems and a learning disability (disgraphya) and as a result got low grades, which made his uncle unhappy. The referral problems were his learning difficulties and behavioral problems. AA and VB recognize here that there are several difficulties that need to be addressed in such a case – the boy's problems with learning – but also his caregiver's approach toward the child and perhaps high expectations. Both authors contribute to the case with their knowledge, VB by her assessment on the learning, and AA with psychotherapy.

Our Peer-Consultation Related to Cases of Trauma

From the above-written vignettes, you can see that most of the cases we as authors work with have some sort of trauma in their histories. Many times, trauma is war-related. So, what does this do to us?

For any of us, the war experiences, or any experience of loss brought by our patients are reminiscent of our own experiences, either during the war or before the war. Cases like these can bring up our own unpleasant memories and feelings related to the war experiences and fears of losing our own family members (even if we didn't).

Still, we as authors believe that our personal histories, including trauma as part of it, can be very beneficial in helping our clients. They help us be more empathic, understanding, and supportive toward our clients. Now, who could better understand a client who went through bombing, unless you yourself went through it? You can read about it in books, you can watch movies, and cognitively understand how bad it is. But you can never *really* understand what a horrible sound it (the bombing) is, and what shaking of the earth it causes and enormous fear unless you experienced this yourself. Who could better understand what being a refugee is alike, unless you yourself had been a refugee; understand what it means to lose a home, experience sorrow and insecurity of what the future brings, and then again relief that you are at a safe place and have hope for a better life? Luckily, we as authors did not experience any tragic losses in the war, but we did constantly fear such loss.

Therefore, as long as we do not become as Cavanagh, Wiese-Batista, Lachal, Baubet, and Moro (2015) would say, "invaded or absorbed by the traumatic scene" (p. 3), the client tells us about it, and as long as we are mindful of our counter-transference, we can use our own experiences at best for our clients.

We had some opportunity to work on our own personal issues during our formal education/training; however, unfortunately, we did not have as much as we felt we needed. Perhaps we need even more awareness on how they can impact the therapeutic process. Now, this is where our peer-supervision takes place. We as co-authors discuss with each other about how a particular case had made us feel. Since there is so much to say, we end up with mutual associations of many events we went through. This instantly makes us feel more relaxed as a result of understanding each other's more or less similar experiences and validating each other's feelings. Such supervision serves us as an entrance to better understanding of ourselves, however, perhaps not as deeply as we would wish.

Both of us authors are characterized by curiosity about cases and sometimes supervision arises spontaneously. As a therapist, I (AA) definitely needed to talk about a case with my peer-supervisor. I needed to express my intensive emotions of sadness, anger, and despair that I felt aroused in me during the therapeutic session. VB's comment: "the way AA asked for my peer-supervision was by simply approaching me and saying to me, 'What a difficult, but an interesting case I had!,' in this way arousing my curiosity about the case. I am there ready to listen carefully."

At other times, we set a specific time at which we hear each other's cases and carefully analyze counter-transference. An example would be a case of a woman who grew up with her distant relatives because her parents died early, and now that her husband died, she is raising her children to be "orphans" as well as she used to be. For example, the first author's (AA) father died early in her life, and therefore, working with the woman can be professionally quite challenging for her. In such a case, peer supervision can be really helpful, where a colleague (co-author VB) is there, ready to listen to her colleague's concerns, reflects and interprets feelings that arise during the therapeutic process, and contributes to making her colleague aware of how her inner state impacts the therapy.

Considering that a professional therapist can be at risk of empathic distress and burnout, and that there is a risk of counter-transference processes (Iberni, Salihu, & Pacolli, 2009), especially when working with cases of clients who went through severe trauma, for us it is peer-support that helps us prevent the risks.

Peer Support/Supervision of Cases of Families of Children With Special Needs

There are very few things sadder than when you hear a desperate mother saying in a session: "sa të jam une gjallë, apet disi, por çka bëhët me këtë fëmijë kur unë i mbylli sytë përgjithmonë?" (As long as I am alive, something can be done, but what will happen to my child once I close my eyes forever (die)?) In this way, a mother expresses her fear and anxiety about what will happen to her child and who will take care of her child with special needs, once she is gone forever. Or another example is when a mother says: "If I knew that my child would be born with a syndrome, I would have had an abortion back then. Then neither my child nor I would suffer so much." Comments like these often transmit feelings of despair on us authors. Many parents and families are not only worried about their child's current situation, but also extremely worried about who would take care of their child once they are gone forever.

From our clinical observation, we can see that families deal with many existential issues. They lack finances to send their children to occupational therapists, speech therapists, and so forth. There is also lack of expertise in this area. There aren't very many experienced experts in this field, whilst new experts are not employed in institutions. Many parents develop anxiety issues not knowing how, when, and where to help their children with their developmental difficulties. Our work often includes psychiatric diagnosis; however, not treatment—until recently, we did not have special training in such treatment. A lot of our work includes work with families of children with special needs.

In order for us to improve our therapeutic skills for treating the above-mentioned cases, we joined (and suggest attending) various training programs. For example, in order to increase the quality of support for children with developmental problems, and help their families, we both joined the training in DIR Floortime. During this training, we had an opportunity to observe each other's sessions and critically comment on how we were using our skills and emotions, for example, our affect to support the child. We give comments to each other on our body posture and our use of gestures in the session, ability to self-regulate, and so on. Reflecting jointly on our own work helps us learn about ourselves and grow professionally, which is a part of our peer supervision.

When working with families of children with special needs, many times, we, as peer-supervisors, also discuss our own values and beliefs about parenting.

Moreover, it is the emotional support that we provide to one another that is essential when dealing with similar cases where as therapists, we feel that perhaps we cannot do much to help the families.

Additional Methods of Peer-Supervision

One of the authors (VB) has had additional training in a few modules of trauma-therapy, which enables her to better help clients who have gone through traumatic events. Sharing her knowledge and experience with another author is part of the peer-supervision; for example, explaining how to best do psychoeducation on symptoms; or demonstrating various stabilization techniques, which would be very helpful to the above-mentioned clients.

When dealing with a complex case, one of the authors (either AA or VB) would also turn to an international supervisor who is willing to provide supervision on a voluntary basis through Skype. Then the author invites another author so that both would have an opportunity to gain from this kind of voluntary supervision. After having Skype supervision, the two authors would sit together and meta-talk about what they learned from the provided Skype supervision. It is sort of like having meta-supervision.

When Supervision Needs Expansion, Including Multiple Systems and Us

The question arises as to how to expand the supervision, especially when multi-systemic approaches from the non-mental health background are needed. We use medical intervention and literature review. Due to the long-term experiences others have in such cases, consulting with local veteran therapists is extremely helpful. They often offer concrete advice on treating a case and offer useful professional material.

Consulting another professional, such as an endocrinologist, is quite essential and time-saving, and is part of the regular procedure when needed. For example, working with a child with diabetes who also has adjustment difficulties in relation to her diagnosis would definitely require a consultation with an endocrinologist to better understand the child's situation.

Another example would be working with a child with epilepsy who also has behavioral problems. In such a case, we consult with a neurologist.

We also consult, for example, when a child is born with organic problems that are unsafe or dangerous as far as prognoses for life whilst the parents are new in their roles as parents, full of energy and enthusiasm for life, and suddenly their dreams of a healthy baby are quenched. Support from supervision helps relieve the stress and anxiety of both the therapist and the parents.

When we want to consult literature, usually we Google what we need, but also use literature (textbooks, journals, and websites) that were recommended to us through various trainings attended. As the literature is mainly in English, the language is sometimes a challenge for some of our colleagues; therefore, the discussions on diverse literature parts are seldom part of our supervision sessions. Although English language is not a problem for the two of us, what is challenging for us is adapting some terms of therapies into Albanian language.

AA also often consults with colleagues who had other trainings, such as training in Art Therapy. Usually, this is necessary for her in a case where it is rather difficult to discover what the underlying problem of the child is. In such a case, AA turns to our colleague who has special training in Art Therapy and who is specialized in assessment through art. They sit together and as a team analyze the child's drawings, drawing hypotheses, and try to best understand the case.

Concluding Reflections

Coming to an end, what does the peer supervision do for us? To make it simple, the supervision proved useful to us in two main dimensions: first, we could offer our patients better treatment. All the experiences shared, advice gained from diverse professionals and materials used increase the quality of the services we provide and, therefore, we could say that the patient receives the best of care. Second, it is us, the professional workers, who profit highly form this initiative. We benefit in both ways; we accumulate the knowledge and new experiences, but as well, we build our professional skills and self-confidence in what we do.

But for me (VB) it is even deeper. It gives me a sense of security, worth, and belonging: *Belonging to a team* who jointly serves day after day the ones in need, and *therefore I am not alone.* I have my colleagues and feel free to call them my friends, who, with their presence and persistent support, make my demanding work an easy task filled with, yes, much *challenge*, but as well as this much *joy*.

References

Cavanagh, A., Wiese-Batista, E., Lachal, C., Baubet, T., & Moro, M. R. (2015). Countertransference in trauma therapy. *Journal of Traumatic Stress Disorders and Treatment, 4*(4), 1–9. Retrieved from: https://www.scitechnol.com/peer-review/countertransference-in-trauma-therapy-rC9q.php?article_id=4611.

Iberni, E., Salihu, M., & Pacolli, S. (2009). Torture and war traumas: Wounded healers or the experience of the therapist. Retrieved from: http://www.krct.org/site/images/documents/reports/researches/en/Torture%20and%20war%20traumas_en.pdf

14

MY GLOBAL TEAM OF FAMILY THERAPY CONSULTANTS

Seven Commandments of My Method[1]

Laurie L. Charlés

Always Where I am Supposed to Be: An Outsider, Looking In

On a cold morning in March a few years ago, I was in the Bekaa Valley, in Lebanon, with a class of 7th graders. So much about the morning visit felt familiar, but also, at the same time, quite strange. Familiar was my fondness talking to adolescents of that age—I find them so refreshing and engaging. Unfamiliar was that the 7th graders were a class of Syrian adolescents, displaced to Lebanon by the war taking place across the border.

I wasn't supposed to be in Lebanon; I was supposed to be in Syria. Overtaken by events, my plans were upended, and well, here I was, in a 7th grade classroom in Lebanon instead of *Damas*. I've learned as a family therapy supervisor/consultant over the years that I must be ready and willing to "go with the flow." Cool. I can do that. Systemic family therapists know how to do flow, a la Csikszentmihalyi (2008), and take it to the systems with which we are engaged. But as a consultant, I need to maximize that capacity. This is particularly true when my consultation projects are far from home. In other words, although I can maximize difference (Chenail, 2011) fairly comfortably in my own territory, I am often not in it.

In Bekaa, I was not in a therapy room, nor a supervision session. I was in a geopolitical space between two countries with histories of war; one ongoing and present, and the other lengthy and over, but fresh. I had not one family system in front of me but multiple systems: each family of those 7th graders, as well as two states, several NGOs, a refugee camp, a religious school, and one organ of the UN.

As systems thinkers, we learn to take cues from where we are, from all the systemic network of players in our midst. We leave our theory at the door when we walk into the room with a family, as Haley put it years ago. What can I borrow from that idea as a consultant? What cues can I take from a place where I hadn't expected to be? How can I immerse in all that is unknown and unfamiliar?

Eat, Sleep, Run

Fast forward a few months later, and I am back in Texas. In addition to my Bekaa project, I also work at a university as a faculty member and clinical supervisor of family therapy graduate students. Walking in the 100-degree heat to my car after supervising my morning family therapy practicum team, I am exhausted but accustomed to this pace on Tuesdays, having learned to discipline myself to the rhythm of the academy. But I can't really perform it all well unless I am also rested, healthy, *en plein forme*. And I can do none of it if I am hungry. After supervising practica I often feel as hungry as I am after one of my 5K runs. I've been a runner for half my life. But these days I find I am running so much more often, and farther, longer. It's how I cope, like Murakami (2008) said, with all the unhealthy things I hear and see.

My supervisees in Texas are very good. They are good in the way you are good when you are new at something: that is, they are curious to learn, they want to do things correctly, they are eager to explore new territory. I find them very responsive to my nudging and modeling, and this makes my work easy, and fun. Watching them transform before my eyes is amazing and powerful. I once had a colleague who liked to say of supervisees that you must "*inspect* not *expect*" them to do well. But I don't agree with this at all. As a supervisor, I am in the *expect* camp. Expect great things, and they arrive. My supervisees in Syria are also very good. But it is a different kind of good, which I find harder to describe.

When I begin a project as a supervisory consultant, I find my commitment embodied in the desire to see a trainee shine. This shine isn't always easy to see, but I've become better at it. Rather, I've become highly efficient. Perhaps it's because of the different pace of global projects; I don't have two years to work with a supervisee—I have six months. Really, I have five or six days, sometimes ten or 12, face to face, and then perhaps six months, via distance. I have a disciplined pace, a rhythm, in these brief projects, too, informed by the assumption that a brief encounter is as powerful as a lengthy one (Slive & Bobele, 2012).

Hyperlinking Worlds (Bava, 2019) is an Everyday Experience

Later in the evening, before I teach my class, I receive a sms from a colleague in Syria. I've been working with a supervision group of Syrian psychologists and psychiatrists for several months. Most of our contact now (we met face to face in Beirut previously) is by email, web conferencing, and sms.

The text from Syria tonight is a picture. I smile broadly when I see it, and then I scroll in and around to capture the detail.

> A beautiful woman with shiny black hair, tight jeans, and sparkly sneakers is sitting on a rusty tractor. Her gaze looks up into the clouds. The tractor is not in working order, but she looks perfect, groomed, ready, as if she is about to join a tractor race. The background around the tractor looks like someone's backyard. I see what looks like a water tank, and parts of a roof, and lots of green trees, bushes, and a deep blue sky.

A few seconds later I get another text from the same person: "My new car!" With an LOL emoji. I laugh again. It is 1:30 a.m. in Syria—a magic hour of robust internet. Unlike me at 1:30 a.m.—sound asleep—the Syrians are wide awake, burning up the internet and using what they can of the sparse electrical grid. I often wake to find assorted messages from them on my phone apps.

An idea pops up. Maybe I can use this picture to start off my lecture tonight? Something attending to both human security and each training context? The Syrian colleagues I support and the clients and supervisees they work with are living in dynamic humanitarian conditions—that is, they work with "people who have survived terrible experiences—natural disasters, famines, war, ethnic cleansing, political oppression, terrorist attacks, rape and other individual assaults" (Ehrenreich, 2005, p. x). I am very careful about attending to the human security of those I am working with in various geopolitical spots across the globe. In many cases, the people I support don't just *work with* those people who have *survived* terrible experiences, they *are* those people. I am both their witness (Weingarten, 2003) and their supervisor.

Tonight, as I discuss postmodern therapies—in particular, Narrative Therapy (White & Epston, 1990), I can show the picture and then have the students write a quick "story" about what they see, imagining conventions of plot, character, and description. I text my colleague to ask her permission. She agrees, enthusiastic to see what happens, and I add the picture to the presentation with a slide of instructions for the students to follow as they observe the photo. The goal is to demonstrate the varied nature of stories, experience our voice as authors, and note the value of many different lines of inquiry of a phenomenon.

The tractor in Syria takes on a new life as a tractor in Texas.

> "She's just become engaged, and her fiancé took this photo of her to capture the moment."
> "She just won a prize at a local fair, she put on her best clothes to show her animals at the fair, and her sister took this picture."
> "She is a selfie queen but doesn't have her selfie stick so had her BFF take the picture of her on the tractor in a small town they passed on their way home."

Do Both the Story-Telling and the Story-Living

I don't realize how many stories I'm a part of until I have dear colleagues say to me at a conference, one after another: "You have so many stories!" But the stories are more than curious anecdotes for me. They are also instructive information about how to live, to work. Sometimes the instruction occurs immediately; other times, it's years later. It often leads to other, unexpected learnings.

When I am in the role of a global consultant supervisor, I am hyperlinking just as Bava (2019) says, and laterally, globally, across countries, part of the free flow of goods, ideas, and people. In Sri Lanka this summer, I did a presentation at an INGO[2] on post-war reconstruction and reconciliation. I shared preliminary analyses of a project comparing post-war memorialization efforts in the Balkans to Sri Lanka's initiatives after their 26-year war. My slideshow was mostly pictures of civil society-state efforts to memorialize each country's post-war story. It was powerful, watching the Sri Lankans in the audience absorb the photos. The audience of *this* place of post war clearly understood *that* place of post war, its concomitant challenges to transitional justice. The photos tell such a story.

Sometimes, stories tell the story. As part of the same project, I was in Bosnia earlier in the year where I had met someone who knew as much about the siege of Aleppo as I did. He had lived through the siege of Sarajevo as a young boy. Over the course of several days, he told me story after story about how he and his mother survived it, lived it. But he only began telling me his stories after he heard my stories about the siege of Aleppo. I only knew what I knew because my Syrian colleagues' stories had been shared with me and then carried by me to Sarajevo and Prishtina and Colombo. Stories brought stories; patterns resonated from one set of wars to another. I am always surprised by how what I've learned from my Syrian colleagues finds and winds its way into my work.

Consultation is Improvisation and Disruption is My Friend

A few weeks after I am in Sarajevo, I am back in Prishtina. It is early summer. I walk to the University Clinical Center in Prishtina to visit my colleagues, Drs. Mimoza and Adelina, and find Adelina working on a presentation. "Will you look through the presentation with me, just as an editor and family therapy expert?" she asks. Her use of the word expert, after so many years of collaboration, surprises me. Adelina is one of only a few women psychiatrists in Kosovo; she is one of even fewer who specialize in child and adolescent psychiatry.

I've known Adelina and Mimoza since 2009; we met during a training and supervision project in their country and have continued to work and train together, often consulting on cases, over the years. I've met their families, their children; I see them as peers, as friends. They introduce me to others as their *Professor* or *Doktoreshi*. They call each other by these terms as well. I call Adelina and Mimoza my experts, actually. Everything I do here in Kosovo now (my project focuses on post conflict reconciliation and family engagement) requires their input. I need their guidance, their critical thinking. I couldn't do what I do or understand what I understand without our discussions. I feel that way about the Syrians, too. And the Libyans. The Sri Lankans. Even the young man I met in Sarajevo.

The next morning, I walk to the family therapy training Adelina and Mimoza are giving at Mimoza's private clinic. I find a group of about 16 professionals on a coffee break, a crowd fittingly representative of Europe's youngest country. Most of the participants are female, with a handful of males sprinkled in. Adelina is half-way through her lecture—the same one I'd looked at the day before.

I'd brought my computer so I could perhaps write a little bit, but Mimoza was having none of it. She asks if I can do a small thing "similar to what we discussed yesterday?" What did we discuss yesterday, I wondered? Mimoza reminds me that she had asked me how I help trainees focus on their own values and beliefs as a way to inform their work or interventions. Mimoza then adds, "The trainees I work with often just want to know what intervention to use, and how to use it. They forget what they bring, their own values." Mimoza then asks, sincerely and with great confidence that I will say yes (which of course I will): "Can you do something on that now?" Well. I prefer to sit and watch her and Adelina "shine." But I will not say no to these two colleagues. I tell her I need fifteen minutes to think of something. "You have five," Mimoza says.

I wasn't sure what was going to come out of my mouth—but I had noticed the day before how the group was from all over the country—one even from a neighboring country—and although they were all based in Prishtina, none but one or two were from Prishtina.[3] I ask the group to divide by three and each group prepare three family scenarios that represent three different areas of the country. As I have so often found in Kosovo, the trainees are engaged, articulate, and fun, and two hours pass by quickly. Their role-plays illustrate a complex set of issues for families in contemporary Kosovo.

At 4 p.m., we clean up the room and say goodbye until tomorrow. "Tomorrow?" I ask, a bit shocked. "Sunday?" "Yes," Adelina replies, looking at me a bit sternly. "We have to do it on Sunday because here in Kosovo people can't take time off their jobs to do a training like this. They have to work Monday through Friday." Oh. Okay. How come I don't know that? Their day off, they will be here doing a continuing-education training. Looks the same as home. But it's Sunday. It's not a conference, which I might attend once a year (and perhaps even get some time off work or per diem to attend). No. This training has to be on private time, on Sunday. Mimoza suggests we meet for a macchiato at 8 a.m. the next morning at a restaurant across from my hotel, and then walk together to the clinic for the training. Mimoza knows how to snag me again—I love Prishtina macchiatos—even at 8 a.m.

Disruption is Innovation and Errors are Perfect Accidents

Sunday, I wasn't surprised when Mimoza asked me again if I had an exercise or activity I could do with the group. This time, I don't ask for 15 minutes. I decide to do a brief exercise I'd been part of several years ago in a group counseling training in Sri Lanka. Mimoza translates my introduction to the activity into Albanian:

This activity is one I learned in Sri Lanka, where they had a civil war for 26 years. In our work, we hear all kinds of families' experiences, and in a war, certainly after a war, our own life and our families, too, are relevant to our work. This exercise is about the many types of feelings that can happen in our work with populations that have experienced traumatic events of war.

Because I don't speak Albanian, I can't describe with precision the micro events that occurred the moment I said, and Mimoza interpreted a translation of the phrase, "traumatic events of war." But I felt something shift in the room, and it became very quiet. The young faces in front of me lost their animation and the chatter stopped; the energy in the room disappeared. My words. They were such ordinary words. I said them in such an ordinary, boring way. But here, right now, on this day, my words carried a weight that I could not know, nor address, without Mimoza.

In a way, I'd stepped right into the request Mimoza had made a few days before: I'd touched on the sensitive area of what she called values—therapists' positionality as having experienced the war, but not quite yet openly talking about their experience of the war. No matter that the war ended nearly 20 years ago. No matter that many of them were children at the time. The stories of the war, lived by their family members, some of whom were fighters, or survivors, or missing, or raped, are present in Kosovo in a way I've never experienced in other FCVs.[4] My words touched something that Mimoza herself had been trying to touch. It was indeed a perfect accident.

I turn around and put my back to the participants. Looking right at Mimoza, speaking in our common language of English, I say, *sotto voce*: "Let's stay inside. I'm not sure what happened, but let's stay inside. The exercise is simple—we pass a pillow around the room as if it is an emotion—an emotion we might feel in our work with families. We are to experience the pillow as if it is the emotion—without using words or phrases, just to feel it." Mimoza nods and when I ask her if it was okay to do this, she says yes. Of course. I trust her judgment; I also feel trusted by her in turn.

The exercise went fine, but it was brief, rushed; there was very little content brought forward by the trainees. Feelings (in the form of a pillow) were passed around from person to person very hurriedly, in contrast to what I'd seen in Sri Lanka where they were handled methodically, in slow motion. Here in Prishtina, some participants described their feelings with words translated to English as "nervousness" and "worry." Some hid the pillow behind their backs. Mimoza and I participated too; she went first, holding the pillow up to the sky and saying the word "Proud," in Albanian. (I thought this was perfect for how I experience both Mimoza and her work in family therapy). I went last. My feeling was translated as the word "Wow." (Even as I write this, the word still fits).

Defer to the Experts and Maintain an Exit Strategy

After the exercise, I ask Mimosa to lead the discussion of the process for the trainees. She doesn't really need my request; she knows what to do. The difference here in Kosovo is the message my shift away sends to the participants. I am the foreigner, the "expert"; typically, foreigners *direct,* they don't *defer.* Accordingly, the Kosovars participate deferentially to foreigners like me. But now, I am deferring to Mimoza. I must defer to her. Demonstratively, openly, declaratively. I agree with Platt and Rajeswari (2014) that operating from a "unidirectional" approach in such a situation risks overtaking cultural knowledge (p. 65). Unidirectional is the last thing I want. I am constantly surprised at all the ways it is at risk of happening.

When I am a consultant to a colleague, particularly in the field inside another country, I am hypersensitive to the fact that I am an outsider, always, no matter how "inside" I may seem. I hold on to both sensibilities lightly, carefully. My consultation process is dynamic, fluid, and the meanings brought forth by my words and the translations of those words are always in flux. They pop up in surprising ways, requiring me to be constantly creative, fluid, awake. The fluidity is linguistic as well as semantic, a matter of interpretation/translation that is both literal and figurative. My method is in a postmodern and qualitative state of mind. As Gardner, Bobele, and Biever (2002) put it about postmodern supervision, "One of the implications of this dynamism is that meanings are transitory" (p. 218).

Mimoza is a seasoned psychiatrist and a family therapist, a leader in mental health training in her country. She is every bit trained as exquisitely as I am—just in a different setting, in a different country, in a different everything. And that different expertise is what we can re-interpret for the trainees. This is the transitory meaning I would like to try to shift. For me, in this moment, it means sitting down and stepping away—literally as well as metaphorically. It's my exit strategy, as my diplomat friends would describe it. The performance of the exit (not a goodbye, which is different) is critical for the audience of young Kosovars, who so often esteem U.S. expertise in ways that discomfit me.

As I watch Mimoza finish up the discussion and regroup the group, I am grateful for so many things. To watch her shine. To see how she brings the participants back to her, to Kosovo, and Prishtina, in their Albanian language. To feel myself disappear, again, *comme d'habitude.*

I head back to my hotel for the afternoon to go to the gym, tired but inspired, reflective. Mimoza walks me part of the way, to see me off. But also, I think it's to process what had happened. We are consulting again.

Quietly walking between the buildings and paths, I share with Mimoza how it felt for me to experience the disruption of my exercise. Such a message these trainees had sent us. Their message was so "meta," as the Syrians would put it. Kosovo is working very hard to bring to fruition public discourse about the war as a vehicle for social change and economic progress—critical for the country's development (Sen, 1999, p. xiii). But how they do this discourse is another matter, entirely their own. I am lucky to witness even a part of it, and I know this. As if reading my thoughts, Mimoza tells me, "I'm glad for what happened. Because I realize how hard it is for them to talk about these things. And that means when a client brings it up, they may not be ready to hear it. And we need to work on that."

Back to the 7th Grade

Today, those 7th grade voices from Syria still ring in my ears. Their faces, their vitality, their intelligence, and their perfect English—I can still feel it all. In that classroom with my hosts and interpreters/translators, I remember we had asked the students which had had members who had left the family—we used the words "left the family," as it was open enough to cover all possibilities. The 7th graders raised their hands; nearly all held up five or six fingers, answering a question we didn't ask. Then they told us, unprompted, what they wanted for their future: "A red Ferrari!"; "To be back in Syria, where I had perfect grades!"; "More time to do Facebook!"; "To be back in Syria, where my parents didn't worry about me being outside like they do here in Lebanon!" And finally, as if their fingers had brought missing family members into the classroom: "To see my brother/mother/sister/father/uncle/aunt/grandmother/grandfather/ friend again."

The past few years of my work as a family therapy consultant supervisor— particularly beginning in the years 2013/2014 when I started to engage in work with Libyans after the February 17 Revolution and with Syrians living in the Syrian conflict—I feel I've been living in a global community of family therapy consultants, colleagues, supervisors. My virtual team pops up everywhere—on my phone, in my email, on social media on my desktop, on websites from their workplaces across the globe, in conversation with some of my global co trainers from the same projects.

My team of family therapy consultants texts me messages, questions, and ideas, as our years of contact go on and our countries' situations change. Our projects together have ended but our systemic work with clients and supervisees hasn't. So, we always have lots to discuss. Photos are often sent in place of words, telling stories that words do not. Last week that photo came from a place in Syria. Pictures of a teakettle, of two smiling faces, and a small glass of very dark tea, with the invitation "It's yours" written in English script. An audio clip accompanying the photo invites, "Come to Syria … so we can talk … more" This is our consultant method, you see. When I was supporting this group of Syrian supervisors via distance, I often sent them audioclips to accompany modules on family therapy. We still do the method, but now the content is invitations for tea.

The stability of my consultation relationships across the globe remains familiar, knowable. I have had a critical mass of supervisees across the globe over a long enough period that they have become colleagues. Now they do trainings, and I watch them shine. I know they shine because I've seen it, sometimes up close as with Mimoza and Adelina, but more often from a distance, in the pictures and stories of their various adventures. Exercises we once did together face to face are repurposed, adapted, interpreted, shifted to fit each context in both form and content. My colleagues continue to bring me into their stories as I bring them into mine. Projects end, or begin, or transform, as war and conflict do—yet our systemic work with families and trainees remains constant. Plot lines shift. We shift with the plot, sms-ing all the way, as we move forward, always forward. Like the 7th graders in Bekaa, my global team of colleagues are fearless. They declare their losses as vividly as they do their hopes about the future.

The teakettle is only a few minutes in my phone before another sms arrives from a second colleague in yet a third geopolitical spot. He sends a selfie, in front of a city monument, with a caption, "Syria in the Middle East!" Messages in Arabic and English rapidly ping back and forth across the virtual coordinates on our globe. A half hour later, a fourth colleague jumps into the conversation, with an Arabic message directed to me but for everyone to see, and, kindly, it's brief and easy for me to translate: "Yalla Laurie! Let's go!" This story of the tea that is waiting, the talking we have yet to do, our "Yalla! Let's go!" is unknowable. But you see, we are primed for it. Ready. Expectant.

Everything I have learned as an American Association for Marriage and Family Therapy Approved Supervisor I use all the time as a global consultant of supervision. But everything I've learned is often still not enough (Green, Shilts, & Bacigalupe, 2001). The ongoing systems consultation via distance and across states (countries), raises new layers of questions. What does supervision and distance support of family therapy professionals in low income and lower middle-income country economies look like over time? During and after war, via sms? How can disruptions of consultation *in situ* transform into innovations for practice? How do expat "experts" show how they defer expertly, declaratively, openly?

I'd like to read more than stories of telling why all these things are important to do; I'd like to read stories showing me how it is done. I'd like to learn what new stories we can generate when exit strategies create great expectations. When tractors turn into teakettles, each a story unto itself as well as a story of those who are lucky enough to be its unexpected witness. I'd like to see lived examples of how basic questions about supervision and consultation retain their unique relational relevance but in often new and unusual ways when carried across the globe. When carried even by a group of 7th graders who become sudden diplomats, voices of the future, arbiters of history for the family therapist unexpectedly in their midst.

Notes

1 I would like to extend my deep gratitude to the Finnish international human rights lawyer, Outi Korhonen—it was in her writing class in Cairo in 2009 where I was first inspired to write up "the commandments of my method."
2 International Non-Governmental Organization
3 Kosovo has a population of 2 million people, 250K of whom live in Prishtina. The city halves in size every weekend, when everyone goes home to their villages.
4 Fragility, conflict, and violence-affected states.

References

Bava, S. (2019). Hyperlinked identity: A generative resource in a divisive world. In M. McGoldrick & K. Hardy (Eds.), *Re-visioning family therapy* (3rd ed.). New York, NY: Guilford.

Chenail, R. (2011). *Ten Steps for conceptualizing and conducting qualitative research studies in a pragmatically curious manner. The Qualitative Report, 16*(6), 1713–1730.

Csikszentmihalyi, M. (2008). *Flow: The psychology of optimal experience.* New York, NY: HarperCollins.

Ehrenreich, J. H. (2005). *The humanitarian companion: A guide for international aid, development and human rights workers.* Warwickshire, UK: Practical Action Publishing.

Gardner, G., Bobele, M., & Biever, J. (2002). Postmodern models of supervision. In T. Todd & C. Storm (Eds.), *The complete systemic supervisor: Context, philosophy, and pragmatics* (pp. 217–228). Chichester, UK: Wiley Blackwell.

Green, S., Shilts, L., & Bacigalupe, G. (2001). When approved is not enough: Development of a supervision consultation model. *Journal of Marital and Family Therapy, 27*, 515–525

Murakami, H. (2008). *What I talk about when I talk about running: A memoir.* London, UK: Vintage.

Platt, J., & Rajeswari, N. (2014). Preparing global-minded systemic supervisees for an international context. In T. Todd & C. Storm (Eds.), The complete systemic supervisor: Context, philosophy, and pragmatics (2nd ed.; pp. 62–84) Chichester, UK: Wiley Blackwell.

Sen, A. (1999). *Development as freedom.* New York, NY: Anchor.

Slive, A., & Bobele, M. (2012). *When one hour is all you have: Effective therapy for walk-in clients.* Phoenix, AZ: Zeig, Tucker, and Thiessen.

Weingarten, K. (2003). *Common shock: Witnessing violence every day.* London, UK: Penguin.

White, M., & Epston, D. (1990). *Narrative means to therapeutic ends.* New York, NY: Norton.

15

A FORWARD-LOOKING APPROACH TO SUPERVISION OF FAMILY THERAPY AND PSYCHOSOCIAL SUPPORT IN PUBLIC MENTAL HEALTH IN LEBANON

Lina Hussein Sadek

Introduction: The Context of Lebanon

Since it was established, the National Mental Health Programme (NMHP) at the Ministry of Public Health in Lebanon prioritized building capacities of frontline staff (nurses, midwives, doctors, social workers, and mental health professionals) in its national strategy to be able to respond to diverse mental health needs in Lebanon. Much training has been developed and conducted to enhance mental health interventions at the primary level, including Mental Health Gap Action Programme (mhGAP), crises management, and Psychological First Aid. Trainings have been carried out in collaboration with national and international universities, the World Health Organization (WHO), and different non-governmental organizations (NGOs) to refine the skills of mental health professionals.

I have been a part of these initiatives over the years in my clinical work in the office of public health in Lebanon, specifically with a focus on family psychosocial support. Dr. Rabih El Chammay, head of the NMHP, considers family therapy as an essential component of this initiative. He noted that "The national mental health programme recognizes the importance of this therapy, especially for our culture and context but we have struggles finding easily scalable training models. In the next mental health strategy, family therapy will have a place" (personal communication, April 15, 2018).

Although conducted training was professional and focused, this wasn't enough; training can never stand by itself without direct supervision which is a must to guarantee the quality of delivered services.

For example, one of the professionally trained social workers at the Amel association, "Tyre South of Lebanon," finds supervision as the key for problems she used to face previously in her daily work. She was always eager about applying received knowledge acquired during the diverse training she had attended with the Ministry of Public Health and NGOs, but she was constantly facing difficulties, not knowing what the best way would be to overcome the lack of supervision. The supervision that was initiated directly following the training on MHGAP made her more confident and competent in dealing with cases; for her, supervision was also a good opportunity that enhanced her personal growth. She can now deal with mild and moderate cases through low-intensity interventions and is more aware of the right paths in referring difficult cases.

In fact, most supervisees experience dilemmas in providing mental health services in the absence of supervision; they had doubts about being able to deal with cases on their own. Supervision helped to put things together in ways that supervisees start to feel more confident about their work.

For example, most of the supervised nurses were anxious whenever they knew that they had a supervisory visit. One of the nurses declared after six months of consecutive supervision that "at first I used to be very anxious whenever I knew about the supervisory visit. This changed in a positive way of being able to deal with cases, knowing my strength, and points that needed to be improved in my work gave me more confidence and played an important role, resulting in building bridges of trust with our patients. We are now providing comprehensive care for the whole family."

Cultural Overview of Families' Roles in Lebanon: Hospitalization and Self Care

In Lebanon, the family role in health and mental health care is very critical. For example, close relatives attend to the patients during admission and all through hospitalization to alleviate the patient's fears and worries and sometimes answer questions on their behalf (Adib & Mikkey 2003). Family members may assume that patients prefer not to know what is happening in their health care or will become more anxious when they know. The patients, having unclear expectations of their disease process, tend to become dependent on the family for their care during and after hospitalization, and assume a sick role even though they could be recovering. The Lebanese family is typically overprotective of the patient in a sense that family members exchange turns in providing care even when a patient is hospitalized (Gebara & Tashijian 2006).

For example, in the author's supervising of one of the cases in a Beirut primary health care center, the trained mental health nurse was not able to deal with one of her cases without the engagement of the aunt. Although both parents were present, the aunt was more dominant and had a direct influence on the decision of the clients. The nurse had to be able to engage the family system with sensitivity. However, doing this type of consultation benefits from family systems training and supervision, which is seen as a critical goal to support mental health outcomes in low- and middle-income countries.

Family caregivers play a major—and perhaps the most important—role in supporting older adults during hospitalization and especially after discharge. For example, in clinical practice, we notice that most patients visiting the clinic are usually accompanied by one of their family members who could be a supporter or even part of the problem. We usually tend to deviate our approach from individual to family approach taking into consideration the client's best interests. Many cases had been observed to respond and improve in a better way when practitioners work with the whole system rather than just with the individual himself or herself; this was more obvious when working with children and adolescents.

In Lebanon, the family is perceived as the core of the society that plays an important and active role in the health care of any family member. Dr. Abbass Makki, Psychology Professor at the Lebanese University and a systemic psychotherapist, compares the family to the human body where each organ works in harmony with the other; any damage in one organ needs the whole body with all its parts to get up and give support to the injured one. This very systemic concept is well known among family therapists. But for us, it is a cultural concept, not a theoretical one. In our culture, patients yield to the wishes of the family that acts as the protector to the extent that patient autonomy is disregarded when disclosing diagnosis and deciding on treatments; the family has the final word (Kim & Flaskerud, 2008). This applies to mental health disorders where stigma is still considered; stigma plays a significant role in receiving treatment or seeking professional help. Stigma is not just related to patients but to the caregivers trained on delivering mental health services as well.

Raising awareness about the need and role of supervision is important in decreasing stigma levels among healthcare providers themselves. For example, following a training that had been conducted to nurses and social workers at primary healthcare centers, the Ministry of Public Health in Lebanon initiated a supervisory phase to refine the acquired skills. In fact, several trainings had been conducted earlier, but it was proven that without supervision, most skills might be lost. Supervision is not clearly implemented in every project; it is something also that is new and may have a type of stigma as workers may feel they are being judged.

For instance, at first, there was lots of resistance and doubt about the efficiency of mental health interventions, as well as doubt about their capability to carry out low-intensity interventions. The supervisors' team at the NMHP, which I was a part of, went through so many phases, working on building confidence. We found that being supervised while working with patients decreased professionals' stress levels day after day and helped them to become more confident and comfortable. Their cases improved and this resulted in more confidence in mental health approaches. We also found that using a sandwich technique, where you praise supervisees for what they did right, then highlight points for improvement related to their work or intervention, and finally, you mention what went very well. In this way you can provide positive, nonjudgmental feedback about their work;

supervision interventions played a crucial role that helps in building their capacities and refining their skills.

Models That Advocate Family Therapy Interventions and Ongoing Supervision in Lebanon

Lebanese culture is family-oriented, whereby family members not only support each other in all aspects of life including health care but where they are also required to preserve family values and integrity (Gebara & Tashijian, 2006). End-of-life practices in Lebanon emphasize the importance of family involvement in patient care and the need to "make the family one of the central elements in the communication protocol" (Gebara & Tashijian, 2006, p. 386). However, these family-oriented cultural values may adversely affect achieving self-care outcomes because this process entails active engagement in self-care behaviors and an assumption of self-care responsibility. Hence, a need exists to understand the perceptions of Lebanese family members of self-care, the ascribed meaning, and the role each plays in achieving care outcomes, such as patient adherence to self-care behaviors for the prevention of disease complications. Supervision is required to support this type of learning in practice; it is a need we must address going forward.

Different models in Lebanon advocate family therapy due to its importance as one of the most efficient approaches that results in the improvement of cases. Most of these models, outlined below, consider family therapy as new and needs more specific trainings followed by supervision to enhance the quality of delivered services. Many models address the need for ongoing supervision, but each of them do it differently. One-to-one supervision is still the dominant approach over others, whereas we can benefit from group and remote supervision, which can save time and resources.

mhGAP and mhGAP-IG

The mhGAP Intervention Guide (mhGAP-IG) for mental, neurological, and substance use disorders for non-specialist health settings is a technical tool developed by the World Health Organization. The Intervention Guide has been developed through a systematic review of evidence followed by an international consultative and participatory process. The model presents integrated management of priority conditions using protocols for clinical decision-making. The priority conditions included in the mhGAP-IG are depression, psychosis, bipolar disorders, epilepsy, developmental and behavioral disorders in children and adolescents, dementia, alcohol use disorders, drug use disorders, self-harm/suicide, and other significant emotional or medically unexplained complaints. According to the WHO, the mhGAP-IG is a model guide and has been developed for use by health-care providers working in non-specialized health-care settings after adaptation for national and local need. It is designed specifically to address the "gap" in human resources for mental health in low and middle-income countries, and is in wide use in Lebanon. The need for ongoing peer supervision and teamwork is pervasive throughout mhGAP.

Example from PAIR Approach: United Nations Relief and Work Agency for Palestinians

All 12 official Palestinian refugee camps in Lebanon are facing serious problems, mostly due to ongoing conflict and unrest, and unfortunate living conditions characterized by overcrowding and inadequate basic infrastructure (NMHP strategy 2015–2020). Among patients approaching medical care in the Burj-Al-Barajneh camp, depression affects almost one-third, 22% have anxiety, and 14% suffer from psychosis. The PAIR approach to psychosocial support was developed by Professor Nimisha Patel (UK) with Professor David Becker (Germany) between 2011 and 2017, specifically for UNRWA staff working with Palestinian refugees.

The PAIR Approach is not a theoretical model nor a set of techniques; it is an overall approach that encompasses a particular philosophy and principles. It is a holistic approach that focuses on comprehensive mental health services. All care providers in UNRWA were trained on PAIR for the purpose of delivering psychosocial support to others in times of crises. Training on the PAIR approach was conducted with health care providers at UNRWA clinic, social workers, and school counselors. Close supervision was carried out as well.

Supervision included pair support groups, which were conducted at area levels every other week, where all counselors at an area level met to discuss difficult cases with their supervisor who provided technical feedback for adequate interventions. It included a focus on appropriate ways and techniques that helped in tackling and resolving each case. During peer support sessions, all counselors benefitted from discussed cases through direct questioning or reflecting on what could be done. At the end of each session, a small summary was used to highlight what went well, what didn't go well, and points needed for improvement.

These principles of PAIR underpin all professional activities of counselors, teachers, nurses, doctors, social workers, and other frontline colleagues. The PAIR approach recommends family therapy and dealing with systems, as it had been strongly proven that working with families may result in decreasing the influence of traumatic events and enhancing wellbeing in patients. Dr. Nimisha Patel declared that PAIR adopt a systemic approach throughout even with individuals and families; it presents assessment forms including genograms, which are standard in any good psychological approach since they help to understand people's experiences in their familial context and relationships within the family. Dr. Patel noted that "family systemic approaches [are] essential especially when working with refugees" (personal communication, April 5, 2018). She considers it crucial to "build capacities regarding family therapy interventions and systemic approaches" (personal communication, April 5, 2018).

Despite long-term training, supervision, and peer support group sessions, we still found it necessary to conduct case conferences for the discussion of critical cases. During these conferences, counselors were asked to prepare cases that they considered to be difficult and present them in the presence of their colleagues. Case management was presented and discussed in the presence of a technical coordinator who provided her technical feedback with respect to presented cases. For example, one of the presented cases was about a young girl whose parents were divorced and she used to live with her stepmother. The girl was at risk of suicide and the counselor was confused as to whether she needed to involve the stepmother in the therapy or not. The technical supervisor suggested that the counselor engage the stepmother, and this resulted in a great improvement for the girl.

It is always necessary to provide technical feedback for some confusing and complex cases. For example, effective recovery-oriented supervision is an important tool for staff to reflect and explore their work practice, and how their personal values, beliefs, and behavior impact on the treatment, care, and support they provide. Supervision sessions aim to increase staff self-awareness and provide guidance so that staff can further enhance their recovery-focused skills and support with whom they work.

Many other trainings since then were tailored at United Nations Relief and Work Agency for Palestinians (UNRWA) to respond to psychosocial (PSS) needs. Counselors were trained on parenting skills curriculum and better learning programs, both of which help lower children's and parents' stress and recommend parents' engagement in therapy. Counselors at UNRWA schools express the importance of family therapy approaches and supervision in dealing with cases, declaring that their abilities in managing cases have improved since they started the training; they added that families in Palestinian society are the key component that help provide support and results in children's wellbeing.

As per the technology revolution, displacement, and war, there was change in gender roles (in society, family, personally) in most of the Arab countries. In Lebanon, this influenced not only Lebanese families but Syrian and Palestinian refugees as well, expanding the capacity of women to deal with family and community stress. Supervision takes on a different character with this contextual change as well and must be sensitive to this societal transformation.

Parent and Child Mental Health

Parents can be a powerful force in protecting children from war-related stress (Tol, Betancourt, Meyers-Ohki, & Charrow, 2013). However, parents also experience increases in stress, trauma, depression, frustration, and shame/humiliation. This can negatively affect parenting, making parents less responsive to children's needs, use an increase in harsh and even abusive parenting, and also increase intimate partner violence. Therefore, this matter also requires a forward-looking approach to the supervision of public mental health service delivery in that area.

Religious Interventions Recommended Family Therapy in Lebanon

Dr. Aida Chikhani, Instructor at the Lebanese University, reveals in her course and throughout her work with families, the collaboration, supported by the church, between family and couple therapy and psychotherapists (personal communication, May 5, 2018). Most of the families in our community are burning with conflicts and are at risk of collapse. Families value a great need to be heard with an open heart and thus comes the role of the church. For this purpose, the church is conducting several trainings to build capacities of some religiously committed couples regarding psychology of the family, mediation, and canon law. These trainings work mainly on preparing them in order to deepen further in understanding of family problems so they can listen actively to couples, primary accompanying families, and to be able to recognize the cases that need to be referred to a psychotherapist for specialized treatment.

Despite good results and positive outcomes, it is crucial to consider clinical supervision and coaching to have a more systemic approach and sustainable outcomes. Clinical supervision results in more oriented interventions and is highly needed to improve the skills of those trained in a systemic approach. It provides them with safe and confidential environments to reflect on and discuss their work, their personal responses, and on their approaches.

Looking Ahead to Expand and Cover All Areas of Lebanon

There is a proposal to establish counseling offices all over Lebanon similar to the ones already existing in some areas; the role of these offices is to provide family therapy approaches to couples suffering from conflicts. Each counseling office has a structure and consists of social worker, psychologist, and trained volunteers who can perform reconciliation for couples. This approach is similar to what some Islamic clerics do when couples come to have a divorce; before completing the procedures they listen to couples and try to figure out a way to avoid separation between them. This is known as reconciliation, and many times a common relative might be included to help them overcome their difficulties. Other times they also ask support from trusted and wise family members. A social worker specialized in family matters is always present at the Islamic court and is ready to provide support to couples. Most of the social workers involved in these approaches are volunteers majoring in social and medical science; they are not employed at the court or specialized in counseling, and this can contribute to a lack organization and less than positive outcomes. More structured training and systematic approaches are needed. There is a plan to include supervision in this initiative. In Lebanon, that means that it would be a psychologist supervising trained couple therapists for the first six months on a biweekly basis to make sure that they are competent and able to manage conflicts between couples and to provide technical feedback whenever needed, as this will refine their acquired skills.

Supervisors should be adequately trained, experienced, and supported to perform their roles. They may not always come from the same professional background as the supervisee although this is strongly advised. Importantly, the supervisor should have the skills, qualifications, and experience and knowledge of the area of practice required to undertake their role effectively. They should also be supported by having their own clinical supervision. This is a need we plan to address in Lebanon.

With respect to the Druze community, family approaches are essential. Structured approaches are designed to help couples throughout their marriages; psychologists and psychiatrists are assigned at their court to support couples suffering from problems. They are working on establishing reconciliation centers to provide adequate support. Most approaches are based on systemic family therapy theories. Municipalities are playing an important role in conducting awareness and prevention sessions for engaged couples who are planning to get married; these sessions aim at building capacities and raising awareness about the importance of the family role, upcoming responsibilities, communication skills, conflict resolution, and many other related topics.

Missionaries' schools in Lebanon are focusing on raising awareness about family morals. Dr. Jean Daoud, a local counseling programme coordinator, raised a proposal to the Ministry of Education to highlight the importance of including awareness sessions in the Lebanese curriculum aimed at preparing adolescents and building their capacities with respect to their roles and responsibilities in the family.

All these approaches are valuable and considered, but we still have to work on the quality of training and supervision provided. Supervision is a tool with which community-managed organisations can build capacity, promote best practice, maintain staff-wellbeing, enhance professionalism, build team cohesion and share experience across the sector. This, too, is part of our forward-looking plan.

ABAAD[1] Training: Systemic Family Therapy

> Participating in family therapy training gave me insights about what was missing throughout my interventions. Engaging family members, and working with them as a system makes cases improve in a significant way.
>
> —*Sarah Amhaz, mental health professional who participated*
> *in the ABAAD training*

In 2016, ABAAD organized systemic family therapy training for professionals working in humanitarian crisis contexts to improve and build their capacities after the eruption of the Syrian crises. During this training, the author had the opportunity to improve her own skills, and later on to lead a team of four, following up with them regarding their interventions using acquired family therapy techniques.

Cross-disciplinary training that focuses on the settings in which mental health care is delivered is consistent with the findings of effective practice in humanitarian mental health care (Kakuma, Minas, Ginneken, Dal Poz, Desiraju, Morris, & Scheffler, 2011). Cross-disciplinary approaches that use existing infrastructures are an effective response to shortages in human resources for mental health, which are pervasive in middle- and low-income countries. For example, Kakuma et al. (2011) noted that all countries of low and middle income have inadequate funding for mental health, and that "all low-income countries and about two-thirds of middle-income countries had far fewer mental health workers to deliver a core set of mental health interventions than were needed" (p. 2).

In the ABAAD project, an expat delivered the training and did the distance follow-up. One of the most useful ways expat family therapy consultants can be involved in humanitarian settings is through the delivery of supervision and clinical consultation (Charlés & Samarasinghe, 2016). Outside subject matter experts can enhance the technical capacity of host country nationals to perform family therapy methods, which increases both access and availability of psychosocial services among local people already in the field (Patel & Becker, 2011).

In the ABAAD project work, and the component of supervision support via distance, participants were able to identify family systems and subsystems involved in the problem to plan according to a therapeutic plan, which helped in achieving our goals. Engaging families in the therapy plan was most of the time a story of success, whereby most elements find harmony missing between the context and culture dominating our country, making it very difficult to improve without family blessings and enrollment. Working with families in the Lebanese PHCs, where poverty is dominant, reveals the importance of family involvement for the improvement of individuals. The supervision support network developed in this training is an example of something we hope to continue.

Conclusion

There is no recovery without family engagement, especially when it comes to a country like Lebanon, where families are still more important than independent individuals. Most national and international strategies and models consider the family as one of the primary resources that can support people throughout their lives. However, such a focus is not useful unless it includes clinical supervision. Ongoing supervision support in family systemic methods is necessary to enhance the quality of delivered services. Family therapy is highly recommended and will always be the corner stone for every successful mental health intervention. Supervision support is a part of that in both the present and the future.

Note

1 ABAAD is the English translation for the Arabic name of the organization, أبعاد. www. abaadmena.org.

References

Adib, S. M., & Mikkey, I. F. (2003). Lebanon (Lebanese Republic) In C. E. D'Avanzo, & E. M. Geissler (Eds.), *Cultural health assessment: Pocket guide* (3rd ed.). St. Louis, MO: Mosby, 409–414.

Charlés, L., & Samarasinghe, G. (2016). *Family therapy in global humanitarian contexts: Voices and issues from the field.* New York, NY: Springer.

Gebara, J., & Tashijian, H. (2006). End-of-life practices at a Lebanese hospital: Courage or knowledge? *Journal of Transcultural Nursing, 17,* 381–388.

Kakuma, R., Minas, H., Ginneken, N., Dal Poz, M. R., Desiraju, K., Morris, J., & Scheffler, R. M. (2011). Human resources for mental health care: Current situation and strategies for action. *Lancet, 378,* 1654–1663.

Kim, S., & Flaskerud, J. (2008). Does culture frame adjustment to the sick role? *Issues in Mental Health Nursing, 29,* 315–318.

Lebanon Ministry of Public Health (2015). *National Mental Health Strategy 2015–2020: Mental health and substance use, strategy for Lebanon 2015–2020.* Beirut, Lebanon: Author.

Patel, V., & Becker, D. (2011). *PAIR approach to mental health and psycho-social support.* Unpublished manuscript.

Tol, W., Betancourt, T., Meyers-Ohki, S., & Charrow, A. (2013). Interventions for children affected by war: An ecological perspective on psychosocial support and mental health care. *Harvard Review of Psychiatry, 21*(2), 70–91.

16

EMBODIED CONVERSATIONS

Partnering with Horses in Clinical Supervision

Shelley Green

Introduction

Nine years ago, I could wait no longer to have horses in my life in a full and significant way. Growing up in Texas, I was obsessed with these beautiful creatures since I first experienced thought and language. They drew me to them like a moth to a flame, as anyone who shares this obsession will understand. My good friend and colleague, Jim Hibel, describes it as a genetic flaw with no known cure and only highly expensive and frequent treatment. As a full-time faculty member in a COAMFTE-accredited program at Nova Southeastern University (NSU), I had very little free time or money to spend on horses. My wise and usually right husband, Douglas Flemons, suggested that I find a way to combine my passion for horses with my love for family therapy teaching and training. He would live to rethink those words, but his suggestion launched the work that has captivated me and, in some ways, taken over my life since 2009. I hold him completely responsible.

Once the idea was floated, it took over my consciousness in a similar way that horses had when I was a ten-year-old Texas girl. I read everything I could find, went to conferences, talked to people, found trainings and workshops, and within a couple of months, approached my department chair, Tommie Boyd, and said, "I want to do this horse thing with our students and maybe some clients." She had no idea what I was talking about but was immediately supportive. The work I will describe in this chapter reflects nine years of exploration, experimentation, creation, frustration, collaboration, and innovation. I have had the great fortune to find talented and passionate colleagues in the equine world, enthusiastic and curious students and supervisees, and a welcoming administrative team at NSU that has supported the ups and downs of creating a complex community partnership with no road map nor precedent.

The historical and current shape of my work includes the development and co-founding of a non-profit equine-assisted family therapy organization, Stable Place (with my equine professional colleague, Valerie Judd), internship and staff placements for ten master's and doctoral family therapy students, two funded research/clinical projects, and clinical service provision of over 1,000 client contacts per year. However, this chapter will focus exclusively on how I have brought horses into a collaborative supervision conversation with family therapy trainees. This focus is where the work began, and it has been a guiding force throughout the expansion of the program.

My earliest forays into this world involved finding a couple of horses, partnering with Valerie, and asking five to six family therapy doctoral students from NSU to come out to the barn and see what they could learn about themselves as therapists and humans from their interactions with horses. From those early days, it was clear that the potential was immense, and the students were intrigued and asking for more. We began offering CEU workshops in the community, which generated more interest, and within a couple of years I had designed and offered the first section of *Introduction to Equine Assisted Family Therapy*—a 3-credit graduate level course in the NSU Department of Family Therapy. That was in 2012; the course has been offered consistently each fall and winter term since, and since 2014, I have also been teaching a second, advanced course each year. The NSU Family Therapy program now offers a concentration in Equine-Assisted Family Therapy.

In this chapter, I describe the rationale for partnering with horses in supervision and training, and I delineate the clinical and theoretical assumptions that guide my approach. I offer examples of specific ways I have brought this unusual partnership into the realm of family therapy supervision and training, and I include student/trainee voices to help illustrate the power of the experiential process and its potential for exploring the self-of-the-therapist.

Horses as Supervision and Training Partners

For most clinical supervisors, the rationale for bringing horses into the supervision process is not obvious. Indeed, the reasons for *not* incorporating horses into clinical supervision may be much more apparent and compelling. Horses are large, high-maintenance prey animals; they are expensive to feed and maintain; they can be unpredictable and possibly dangerous; and they require knowledgeable, trained professionals to manage them effectively. They don't fit into an air-conditioned therapy office, and they don't travel easily. However, on the plus side, they are beautiful, intriguing, social, and herd-based. Being in their presence invites quiet contemplation and mindful awareness of what we bring to a situation (emotionally, physically, and in terms of our intentionality). As prey animals, horses are exquisitely attuned to their immediate surroundings—centuries of survival and adaptation have developed their observational skills such that they respond instantaneously to any perceived threat. Horses will always take care of their own needs for safety and survival first; thus, in order to connect and build a collabora-tive relationship with them, humans must create and maintain a safe space so that the horse can choose to become a part of the process. This creates an interesting context for exploring the skills and personal qualities that developing clinicians bring to the therapy room given the rather obvious parallels with the therapeutic process.

Clinical and Theoretical Assumptions

Because the equine coursework that I have developed is housed within the Family Therapy graduate program at NSU, the clinical approach is consistently grounded in the systemic, brief therapy traditions that are the hallmark of our education and training at NSU (Cade & O'Hanlon, 1993; Green, 2014, 2011; Green & Flemons, 2018; Flemons & Green, 2014, 2017; Watzlawick, Weakland & Fisch, 1974). Clinical conundrums are conceptualized from a strengths-based perspective that prioritizes the honoring of clients' solutions and resources and emphasizes a non-normative and non-pathologizing stance (Green & Flemons, 2018). I am similarly informed by this relational approach when developing equine-assisted training and supervision activities (Green, 2013, 2014, 2017, 2018, 2019; Green, Rolleston, & Schroeder, 2018; Green, Schroeder, Rolleston, Penalva, & Judd, 2018). My goal is to create a context where students and super-visees can maintain an openness to learning about themselves, both personally and professionally, while interacting with horses in an experiential group setting. This requires a level of vulnerability and trust that is not unlike that which our clients experience in session. By maintaining a focus on strengths and resources and avoiding pathologizing conceptualizations, I attempt to create a generative context in which students can explore their personal assumptions, examine their responses to the horses and to each other as well as the values that inform those responses, and experiment with new ways of relating through their interactions with the horses.

My own clinical stance and personal values inform the ideals that I believe are essential in developing thoughtful, self-reflective, and mindful therapists who offer their clients a safe place to address life challenges. In order to create this generative context for their clients, therapists must be able to:

- Develop rapport
- Build trust
- Create a collaborative and respectful relationship
- Consider their beliefs about therapist intentionality
- Examine their assumptions about movement, change, direction, leading/ pacing
- Attend to ethical and legal responsibilities
- Maintain safety

Managing these complex demands requires a level of self-awareness and self-reflection that must be intentionally explored and developed. Attention to the self-of-the-therapist is foundational in our equine coursework, and it is always informed by a systemic, relational perspective. Rober (1999) noted that within the family therapy literature, the notion of "self" doesn't imply that the self is a separate entity, but, rather, refers to "the experiencing process of the therapist—in other words, to his [or her] feelings, intuitions, fears, images, ideas, and so on" (p. 4). This view of the self-of-the-therapist as an experiencing process resonates with a relational framework for training therapists and is particularly relevant given the experiential nature of our equine-assisted approach. Timm and Blow (1999) define self-of-the-therapist work as "the willingness of a therapist or supervisor to participate in a process that requires introspective work on issues in his or her own life, that has an impact [on] the process of therapy in both positive and negative ways" (p. 333). Such introspection is generated organically through the equine-based activities designed specifically for this purpose. In the following section, I describe some of the activities that have had maximum impact on our student trainees and will include transcripts of student reflections on their experiences.

Equine-Assisted Supervision/Training Activities and Goals

The two courses that I have developed are both taught as hybrids: in a 15-week term, every other week's class is held at the barn. During classroom days, students become familiar with the literature regarding equine- and other animal-assisted therapies and also process their barn-day experiences. In the Advanced Class, the curriculum includes an intentional focus on the self-of-the-therapist, and the course readings address this topic specifically. During barn days, our work is entirely experiential. For three hours, students are engaged in hands-on activities with the horses that are designed to address some aspect of their professional and personal development. Some examples of these activities and their related target issues/themes include:

- Catching a horse and leading it around a paddock: Themes include connecting with a client; developing trust and rapport; collaboration; considering pacing/leading. In this activity, students often find parallels between their way of approaching the horses and their typical ways of approaching new clients (i.e., being proactive versus giving the client space; level of intentionality and directiveness; and attention to pacing/leading with the client).
- Listening for the horse's heartbeat: The heartbeat can be difficult to hear, and often the moment of hearing it is quite powerful for the students, leading to discussions about how we have to position ourselves in session to hear difficult client experiences or stories that haven't previously been shared.
- Cleaning a horse's hooves: This activity requires that the student lift one hoof, thus asking the horse to be a bit off balance. Metaphors of support, balance,

connection, and vulnerability are abundant in discussions of this activity. This exercise can also be quite intimidating for students who have never been around horses, as asking a horse to lift a heavy hoof requires responsiveness from the horse and a significant level of confidence from the human.

As we invite students into these activities, we bring awareness to a shared assumption (and repeated observation) that participants typically "show up at the barn like they show up in life." This is a common theme in equine-assisted work, and we find it to be a useful understanding as we continually experience students' finding parallels in their clinical behavior and appreciating the richness of exploring new ways of connecting and relating. Below I present in greater depth some of the activities that have been most compelling for our students, along with their reflections on the impact of these experiences.

Blindfolded connecting. In this exercise, typically conducted the first barn day of the Advanced Class, students are individually blindfolded and then led to a horse and given the following instructions: "Find a way to connect with and learn about your horse in any manner you choose. And when you feel comfortable, find a way to create movement with your horse." The instructions are not elaborated on further; an Equine Specialist (ES) is at all times holding the horse on a lead rope and monitoring horse and human safety. The student is free to reach out to the ES for assistance or guidance at any time and may speak freely with the ES throughout the experience (although often, the entire experience occurs in silence). My goal for this activity is to invite students to learn to connect with the horse utilizing non-verbal communication and to let go of their typical assumptions about how to build trust, learn about another being, and find ways to connect and collaborate. My observation is that students find the silence and the absence of visual cues to offer an intensification of their other senses; they become fully present and mindfully aware of their proximity to the horse, attending to each movement and footstep. This heightened awareness serves them well as they explore how they can approach clients with fewer assumptions and greater attunement.

Rana: I went to the horse wearing my curiosity hat and nothing else. I was stunned (by) how empathy and curiosity together became a successful recipe to connection and change. Actually, being blindfolded really helped me to be more sensitive to my other senses and to be in the zone, flowing with the horse, not thinking who will take the next step or where are we going. Instead, curiosity took the wheel.

Cristina: I was relaxed, not too worried about the movement part but I was focused more on the connection between us. It makes me think of when working with clients, we are in the dark, we do not know much about them or their story. However, we have to co-create change and lead them in the right direction, and that is being made by joining, by creating that trust, where they can be vulnerable and be open for change.

Mark: In my mind, we go into the therapy room blindfolded and connect with the clients in a way that they will lead us in certain ways and trust us enough to follow us in other ways. Having the space to move (literally and figuratively) is something that was meaningful to me. For me, with more space comes more options for maneuverability. I also found myself being more mindful of the horse. I utilized the horse as a center for my mindfulness during the session.

Labeling. This activity is also conducted early in the semester of the Advanced Class. Students are provided with non-toxic, water-based paints and asked to depict on one side of the horse any labels that have been applied to them (or that they have applied to themselves) that they are not comfortable with. They can depict these labels in any way (images, words, etc.), and can include as many labels as they wish. After discussion of these initial labels, they are asked if they would like to remove the labels from the horse (they are provided with a bucket of water and a sponge) or alter them in any way and then are asked to depict labels with which they resonate or embrace. This activity simultaneously allows therapists to understand this experience from a client's perspective, and, as well, to explore how their own and others' ideas about themselves (personally and professionally) contribute to or detract from their ability to be fully present in the therapy room. The level of intensity and vulnerability inspired by this activity is frequently surprising to the participants, and they explore ways to fully embrace the strengths they hope to bring into the clinical setting.

Amylie: It was somewhat nerve-racking to think about the implications of placing my thoughts and feelings onto the horse; it felt as if I was going to hurt one of the horses with my negative thoughts by attaching my label to them, and yet I never really think about how I hurt myself by applying the label to myself in my mind. It was also difficult knowing that I would be sharing these thoughts with my cohort but at the same time, there was a freedom in that vulnerability. By accepting the help and, as Herb [one of the Equine Specialists] put it, "structure" of the halter, a really big change happened in myself and in Casper (her chosen equine partner). By asking for help and accepting help, the chaos of the day seemed to dissolve and suddenly everything seemed much more calm and orderly. I really learnt so much about humility in that moment and how as therapist, a big part of what we do is just be there with our clients when aid and change is difficult to allow, ask for, and accept.

Caitlin: I found that I remain ... my own worst critic and that I really should take the advice I have/would give any client. I will now work on reframing the following concepts in my mind: Asking for help and being more emotionally vulnerable/open (to appropriate people). This will not only help me grow, but it will provide others the opportunity to help me (which judging from our conversation, at least other therapists love to do) and improve/strengthen my relationships.

Risky Crossings. A large tarp is laid out on the ground and students are asked to find a way to lead a horse across the tarp. This presents several layers of difficulty, depending on the weather, wind, distractions, and the horse's reaction to walking across an unstable, noisy surface. Metaphors of fear, risk-taking, connecting, building trust, and developing collaboration are all possible within this conversation. My intention for this activity is to explore how the participants conceptualize risk, how they might invite a client into walking through difficult conversations, how they would invite trust and maintain a strong, guiding presence throughout those conversations, and how they might respond to clients' experiences of danger or risk. The horses provide a large and compelling example because they may have a very strong, immediate, physical response to the noises and distractions that accompany their walk across the tarp.

Rana: Sometimes I purposefully choose not to go to "a dark place" with the client because it's scary to me, too, so I play it safe by going around the problem instead of facing it with my safe curiosity. This can be not physically safe for the client, especially if the client is facing a serious problem. I guess it would be helpful if I utilized the emotional safety part for the client to feel safe to talk and share and connect, but that doesn't mean that this kind of safety is enough.

Triggers. This activity was originally developed by our Stable Place team for the substance abuse groups that we work with (see Green et al., 2018). The exercise involves the use of a range of dressage or lunge whips (short to long) that can be used as a tool of communication for the horses. An ES initially enters the arena and demonstrates the effect on the herd of introducing whips of varying lengths in different ways; they may point or gesture with them, swing them, raise or lower them, tap the ground or their own leg with them, or even simply place them on the ground (they do not touch the horses with them). Then each participant is allowed to enter the arena or paddock and discover ways to interact with the horses using one or more of these tools. Students experiment with creating varying levels of energy with the horses based on their selection of a whip and on their method of using it. We use this activity with substance abuse clients to help create new conversations with them around the things that "trigger" a response to use or relapse; during our supervision sessions, the same activity is utilized to explore therapists' comfort levels with introducing different levels of intensity and movement within a session, and how these choices impact their ability to connect with their clients and "move" the session.

Mark: In my therapeutic experience, I have the "trigger" (idea) that I cannot connect with people in a chaotic setting, but in my life, I have connected the most with people during some chaotic times. I reflected on these chaotic times and saw that during these times, people seemed more vulnerable. So why am I not comfortable and able to embrace the chaos in a therapy session? It could be a good rapport-builder if used correctly. The clients are potentially stepping out of their comfort zones and that can be punctuated. I believe that I will have more awareness in sessions and learning how to use chaos as a rapport-builder rather than something negative that must be brought back to manageable levels all the time. Chaos can be good.

Round Pen. This is often one of the most powerful activities for the class, and it is offered at the final session of the Advanced Class. During this exercise, the students are invited to experience the Monty Roberts's *Join-Up* method (Epston, 2011; Roberts, 2002) in the round pen with one horse and one ES. The ES briefly demonstrates how to communicate with the horse to create forward motion within the round pen, and then how to invite the horse to turn inward and move in the opposite direction around the pen. After some time, the student is offered the opportunity to turn away and find the horse "joining up" in the center of the round pen. The beauty of this activity is in the freedom it affords; each student and her or his horse finds a unique way to connect and "dance" together. For some, the process is sticky, challenging, and at times, chaotic. For others, the dance is fluid and graceful, allowing both horse and human to enjoy the rhythm and pattern of a connected relationship. Each student takes something different from this activity, and we utilize group observation and processing to help punctuate the strengths observed in each horse/human process.

Mark: Thinking back to my experience in the round pen, I see growth in myself in equine work and as a therapist. My thoughts going into the pen were to "have fun" and enjoy being in the pen. With that in mind, I was able to go in and have a conversation with the horse pretty easily. Where I moved, they moved and when I stopped, they stopped, and it felt pretty good to have that connection. Though I saw my own growth, I could see that there was more I could do and learn for future sessions. I saw this as how I see sessions and how I may need to work on sitting in a higher anxiety environment, potentially inciting a little anxiety within the client. I see this as being a way to bring a change within the clients. I also value the times where the client and I "jam" together and have a conversation.

Tyrone: The horse stayed completely still, and I internally initially felt some sort of discouragement and a little worry of "what if I can't get the horse to react in ways the others did?" A little over five minutes into a heated stare-off, I quickly remembered that there is no right or wrong and that each of our experiences would be completely different. Upon shifting my perception, I was able to see that I did create movement. Though it may not have been physical, the horse was mentally connected with me throughout my time in the round pen. His attention was completely fixated on me and the direction I decided to move for the entire time I was doing the round pen exercise. I immediately remembered intentionality. Walking in with a purpose would have made a difference. Though I had a personal purpose, I am sure the horse sensed that I was unsure and a little untrusting of how he would react.

Rana: I have had sessions where the client just does like what the horse did and just is themselves and talks about their stories, and there are sessions where the spotlight is about shifting and changing. This was very useful for me to experience, to be always aware of my intentions and what I am bringing to the session. The image of the horse will always remind me to be kinder to myself and to be patient with my own process and timing!

Conclusions

These examples provide only a brief glimpse into our work at the barn, but I hope they reflect the generative conversations that become possible when students leave their conventional settings of talk therapy and "talk supervision" and enter into an experiential process with our horses and each other. These experiences allow the participants to try something different in the moment, in their interactions with a 1,000 lb. animal, and to experience *in their bodies* as well as their minds, the impact of that difference.

We utilize similar equine-assisted activities in training a wide range of professionals, including anesthesiology-assistant students, financial-planning consultants, agency staff, university administrators, and high school teachers and administrators. In such trainings, our conversations are adapted to the particular context of those we are training, but we find the richness of the experience remains and the metaphors abound. Of course, our primary focus is conducting equine-assisted clinical sessions with individuals, couples, families, and groups. We work with varied populations and presenting issues, including at-risk and incarcerated youth; foster care children; adults in residential substance abuse treatment; individuals and families experiencing the aftermath of trauma (including those affected by the Parkland shooting in the spring of 2018); veterans; those dealing with illness, grief, and loss; as well as couple and family communication and conflict resolution. In every case, we find that the horses bring a powerful and generative presence to the therapeutic and training context, and we are so grateful for their partnership.

Through experiential processes with the horses, our supervisees and our clients have an embodied conversation that lingers long past the last day at the barn.

References

Cade, B., & O'Hanlon, W. (1993). *A brief guide to brief therapy*. New York, NY: Norton.

Epston, D. (2011). The corner: Innovative services. *Journal of Systemic Therapies*. *30*(3), 86–95.

Flemons, D., & Green, S. (2017). Brief relational couple therapy. In J. L. Lebow, A. L. Chambers, & D. C. Breunlin (Eds.), *Encyclopedia of couple and family therapy*. New York, NY: Springer. Retrieved from https://doi.org/10.1007/978-3-319-15877-8

Flemons, D., & Green, S. (2014). Quickies: Single-session sex therapy. In M. Hoyt & M. Talmon (Eds.), *Capturing the moment: Single session therapy and walk-in services* (pp. 407–423). Bethel, CT: Crown House Publishing.

Green, S. (2011). Power or pattern? A brief, relational approach. *Family Therapy Magazine*, *10*(6), 9–11.

Green, S. (2013). Horses and families: Bringing equine assisted approaches to family therapy. In A. Rambo, T. Boyd, A. Schooley, & C. West (Eds.), *Family therapy review: Contrasting contemporary models*. New York, NY: Taylor and Francis.

Green, S. (2014). Horse sense: Equine assisted single session consultations. In M. Hoyt & M. Talmon (Eds.), *Capture the moment: Single session therapy and walk-in service*. Williston, VT: Crown House Publishing.

Green, S. (2017). Equine assisted psychotherapy. In J. Carlson & S. Dermer (Eds.), *The SAGE encyclopedia of marriage, family, and couples counseling* (pp. 552–554). Thousand Oaks, CA: SAGE.

Green, S. (2018). Partnering with horses to train mental health professionals. In K. S. Trotter & J. Baggerly (Eds.), *Equine assisted mental health interventions: Harnessing solutions to common problems* (pp. 251–256). New York, NY: Taylor and Francis.

Green, S. (2019). Equine facilitated psychotherapy: Partnering with horses to provide mental health services. *Horse Industry Handbook*. McDonald, NM: American Youth Horse Council.

Green, S., & Flemons, D. (Eds.) (2018). *Quickies: The handbook of brief sex therapy* (3rd ed.). New York, NY: Norton.

Green, S., Rolleston, M., & Schroeder, M. (2018). Equine assisted therapy with couples and families in crisis. In K. S. Trotter & J. Baggerly (Eds.), *Equine assisted mental health interventions: Harnessing solutions to common problems* (pp. 238–248). New York, NY: Taylor and Francis.

Green, S., Schroeder, M., Rolleston, M., Penalva, C., & Judd, V. (2018). Triggering transformations: An equine assisted approach to the treatment of substance abuse. In K. S. Trotter & J. Baggerly (Eds.), *Equine assisted mental health interventions: Harnessing solutions to common problems* (pp. 161–168). New York, NY: Taylor and Francis.

Rober, P. (1999). The therapist's inner conversation in family therapy practice: Some ideas about the self of the therapist, therapeutic impasse, and the process of reflection. *Family Process*, *38*(2), 209–228.

Roberts, M. (2002). *Horse sense for people*. New York, NY: Penguin.

Timm, T. M., & Blow, A. J. (1999). Self-of-the-therapist work: A balance between removing restraints and identifying resources. *Contemporary Family Therapy*, *21*(3), 331–351.

Watzlawick, P., Weakland, J., & Fisch, R. (1974). *Change: Principles of problem formation and problem resolution*. New York, NY: Norton.

17

SUPERVISION REFLECTIONS FROM A NON-WESTERN FAMILY THERAPIST IN AN INTEGRATED PRIMARY HEALTHCARE SETTING

Saeid Kianpour

In this chapter I illustrate my experiences as a non-western family therapist in an integrated healthcare clinic through my own sociocultural, political, and historical lens, and explain my experiences in a supervisory context. Before narrating my story of extraordinary supervision, I would prefer to define my identity as a non-western family therapist in more detail. I believe the term *non-western clinicians*, including family therapists, refers to those whose sociocultural and political developmental experiences are different from, or in some cases against, the dominant cultural norms and values in western countries, particularly those of the US. I grew up in a family in which my father used to be a Marxist when the Islamic revolution was happening, as many people used to be with plenty of other different revolutionary groups with various ideologies who made the revolution happen in 1979. A few years after the revolution, my father started to walk away from his Marxist beliefs and gradually approached Islamic ideology, creating a more eclectic worldview that was almost against imperialism, a dominant sociocultural and political state in the west, especially the US. Thus, I was exposed to interpreting political affairs and incidents when my father, my brother, and I used to discuss politics most of the time. Based on my experience, by non-western, I mean not only my geographical place of birth, which is Iran, but mainly my sociocultural and political worldview as different from dominant western cultural norms and values, which basically come from capitalism.

Furthermore, since moving to the US as a non-western student and then studying a doctorate in MFT, becoming a family therapist, always there has been a feeling, presumably fear, in me about white supremacy. This feeling is rooted in a fact that although I am white, I am not Caucasian, that is, I do not have European origin. Also, because I came from the Middle East, where it is claimed that all terrorist groups come from, talking and discussing my sociocultural and political worldview is dangerous or might be perceived offensive as seen in others' reactions. Thus, it was difficult for me to talk about my values, emotions, or worldview not only among friends, but in professional contexts such as supervision. Therefore, extraordinary supervision for me begins when I am not sure how to share my inner voices/conversations in supervision consistent with my thoughts and emotions, which are colored by my cultural and political beliefs about clients.

My inner conversations and the elements of my self-of-the-therapist can be illustrated through working with clients who provoke intense emotions. For instance, a 28-year-old veteran who served in Iraq shot a young girl in the head in addition to shooting many other innocent citizens. Another example could be a veteran who participated in Operation Eagle Claw in 1980, ordered by President Jimmy Carter, to attempt to end the Iran hostage crisis. These examples are potentially able to provoke intense emotions and feelings in supervisees or family therapists whose sociocultural development and background are tied to them and create emotional and ethical dilemmas for them. Thus, extraordinary supervision begins when I am not sure how to conceptualize or fit clients into my cultural schemes, avoid sociocultural and political biases, and feel supported in a safe supervision context in order to evaluate and explore these biases. Otherwise, I may need to rely merely on self-supervision. By creating a safe environment, supervisors and supervisees should be able to discuss their values and beliefs as they are important in therapy. In this context supervisees become more confident and able to involve their self-of-the-therapist in the process of therapy.

I see supervision as a juncture in which I, as a supervisee, interact with my supervisor regarding my clients and create a triad for each case. Through such a three-part relationship, I am able to not only evaluate my own/personal sociocultural and intellectual biases and experiences, but also to facilitate the indirect relatedness of the supervisor and client. Thus, I will be able to create, develop, or add new meaning to clients' presenting problems or understand how biases and experiences influence perceptions of clients.

My Definition of Supervision in an Integrated Healthcare Setting: A Non-Traditional Context

When I was preparing the first draft of this chapter, I was a doctoral behavioral science intern at Indiana University-Family Medicine Residency Program. I saw clients and had weekly supervision in an integrated primary healthcare center. Most of my clients had a low socioeconomic status with a high rate of psychiatric disorders such as anxiety, depression, different types of personality disorders, and bipolar disorder. I was new in the field of Medical Family Therapy (MedFT). McDaniel, Doherty, and Hepworth (2015) defined medical family therapy as a systemic approach that sees the interactions between mind, body, family relationships, and the larger community world and the ways they all together affect individuals' health, an approach that is called *biopsychosocial* in medicine. They also believe that medical family therapists see the connection between their own experiences of illness and those of their clients in order to include the self-of-the-therapist and its influence on the process of therapy (McDaniel et al., 2015). A similar process takes place in supervision when supervisees may be asked to share their stories of illness or asked to illustrate their individual or family experiences of illness in genogram formats and discuss their effects (Speice & McDaniel, 2016). I see this process as extending beyond "illness" to other factors, such as the supervisees' values and beliefs, which enter not only therapy relationships but also supervisory relationships. In other words, I believe both my experiences of illness as a family therapist and my sociocultural development and experience affect the process of therapy. Furthermore, a similar, reciprocal influence or connection is co-created in supervision in which my sociocultural development and experience as a supervisee and those of supervisors interact, establishing a supervisory alliance, and creating either safe or conflictual learning contexts. Here, I borrow some concepts from existential-phenomenological supervision in order to develop my ideas regarding supervision and also to conceptualize my experiences in this context. The intersection of sociocultural experiences between supervisor, supervisee, and client takes place in supervision that creates a triad in which the supervisee mediates or facilitates the indirect relatedness between the other two.

Indeed, supervision is a juncture in which supervisees are challenged to articulate their inner conversation, evaluate the relatedness and their understanding of clients and their presenting problems. Such an interaction is a developmental process in supervision, facilitating the development of supervisees' competence, skills, and knowledge of therapeutic models; strengthening their state of being; or may empower and giving voice to their self-of-the-therapist. This juncture is not developed in the air but in relationship: *Mitwelt*, in which individuals are related to the world through interaction, in which meaning-making processes also are developed. Individuals may not be understood in isolation, meaning in supervision, the supervisors and supervisees deal with a particular type of relationship in which their understanding of the matter—the meaning-making process—is grounded (de Plock, 2009). To me, it means I should feel safe enough to express my inner conversation and self-of-the-therapist in the supervision in order to evaluate my thoughts and emotions in the therapy process.

Borrowed from de Plock's (2009) definition of existential-phenomenological supervision, the client's narratives of being/meaning reported by the supervisee, the supervisee's experience of being in relation to the client's narratives in therapy, and the lived experience of the supervisory encounter conceptualize the supervision in the form of a triad of supervisor-supervisee/therapist-client, in which a new meaning emerges from the intersection of their sociocultural experiences. From my own personal lens, the juncture of these sociocultural developmental experiences leads to the advent of a new meaning in supervision when the type of supervisory relationship helps me to understand my experience of being in therapy.

Having isomorphism in mind, supervision can be like therapy wherein the relational patterns are mirrored over contexts. That is, the supervision process often reflects for me the issues played in the relationship between me, as a supervisee, and my clients in therapy. For me, isomorphism emphasizes the importance of the process in which my supervisor could observe the juncture or a new meaning emerges from the intersection of our sociocultural experiences (Rober, 2017). The supervisors' attention to the here-and-now or the process in supervision provides a safe supervision culture in which a supervisees' inner conversations are articulated and their not-yet-said can be said (Anderson & Goolishian, 1988; Rober, 2017).

Thus, in order for me to express my not-yet-said or self-of-the-therapist in supervision, I try to provide myself with some moments of self-reflection and introspection (Aponte & Kissil, 2014). By providing an opportunity to be aware of my personal vulnerabilities and emotional and intellectual experiences in the therapy, supervision could strengthen my confidence to bring my self into the therapy process. If I, as a supervisee, am an active participant and part of a system (family) with which I am working, considering the self-of-the-therapist in the therapeutic relationship is an important element, because not only my emotions and intellect, but also my spirituality, cultural values, and social and political viewpoints are involved in the therapeutic context (Aponte & Kissil, 2014). I believe without such understandings of one's self, conflict between clients' and therapists' (or supervisees' and supervisors') values or essential understandings of the world may not be resolved or even recognized.

My Experience of Supervision

I attended one to two hours of individual supervision per week including individual, video, and live supervision. This was an essential part of my clinical practice at the Family Medicine Clinic as it was co-created in a supervision contract. I usually prepared a few questions or concerns about a client before the supervision session and then discussed them in detail in the session. A similar process often took place for video supervision in which some parts of a recorded encounter were selected and watched while discussing my questions, concerns, or therapeutic approach, and the client's presenting problem in details. When we had live supervision, I briefly went through the case with my supervisor before meeting the client(s) and discussed what I needed her to focus on; after the encounter, we discussed the weaknesses and strengths of the whole session.

Having said that, there were many occasions when I might think that our supervision and discussion did not fit into the way I perceived and experienced the client, or at least I thought I might not benefit based on my values in the supervisory context. There was not enough room or opportunity to explore the juncture where I hoped to make sociocultural and political connections in order for my inner conversation to find words for expressing myself. I believe it happened when our sociocultural and political experiences contradicted each other and led to a different perception of a client and a supervision experience with an unclear resolution. In such instances, self-supervision could be an alternative, playing a big role in my clinical practice. I use self-supervision when I am self-sustaining (Rober, 2017), helping me to feel competent enough and confident to use my own ideas. Through this practice, I also dig into the back of my mind to find connections between clients' experiences and mine in order to learn and see the world from the clients' eyes and improve their outcomes.

Mark, a Veteran

Mark is a 28-year-old veteran, referred for counseling due to high anxiety. Mark primarily came to the clinic because of hypertension, but later complained about alcoholism and smoking. For a few weeks, every time he came to the clinic to measure his blood pressure, it was unbelievably as high as 200/160. Most of the time, he was not showing any symptoms or expressing any complaints, just saying, "my blood pressure spikes, I should be dead already." He reported that he used to drink a gallon of whiskey, but still smokes almost two packs of cigarettes per day. He complained a lot about his job circumstances and how running a personal business and dealing with different issues was hard and anxiety-provoking. In addition, his family history seemed very tough. As he reported, he was raised in Detroit where he witnessed and became familiar with various kinds of crimes. He lived with his mother until ten years of age, never saw his father, and then was taken care of and raised in foster care until age18 when he joined the Army. After having a few dramatic experiences, he believed that the Army needed someone like him who did not have any familial affiliation or a stable role model during childhood to teach him the "right behaviors" and to be "heartless in the battle," and that he was a good candidate for them.

Mark's story began from when he reported an incident in Iraq, where he served for a few months. He found himself in a situation wherein he was confronted with a so-called *possibility* of shooting an 11-year-old girl in the head as part of his duty and service. It was a silent moment of consternation and perplexity for me as a family therapist who not only originally came from the same region, but also is always politically against the US policy in the Middle East and seeing the outcomes of such policies for both American people—including soldiers and veterans—and the innocent people of Middle Eastern countries. At the time, I was bombarded with many questions, embraced with intense emotions such as why did this guy shoot a young girl in the head? Why did he follow the order? What was he thinking when he fired his gun? And why should I help this guy?

Supervision

My supervisor and I had several supervision sessions discussing Mark's presenting problem as well as my perception of him from different perspectives. Due to the sensitive nature of Mark's experience in terms of politics, and my sociopolitical development as his therapist, I expected that some disagreements could rise up in supervision; at least, it became too difficult for me to express my inner conversation in supervision. I still believe any disagreement or emotion allowing me to not feel safe in supervision could create a frustrating context in which I felt I am an outsider who could not communicate with both my supervisor and Mark. A potential disagreement that took place at the first supervision session was that my supervisor mentioned that Mark had to follow his commander's order and so what he did is understandable! Such a statement may make sense in the military when a soldier is ordered and so is obligated to do an action. Soldiers are told that they cannot refuse the order; otherwise they will be suspended or punished. I had similar military training when I was serving in the Iranian Army where "in the Army, there is no 'why'" was the first lesson we learned as soldiers. But the main point, from my perspective, was the moral aspect of Mark's action, which I believed he was suffering from the most. He followed the order and shot the girl, leaving him with overwhelming feelings of guilt and destructive behaviors. He could have been suspended and punished but not kill a young girl and make her family mournful. This may be the main reason why I felt involved emotionally, intellectually, and ethically.

Through most of our supervision sessions, my supervisor reflected and emphasized more on Mark's life style and how I could help him decrease his anxiety by equipping him with essential tools and coping skills. These coping strategies encompassed quitting smoking by seeing the pharmacist in the clinic, enrolling in a smoke-cessation program, and other ways he could go in order to deal with his demanding workload in a fast-paced environment. Examples included having healthy sleep hygiene, creating a timetable in order to organize his obligations and meetings at work, and practicing deep-breath exercises or mindfulness meditation.

Despite these valuable strategies for addressing Mark's anxiety and physical problems, however, such a biopsychosocial approach to therapy might not be ideal for me to answer my questions or help me to overcome my emotional and intellectual struggles in therapy with him. In other words, there was no room for me to actively and purposefully make use of my self-of-the-therapist in supervision in order to uncover my sociopolitical development and experiences to address my emotional struggles with Mark. Therefore, my inner conversation prevented me from taking a very first step to help Mark and ideally use my supervisor's behavioral techniques in therapy. My supervisor's belief regarding removing Mark's responsibility over what he did in Iraq conflicted with my moral and political beliefs. Consequently, I assumed that supervision was not a safe environment for such discussions and could not empower a realistic confidence within me in order to express my not-yet-said emotional struggles and self. From a more isomorphic lens, when I could not process these feelings in supervision and find the juncture of sociocultural developmental experiences to express myself, I was not able to bring them up in therapy, and the client could not bring them up, either

Through self-reflection and introspection, what helped my self-of-the–therapist to be expressed in the therapeutic relationship was *Mark's current status*, the fact that he felt regretful for what he did. Mark mentioned in therapy that he regretted what he did and felt guilty. Such a feeling even made him leave the Army and start a new personal business. I could see how he was remorseful, and a first step for him to ease his feelings of resentment and sorrow was to change his life; at least he would not kill more innocent civilians. His decision and sorrow were based on an insight that happened to him later about why someone like him was recruited to the Army. He knew it was his responsibility no matter that he was ordered by his commander. Such an attitude and talking about it in detail even motivated me to be more professional and continue therapy with Mark while addressing my emotional, intellectual, and ethical struggles adequately. It also helped me to have enough confidence to use my self-of-the-therapist without being worried about my inner conversation. It was through our discussion in therapy that we made the connection between our sociocultural experiences letting, Mark, and me, to make new meaning out of his experiences.

Scott, a Medical Resident

Although our clinic provided brief and short-term psychotherapy services, I had very few clients such as Scott, who was seen every other week for a few months. Scott was a very successful medical resident who was referred to therapy mainly because of anxiety and depression. He was also a musician and performed with a local orchestra. Scott complained about performance anxiety and the fact that everyone was looking at him while performing; he was afraid that he would be letting them down by making very "bad and ridiculous" mistakes. He was also a religious believer and usually sang at his church but never felt anxious while singing or experienced a similar feeling as when he performed in the orchestra. Another presenting problem reported by Scott was about pornography and his inability or struggle in initiating and maintaining an intimate relationship. In addition, in very rare intimate relationships he had had, he was often suffering from sexual impotency. He considered himself a religious and virtuous person who tried to pray and closely watch his own behaviors. However, his pornography use, a behavior against his moral and religious values, increased his anxiety, having him stuck in a vicious cycle. He was also very selective in dating, trying to meet those who also were believers, who followed and respected his moral and religious values and dating rituals, which were based on his values. He believed in marriage and did not want to have a premarital sexual relationship, although he had experienced one for a very short period of time. One of the only things he thought he was missing in his life was marriage because he had every other thing he needed, such as an apartment or car—everything except a partner and a family of his own. Nevertheless, he was a goal-oriented, successful medical resident, according to him, who could do his academic and clinical practice without stress. We had 14 therapy sessions over five months.

Scott was among those clients for whom I had several supervision sessions. His presenting problems were discussed in supervision from different perspectives. Probably the most highlighted aspects of supervision were exploring the connection between my sociocultural and developmental experiences and his, followed by my supervisor's comments and input. Scott's moral and religious values as a Christian about intimate relationships and marriage were close to mine as a Muslim. Exploring such a connection in supervision helped me to reveal and freely express my inner conversation regarding the immorality and prohibition of sex outside of marriage in Abrahamic religions. Scott believed in such a prohibition but hesitated to express or practice it mainly due to ongoing western societal and cultural norms and forces. Supervision provided a safe setting in which I was confident enough to use more of my own beliefs through narrating personal stories that fit into Scott's narration of marriage. It helped to provide a safe therapeutic environment for Scott to freely talk about his own values although they might not be common in the society. Although my supervisor's sociocultural experiences or ideology were not aligned with mine and Scott's, or in some cases contradicted, there was enough room for me to express my narratives of religion and marriage.

Another supervision discussion that helped me to track and explore the roots of Scott's anxiety was about his family of origin. Asking about Scott's parents and the environment wherein he was raised significantly contributed to the therapeutic outcome. According to him, his mother's obsessive-compulsive disorder during his childhood made Scott a very structured, perfectionist person. His lifestyle and high expectations about life in general made him an individual with whom it was difficult to interact, as he thought about himself. One of the homework assignments offered in supervision, which could challenge both his perfectionism and dating style or interacting and meeting people in general, was to ask him to experience speed dating somewhere in town. Although such an assignment or idea was not consistent with either of Scott's and my moral values, it could be a step toward narrating a different story about dating and adjusting to a not-perfect but fast-paced situation. His experience of speed dating was very challenging for Scott. The idea was also challenging for me, who recommended it in therapy. I just imagined if I was in Scott's shoes and was recommended to try speed dating, I would never try because the whole idea and reasons behind it were against my values. Speed dating could lead me to be involved in other behaviors such as drinking or hanging out with people who may not have the same values as mine, which can make this experience a tough one. Although he had some difficulty accepting the idea, it had him do more self-reflection and introspection in order to identify his way of approaching potential partners, and to be less critical of himself when he failed in any relationship.

Watching videos of therapy sessions in supervision and discussing Scott's narration of his speed-dating experience revealed that he did not have enough opportunities to meet or date intimate partners as much as he needed. He was an inexperienced young man who needed to focus on building a new set of communication skills. Furthermore, this assignment helped Scott to realize that in speed dating, and finally in a potential intimate relationship, he might not have enough time to focus on self and evaluate or criticize himself, but he could let himself fully concentrate and listen to the partner, which could make a difference.

By creating a safe environment wherein my supervisor and I were able to briefly discuss Islamic and Christian beliefs and theology in supervision and make connections between my sociocultural experiences and those of Scott, supervision played an important role in making me confident to involve my self-of-the-therapist in the process of therapy. I believe one of the main reasons I was able to express myself in therapy was the supervision context in which my values were respected. The expression of my self-of-the-therapist in therapy was just a reflection of sociocultural juncture in supervision. I believe not having a fear to talk about my values in supervision, although they may not be acceptable in the US culture, was a privilege I had in supervision that let us connect our different sociocultural experiences and avoid conflict.

References

Anderson, H., & Goolishian, H. (1988). Human systems as linguistic systems. *Family Process,* 27, 371–393.

Aponte, H. J., & Kissil, K. (2014). "If I can grapple with this, I can truly be of use in the therapy room": Using the therapist's own emotional struggles to facilitate effective therapy. *Journal of Marital and Family Therapy, 40*(2), 152–164.

de Plock, S. (2009). An existential-phenomenological inquiry into the meaning of clinical supervision: What do we mean when we talk about Existential-Phenomenological Supervision? *Journal Society for Existential Analysis, 20*(2), 299–318.

McDaniel, S. H., Doherty, W. J., & Hepworth, J. (2015). *Medical family therapy and integrated care* (2nd ed). Washington, DC: American Psychological Association.

Rober, P. (2017). Addressing the person of the therapist in supervision: The therapist's inner conversation method. *Family Process, 56*, 487–500.

Speice, J. & McDaniel, S.H. (2016). Training the medical family therapist in an integrated care setting. In K. Jordan (Ed.), *Couple, marriage, and family therapy supervision* (pp. 371–389). New York, NY: Springer Publishing Company.

INDEX